The Wager Disaster

Also by C.H. Layman

Man of Letters
The Falklands and the Dwarf (with Jane Cameron)

The Wager Disaster

Mayhem, Mutiny and Murder in the South Seas

Rear Admiral C.H. Layman, CB, DSO, LVO

UNIFORM
PRESS

Uniform Press Ltd
66 Charlotte Street
London
W1T 4QE

www.uniformpress.co.uk

Published by Uniform Press Ltd 2015
Text Copyright © C.H. Layman 2015

ISBN 978-1-910065-50-1

10 9 8 7 6 5 4 3 2

Book design by Felicity Price-Smith
Printed in Spain by Graphycems

For Amanda, with my love

Editor's Note

I have modernised punctuation, spelling, place names where I can, and eighteenth-century abbreviations such as 'tis, 'em, look'd etc. In a very few places I have corrected mistakes or changed an unimportant word in the interest of continuity. Of the several different spellings of the First Lieutenant's name I have settled on Baynes. The long-boat after lengthening was sometimes called a schooner. The term vessel was also used. I have retained *long-boat* for simplicity and clarity, and standardised the names of the other boats as in Appendix A.

CONTENTS

APPENDICES

FOREWORD

by H.R.H. The Duke of Edinburgh

It does not often happen that a sub-plot can be said to have overshadowed the main drama. Yet this remarkable story of the fate of the supply ship for Commodore Anson's expedition into the Pacific in 1741 is far more gripping than the record of his more conventional activities in the war against Spain in that part of the world. In most accounts of the expedition, the only mention of HMS *Wager* is that she was the supply ship for the small squadron and that she was wrecked in a gale on the coast of southern Chile.

But thereby hangs this tale – and what a tale! Told largely in the words of the participants themselves, it reveals a drama of misfortune, unimaginable hardship, super-human endurance, mixed with extremes in human behaviour, both heroic and despicable, and a small boat journey of epic proportions.

Only 36 of the original crew of about 140 made it back to Britain, but one good thing came out of it in the end. Fortunately, Commodore Anson, who later became an Admiral and served on the Board of Admiralty until his death, took the trouble to learn as much as he could about the story, and to apply the lessons of this tragic drama to the improvement and modernisation of the Royal Navy as a whole.

DRAMATIS PERSONAE

Commission Officers (later called Commissioned Officers)

Captain Daniel (Dandy) KIDD,
>   commanding HMS *Wager* until his death in January 1741

Acting Captain David CHEAP,
>   commanding HMS *Wager* from January 1741

Lieutenant Robert BAYNES (sometimes spelt Beans or Baines),
>   First Lieutenant, second in command

Warrant Officers

Thomas CLARK, Master, responsible for navigation

John BULKELEY, Gunner

John KING, Boatswain; responsible for rigging, sails, boats etc.

John CUMMINS, Carpenter

John YOUNG, Cooper

Dr ELLIOT, Surgeon

Thomas HARVEY, Purser; responsible for provisions

Petty Officers (junior to Warrant Officers)

Midshipman the Hon John BYRON

Midshipman Alexander CAMPBELL

Midshipman Isaac MORRIS

Midshipman Henry COZENS

John JONES, Mate, assistant to the Master

Others

Robert ELLIOT, Surgeon's Mate; no relation to the Surgeon

Embarked Marine Contingent

Captain Robert PEMBERTON

Lieutenant Thomas HAMILTON

Dr Vincent OAKLEY, Surgeon

PART 1

Setting the Scene

SHARED HERITAGE
AT THE END OF THE WORLD

By Chilean maritime archaeologist Diego Carabias Amor, Director of the Wager Research Project.

The remarkable story of HMS *Wager* has been recognised many times in the past as one of the most extraordinary episodes in the literature of the sea, being a dramatic and powerful tale of violence, disorder, affliction and endurance. This combination of human qualities made the survivors' narratives eighteenth-century best-sellers. Indeed John Byron's account, published for the first time in 1768, and perhaps the best known of them, was some years ago placed on UNESCO's International Collection of Representative Works.

Other aspects of this saga are less well known. For example, survivors' accounts provide valuable and privileged first-hand ethnographic information about the maritime-oriented indigenous groups of Western Patagonia during the Spanish Colonial period: the Chonos and the Kawéqar. The Chonos, in fact, were assimilated and became extinct during the following decades. Today, the descriptions by the *Wager* officers of their contacts with the Chonos and the Kawéqar are essential reading for any scientist or scholar who wishes to study these ancient inhabitants of Patagonian coastal waters.

Moreover, shipwreck archaeological sites represent an important category of our Underwater Cultural Heritage. Ships, being long-distance vehicles for the transport of people, goods and ideas, go well beyond normal cultural boundaries. Shipwrecks are often relevant both to the country of origin and to the coastal state where they are located, and imply joint responsibilities. Shipwreck sites are unique, vulnerable and valuable cultural resources, and with scientific research they can provide us with substantial information about our past. If they are not properly managed, they may be lost for ever. There is, happily, an increasing international awareness of the urgent need to protect them, and the UNESCO Convention on the Protection of Underwater Cultural Heritage is a fine example of this broad effort.

The loss of the *Wager* also had important consequences for colonial southern Chile, and contributed significantly to the geographic and

The shared heritage of Britain and Chile.
It is highly likely that this cannon in the main street of Maullin (a town on the mainland just north of Chiloé) was salvaged from the wreck of the *Wager*.

cartographic knowledge of Western Patagonia and its indigenous inhabitants. For some years after the ship was wrecked in 1741 there were expeditions to salvage the wreck, and this sparked missionary zeal to convert to Christianity the native peoples discovered there. So the *Wager* played a decisive part in social construction and surveying of Western Patagonia in a multi-ethnic context, relevant both for the Spanish and the local people of the area.

The process through which significance and meaning is attached to places is dynamic and multi-layered. Although the material remains of the *Wager* were forgotten for many years, two completely different and independent expeditions coincided 265 years afterwards in the isolated islands where the ship was lost, one a party of British exploration divers and another a group of Chilean maritime archaeologists. Although with different aims and approaches, both were interested in the *Wager* story. Their collaboration made possible the discovery and study of the archaeological remains of this drama – a process that is just beginning.

The historical account now published in this book, based on a thorough research of archives in England and Chile, provides new insights that broaden our perspective. For this story of a ship, lost at the end of the world, was to become a legacy for the whole of humankind.

Chapter 1

THE CAPTAIN WRITES FROM JAIL

This letter is from a British naval captain in Santiago who had been taken prisoner by the Spanish.

To Richard Lindsey Esquire
Buenos Aires
26th February 1744

Dear Sir…

His Majesty's ship the *Wager*, under my command, was lost in the night between the 13th and 14th May in the year 1741, upon rocks that lay four or five miles distant from some islands that lay near the coast of Patagonia,[1] in the latitude of 46 degrees and a half. The weather was at that time (and had been for almost ten weeks before) extremely bad, the night very dark, and the ship without a mizzen-mast, having lost that some time before in coming round the Cape. My ship's company at that unhappy juncture were almost all sick, having not more than six or seven seamen, and three or four marines, that were able to keep the deck; and they so fatigued with the excessive length of the voyage, the long course

---

1. This is Pacific, not Atlantic, Patagonia.

of bad weather, and scarcity of fresh water, that they were very little able to do their duty.

As for myself, I had enjoyed but a very indifferent state of health from the time of our leaving Britain, being seldom free from the rheumatism, or asthma; and to heighten my misfortunes, on the afternoon before the ship was lost, as I was walking along the deck with a design to go upon the forecastle in order to give some directions about repairing of four of the chain-plates that were broken by the excessive labouring of the ship, I was thrown down one of the hatchways, and was so unlucky as to dislocate the upper bone of my left arm. I was taken up very much stunned and hurt with the violence of the fall and dislocation, which cost the Surgeon two or three hours of trouble to reduce, and bring me to myself.

I then sent for my Lieutenant and Gunner, and told them of the danger we were in, and gave them such orders as, had they been complied with, would in all probability have saved the ship. But my Lieutenant, regardless of his charge, went (as I was afterwards informed) to his bottle, without giving himself any farther concern about the preservation of His Majesty's ship. The Surgeon, contrary to my knowledge, laid me asleep with an opiate, telling me it was only something to prevent a fever. So that I knew nothing of what was doing in the ship from seven o'clock at night till half an hour past four next morning, the time when the ship first struck, although my Lieutenant had orders, and his duty required him, to keep every body upon deck that was able to stir out of their hammocks, and to inform me if we had any ground with the lead, and of the winds and weather. It is surprising strange that in all that time neither he nor any of my officers should come and wake me.

We struck, as I told you before, at half an hour past four, and from that time until seven ran through breakers, with rocks above water close on each side of us, very often striking, and expecting the ship every moment to go to pieces. For the third stroke broke the rudder, and made such a hole in her bottom, that she was in an instant full of water up to the hatches. However, it pleased God that at break of day she stuck fast on a rock near the land, which proved an island, in sight of the Cordilleras,[2] where my first care was to securing a good quantity of arms, ammunition and some provisions.

You cannot well conceive, nor can I easily recount to you, the repeated troubles and vexations that I met with for the space of five months after the ship was lost, from mutinous and disobedient men, headed by all my officers; being for most part of that time lame of an arm, and ill of the rheumatism. I endeavoured, both by fair means and force, to bring them to reason and a sense of their duty. I even proceeded to extremities, when other means proved ineffectual; and I firmly believe I should have got the better of them had it not been for the behaviour of the Captain of the Marines, who (lost to all sense of honour or the interest of his country) came into all their measures. The consequence of which was, that about four days before the long-boat was ready to sail (which I had built with a design to join the Commodore at the rendezvous, or in case of not finding him to act as occasion should offer) they surprised me whilst asleep, bound my hands, and put me in close confinement under a guard of six or eight men and an officer; and at the same time making a prisoner of Mr Hamilton, who was the only man among the marine officers that during all this unfortunate affair behaved himself with either honour, courage, or steadiness.

I am afraid of tiring your patience, and shall therefore be as concise as I can. They sailed on the 14th October 1741, saying when they went off, with the utmost insolence and inhumanity, "that I might take my leave of Englishmen, for I never would see any more of them than what they left with me": who were only Mr Hamilton, Mr Elliot my surgeon, who refused to go on board except they submitted themselves to my command, and seven men more that were upon an island, about five or six miles distant from us. They likewise left a very small quantity of extraordinarily bad flour, and a few pieces of salt meat. Their design, as

---

2. A mountain range, part of the Andes chain.

well as I could be informed, was to sail through the Straits of Magellan, for the coast of Brazil.

About five or six days after the long-boat sailed, Mr Byron and another of my midshipmen, whose name is Campbell, returned to me in the barge, bringing with them six seamen whom they had prevailed upon to leave the long-boat, which was at anchor about six or eight leagues to the westward. I then began to conceive great hopes, and set about repairing the yawl, which they had left on the beach all in pieces. Which when done, as soon as the weather would permit, we sailed, coasting along to the northward. Our resolutions I cannot so well communicate to you in a letter; I leave you to guess them; for I had then 18 men very well armed, and two boats.

It would be endless to enumerate the many dangers, hardships, and difficulties that we underwent. Let it suffice to tell you that our number was at last reduced to 11, viz. we four that are here, my Surgeon, who died of hunger and the hardships we underwent, and six seamen, with only one boat, for the other we lost in bad weather.

I wish I could forget the rest of our story, for really the barbarity of these six villains shocks me yet; who one day (as I was gone out to pick up sea weed or anything I could find to satisfy my hunger) ran away with the boat, carrying with them all our arms, ammunition, the few clothes that we had saved, and in short everything that could be of the least use to us. What could provoke the villains to so foul a deed I cannot tell, except it was their cowardice. We had now nothing but a scene of human misery before our eyes, and must infallibly have perished of hunger in a very few days, had not Providence sent some Indians to our assistance, who undertook to pilot us to the island of Chiloé; for I was now reduced to the infamous necessity of surrendering myself a prisoner, which you know sir, is the greatest misfortune that can befall a man.

It is impossible for me to describe to you the condition that we were in when we arrived at the island of Chiloé, for it really surpasses all description. I shall only say this, that if half the number of lice that we had about us had been armed men, we could not easily have been got the better of. Nor could it well be otherwise, for we were three months with the Indians, in a most rigorous climate, exposed to the inclemency of the weather, without meat, without clothes, and living in a dirtier manner than the Hottentots.

We were at Chiloé seven months before we could have an opportunity of a vessel to Valparaiso, where we arrived 19th February 1743. And on the 25th we were brought to Santiago, by order of the President, Señor Don Joseph Mansa, who seems to be a gentleman of distinguished honour and merit.

It would be very ungrateful in me if I did not do justice to your friend, Señor Don Manuel de Guiroir, who with great politeness and humanity offered me what money I wanted to supply my necessities. I only took 600 pieces-of-eight from him, for which I gave him bills on Mr Compton, His Majesty's consul-general of Portugal, payable in Lisbon. However, as we came here all in rags, that (you know) goes but a very small way. I have received 850 pieces-of-eight, which they say is the amount of what is sold of the cargo you mention, and should have sent you bills of exchange before this time had not Don Manuel told me that it was absolutely necessary to defer them, until such time as he went; which he says will be about a month hence.

I am sure that I have quite tired your patience, but I must beg your indulgence a little longer. I assure you, without compliment, that I am extremely glad of commencing an acquaintance with any relation of my Lord Crawford's, to whom I have the honour to be very well known; and I am sorry to tell you that when we left Britain he was very ill of the wounds which he received at the battle of Belgrade, where he behaved himself with great bravery.

I have been informed, since my arrival here, that my mutineers in the long-boat were seen in the mouth of the River Plate, with only 25 or 30 men in her. If this be true, one half or more of them are dead for they were in all 62 when they left me. If you know anything particularly of them, or of three more of my men who are said to be in the hands of the Governor of Buenos Aires, conducted thither by land by some wild Indians, pray be so good as to let me know, particularly their names.

You know it is the unhappy fate of a prisoner at discretion[3] that he cannot make articles[4] for himself. I therefore cannot tell you anything of our destiny. However I have this comfort, that I did everything in my power to prevent our falling into their hands, and for the rest must have patience until God sends a peace; which I hope will be for the honour of Great Britain. Let the fate of particular persons be what it will, but let the honour of our country be immortal. I have still strong hopes of seeing it; and it will add much to the pleasure if we should happen to go together. I must confess to you that every day here seems to me an age, though I must at the same time own that my misfortunes are greatly softened by the good offices of our friend and countryman, Mr Gedd; of whose kindness and civility I cannot say too much.

I will not add to the exorbitant prolixity of this letter by making apologies for it; but conclude, with great truth and sincerity,

Dear Sir,

Your most faithful humble servant,

David Cheap

This letter raises a number of intriguing and bizarre questions. What was HMS Wager *doing off the coast of Chile in 1744, apparently so far away from British interests and possessions? Was it not a major navigational error for the ship to be set so far inshore? And what does Captain Cheap mean by the words "I even proceeded to extremities" when trying to control mutinous and disobedient men? To address these questions, and many others, we must go back five years to the start of Britain's war with Spain.*

---

3. On parole.
4. Rules or conditions.

Chapter 2

PREPARATIONS FOR WAR

It is 1740, and Britain and Spain have been at war for a few months. An experienced naval captain, George Anson, is appointed Commodore and Commander-in-Chief of a small squadron to "annoy and distress" the Spanish in the Pacific. His ships, which include H.M.S. Wager *as stores-ship, are with difficulty fitted out and manned in Portsmouth and Deptford by an over-stretched naval administration, and their departure is delayed. They eventually sail too late for Cape Horn and the most hostile of sea passages anywhere in the world.*

The story of the *Wager* disaster begins with some admirably clear and flexible orders, probably drafted by the First Lord, in the name of King George II:

> (signed) George R
> Instructions for our trusty and well-beloved George Anson, Esq., Commander-in-Chief of our ships designed to be sent into the South Seas in America. Given at our Court at St. James's the 31ˢᵗ day of January 1740, in the thirteenth year of our reign.
> Whereas we have thought proper to declare war against the King of Spain, for the several injuries and indignities offered to our crown and

people, which are more particularly set forth in our declaration of war, we have thought fit to direct that you, taking under your command our ships, should proceed with them according to the following instructions. You are to receive on board our said ships five hundred of our land forces, and to proceed forthwith to the Cape de Verde Islands, and to supply your ships with water and such refreshments as are to be procured there; and you are from thence to make the best of your way to the Island of St Catherine on the coast of Brazil, or such other place on that coast as you may be advised is more proper, where you are again to supply your ships with water and any other necessaries you may want that can be had there. And when you have done so, you are to proceed with our ships under your command into the South Sea, either round Cape Horn or through the Straits of Magellan, as you shall judge most proper, and according as the season of the year and winds and weather shall best permit.

When you shall arrive on the Spanish coast of the South Sea,[1] you are to use your best endeavours to annoy and distress the Spaniards, either at sea or land, to the utmost of your power, by taking, sinking, burning, or otherwise destroying all their ships and vessels that you shall meet with, and particularly their boats, and all embarkations[2] whatsoever, that they may not be able to send any intelligence by sea along the coast of your being in those parts.

In case you shall find it practical to seize, surprise or take any of the towns or places belonging to the Spaniards on the coast, that you may judge worthy of making such an enterprise upon, you are to attempt it; for which purpose we have not only ordered the land forces above mentioned, but have also thought proper to direct that an additional number of small arms be put on board the ships under your command to be used, as occasion may require, by the crews of the said ships, or otherwise, as you shall find best for our service. And you are, on such

1. The Pacific Ocean.
2. Vessels.

occasions, to take the opinion of the Captains of our ships under your command at a Council of War: of which Council of War, in case of any attack or enterprise by land, the Commander of our land forces shall also be one; which said land forces shall, upon such occasions, be landed according to the determination of the said Council of War. And as it will be absolutely necessary for you to be supplied with provisions and water, when and where they can be had, you will inform yourself of the places where that can most conveniently be done; and as we have been informed that the coasts of Chile, and particularly the island of Chiloé, do abound with provisions and necessaries of all sorts, you are to call there for that purpose.

As it has been represented unto us that the number of native Indians on the coast of Chile greatly exceeds that of the Spaniards, and that there is reason to believe that the said Indians may not be averse to join with you against the Spaniards in order to recover their freedom, you are to endeavour to cultivate a good understanding with such Indians as shall be willing to join and assist you in any attempt that you may think proper to make against the Spaniards that are established there …

But where the Spanish ships in their passage between Panama and Lima do usually stop, it will be proper for you to look into those places, and to annoy Spaniards there, as much as it shall be in your power. And if you shall meet with the Spanish men-of-war that carry the treasure from Lima to Panama, you are to endeavour to make yourself master of them.

When you are arrived at Panama you will probably have an opportunity to take or destroy such embarkations as you shall find there. And as the town itself is represented to be not very strong, especially as it has been lately burnt down, you are, if you shall think you have sufficient force for that purpose, to make an attempt upon that town and endeavour to take it, or burn and destroy it, as you think most for our service.

And as you may possibly find an opportunity to send privately overland to Portobello or Darien, you are by that means to endeavour to transmit to any of our ships or forces that shall be on that coast an account of what you have done, or intend to do. And lest any such intelligence should fall into the hands of the Spaniards we have ordered you to be furnished with a cipher in which manner only you are to correspond with our Admiral, or the Commander-in-Chief of any of our ships …

Britain's war with Spain had been in force for three months, and has been called "the War of Jenkins' Ear". A merchant ship, the *Rebecca* of Glasgow, had been stopped by the Spanish some years before and plundered; the ship's company had been maltreated, and the Master, Captain Jenkins, claimed he had had his ear cut off. The ear, pickled and presented to Parliament by Captain Jenkins, outraged public opinion which the MP-Admiral Edward Vernon in the House of Commons did all he could to inflame. There was much talk of the Catholic threat and a Spanish invasion, and a Jacobite-Catholic rising in Scotland, supported by France and Spain, seemed entirely possible. Moreover Spanish trading restrictions were hampering British trade, and no doubt the immensely rich Spanish colonies in the West Indies and in Central and South America were also in everyone's mind. The government, headed by Robert Walpole, had reluctantly decided that war was unavoidable.

In this unsettled scene the Royal Navy, as so often in its history, could offer the nation stability and protection, as well as the possibility of taking the initiative against a powerful and aggressive enemy.

With hindsight it is easy to see that for Anson's expedition – given sound ships, experienced crews and soldiers, surprise, and provision against disease – there would have been an excellent chance of causing havoc in the almost undefended Spanish Pacific colonies. But all was not well with the Navy, and almost none of those elements for success were achievable. Certainly there were resolute officers and some fine ships, but the administration was overstretched and haphazard in many crucial respects, and recruitment based on the press-gang was a constant problem.

In the summer of 1740 Portsmouth Dockyard, Spithead and the Solent were all crowded with ships as the Navy prepared two large fleets. One

The eighteenth-century press-gang at work.
The system was more unpopular, and less efficient, than twentieth-century conscription.
But in wartime both were necessary.

was intended for the North Atlantic and Mediterranean, to intercept and capture shipping going to and from Spanish ports. The other was to head for the West Indies to exploit Admiral Vernon's recent and stirring success at Portobello. Fitting out, storing and manning these two large fleets and their auxiliaries meant that all the support services were working at full stretch.

Anson was aged 42 and a much-respected Captain with a reputation for being firm, uncommunicative, humane, calm, and highly professional. He was allocated six warships and two victualling ships (pinks) for his small squadron with its secret mission to the Pacific Ocean:

Centurion (Commodore George Anson), 4th rate, 60 guns, 400 men
Gloucester (Captain Richard Norris), 4th rate, 50 guns, 300 men
Severn (Captain the Hon. Edward Legge), 4th rate, 50 guns, 300 men
Pearl (Captain Mathew Mitchel), 5th rate, 40 guns, 250 men
Wager (Captain Daniel Kidd), 6th rate, 28 guns, 160 men
Tryall (Captain the Hon. George Murray), sloop, 8 guns, 100 men
Anna, pink
Industry, pink

With respect to preparing and fitting out this comparatively small squadron for what was known would be an extremely challenging operation, it is fair to say that just about everything went wrong. The other two fleets, both to be commanded by admirals, numbered 33 ships of the line,[3] and there were no less than 120 merchant ships to be organised into three convoys for North America, and the Eastern and Western Mediterranean. It is perhaps not surprising, but still highly regrettable, that top priority for stores, men, and dockyard support went to the larger fleets. Anson and his captains battled desperately against reluctant dockyard officials to get their own ships ready. The situation was urgent in that it was considered essential to get round Cape Horn in the austral summer; sailing conditions in

---

3. Ships of the line were 1st, 2nd and 3rd rates; that is, ships of 70 guns or more.

that area are always vicious, but in winter they were thought to be nearly impossible.[4] A sailing date of June or July was desirable, but the squadron was delayed long after this. Moreover the longer the delay the less likely secrecy could be maintained, and indeed the Spanish heard about the expedition very quickly through their spies, and had time to warn their colonies and send a squadron of their own under Admiral Pizarro to intercept Anson.[5]

It is intriguing to see how efficient the intelligence services were at that time, and how difficult it seems to have been to keep a secret. The decision to send the expedition was made on 7th December 1739. On 30th January 1740 the French Ambassador at Madrid received a report – clearly based on an overheard conversation – "There are letters from England which report that they are sending six frigates under the command of M. Hanson, which are under orders to round Cape Horn and enter the South Sea." And on 7th August 1740 Anson was informed that intercepted Spanish letters made it clear that the Viceroys of Peru and Mexico had been accurately informed of the size and intent of his squadron, and warned to be on their guard. In addition the English Press reported the slow progress of getting the squadron ready. On 19th July the *London Evening Post* informed readers and spies, "Commodore Anson and the ships under his command, it's said, are actually victualled for two and twenty months, and the sea and land officers on board have great lucrative expectations from the expedition that they are to be employed in."

If dockyard officials and naval administrators were not seized with the urgency of the situation, the captains of the ships of the squadron certainly were. They wrote dozens of strongly-worded letters to press for

4. In fact, it is now known that the winds are often less unfavourable in the winter months, but neither Anson nor anyone else knew this at the time. March, when the squadron actually started its battle round Cape Horn, could well be the worst month of all.

5. Pizarro's squadron, which out-gunned Anson's, left Spain as Anson was leaving the Channel. The two squadrons narrowly missed each other on two occasions. The Spanish ships were dispersed trying to round the Horn, and they suffered shipwreck, weather damage, mutiny, and disease. Only one, the flagship *Asia*, could be made sufficiently seaworthy to return home five years later, when her adventures will feature later in this story.

the timely readying of their ships, letters that still survive in Admiralty files. Captain Kidd of the *Wager* seems to have been the most active of all. We find requests for storerooms, accommodation, soldiers' beds, iron ballast, a pinnace, a six-oared boat, surgeons' necessaries for six months, oil and paint. He asked for an adjustment to the position of his after capstan, and made the point that the orlop[6] had to be finished before he could embark his cables. He protested that although the Board had sent the necessary orders, dockyard officials "have not understood them" – a neat way of trying to put a bomb under a dockyard department. He requested his allocated deal cutter to be provided, a boat which seems to have been shanghaied by another ship. All this will seem familiar to any captain who has battled with dockyards and bureaucracy endeavouring to get his ship ready for sea.

It is 1739, and naval dockyards are working flat out to prepare a large number of ships for the war against Spain.

6. The highest deck that runs the whole length of the ship.

And in spite of all this activity the *Wager*, a converted East Indiaman, was never ideal for this projected voyage around Cape Horn through the world's most hostile seas. Built in Rotherhithe in 1734, she was bought by the Navy for use as a stores-ship, and after a fairly extensive refit at Deptford emerged as a 6th rate. She was named after the First Lord of the Admiralty, Admiral Sir Charles Wager, himself a highly successful veteran of a previous conflict with Spain. He was the prime mover behind the planning of the expedition, and he more than anyone else had been responsible for the drafting of Anson's instructions.

The *Wager* was broader in the beam than purpose-built 6th rates, which made her more commodious for stores and passengers, but less handy in a rough sea and less able to head into wind. Square riggers in general could not expect to head closer to the wind than six points or about 68 degrees, but it is likely *Wager* could not even achieve this.

Her role was to carry naval and military stores for the whole squadron, and of course to support with her 28 guns whatever naval action might occur. Her naval stores included victuals for the squadron, bulky careening gear, merchandise in bales for trading with disaffected Indians, and a significant quantity of brandy and wine. Her military stores were for the squadron's land forces, whose role was to create mayhem among the Spanish settlements. These included four eight-pounders, twenty 4.4 inch mortars, much ammunition, muskets, tents, spades, axes, wheelbarrows, and 10,000 sandbags – all equipment necessary for operations on shore.

She was therefore deeply laden and cluttered below decks, and in Byron's words, writing later when he was himself an experienced Commodore, "a ship of this quality and condition could not be expected to work with that readiness and ease which was necessary for... those heavy seas which she was to encounter."

As the sailing date approached Anson found that his squadron was some 300 seamen short. He informed the Admiralty, who told him to apply to Admiral Norris, commanding the Atlantic Fleet, for what he needed. But Admiral Norris was short of men too, and declined to help.

Admiral Sir Charles Wager was First Lord of the Admiralty at the outbreak of war with Spain in 1739. "A man of great natural talents, improved by industry and long experience", he probably drafted the instructions for Anson's squadron to "annoy and distress" the Spanish in the Pacific Ocean, waters they regarded as their own. HMS *Wager* was named after him.

Anson eventually was sent 69 seamen (half from the sick bay ashore and local hospitals) and about 100 Marines.

Anson's official orders had included, "You are to receive on board... 500 of our land forces," but they were not forthcoming either. In a crass decision that ranks high in the long annals of culpable bureaucratic stupidity, the Government sent 500 men from the "Corps of Invalids," out-patients from Chelsea Hospital who, from age, wounds, or other infirmities, were considered incapable of service in the Army. Anson protested vigorously that these men were entirely unsuitable for the mission, and he was supported by the First Lord of the Admiralty himself,[7] but to no avail. Anson's own account at this point states, "(Sir Charles Wager) was told that persons, who were supposed to be better judges of soldiers than either he or Mr Anson, thought them to be the properest men to be employed on this occasion."

Of the 500 Invalids, those capable of walking deserted before they could be embarked. Some 259 of the most decrepit were hoisted aboard the ships of the squadron because, accounts say, they could not even climb the ladders to reach the deck. Most of them were over 60 years of age, some over 70; and it is almost certain that they all died on the voyage. Anson's *Voyage*[8] comments:

> It is difficult to conceive a more moving scene than the embarkation of these unhappy veterans. They were themselves extremely averse to the service they were engaged in, and fully apprised of all the disasters they were afterwards exposed to, the apprehensions of which were strongly marked by the concern that appeared in their countenances, which was mixed with no small degree of indignation, to be thus hurried from their repose into a fatiguing employ to which neither the strength of their bodies nor the vigour of their minds were in any way proportioned, and

7. It is possible that the First Lord had originally nodded agreement to this arrangement.
8. Written under Anson's direction.

Desertion was a constant problem in the days of the press-gang navy. The *Wager* men on this list (including one called Robinson Cruzoe) have R (= Run or deserted) written against their names. They absconded in the weeks prior to the ship's departure in September 1740.

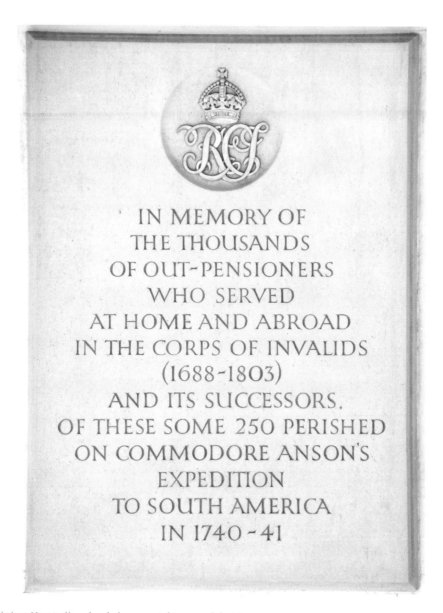

IN MEMORY OF
THE THOUSANDS
OF OUT-PENSIONERS
WHO SERVED
AT HOME AND ABROAD
IN THE CORPS OF INVALIDS
(1688-1803)
AND ITS SUCCESSORS.
OF THESE SOME 250 PERISHED
ON COMMODORE ANSON'S
EXPEDITION
TO SOUTH AMERICA
IN 1740-41

Chelsea Hospital's melancholy memorial to a cruel decision.
Five hundred Chelsea Pensioners were ordered to Portsmouth to make up the Land Force for Commodore Anson's expedition. Anson protested that these men, mostly aged between 60 and 70, some with missing limbs, were entirely unsuitable, and deserved better of the country they had served. The First Lord of the Admiralty agreed. Both were over-ruled. Those pensioners who could walk deserted on the road to Portsmouth. The remaining 250 all died of disease, hunger and exhaustion on the voyage.

where, without seeing the face of an enemy... they would in all probability uselessly perish.

Two hundred and ten marines, raw recruits and probably pressed, made up the number.

The *Wager* therefore sailed short-handed, and with her living spaces severely overcrowded by an extra 142 marines and pensioners and a large quantity of stores for the whole squadron.

Adverse winds caused further delays. Anson's squadron finally departed, much too late, on 18th September 1740. The *London Daily Post* duly told the world, "Yesterday sailed from St Helen's Commodore Anson in the *Centurion*, in company with the *Severn, Gloucester, Pearl, Wager*, and *Tryall*, for the Great South Sea."

Soon after this Captain Kidd died of some unknown cause. Later it was alleged that with his last breath he had foretold that the voyage of the *Wager* would end in "poverty, vermin, famine, death, and destruction," but this looks suspiciously like second-guessing by superstitious yarn-spinners. He was relieved, after some further adjustments, by the *Centurion*'s 47-year-old Scottish First Lieutenant who was now given a temporary promotion and appointed to his first command, Captain David Cheap.

On board the ill-fated *Wager* with Captain Cheap were the sixteen-year-old Midshipman Byron, grandfather of the poet; two other midshipmen, Morris and Campbell; the austere and uncompromising Gunner, Mr Bulkeley; and the Cooper, Mr Young, a man with a perceptive wit and a fluent turn of phrase. These men, who took part in one of the most dramatic catastrophes in the history of the Royal Navy, now tell their story.

A story well known in its time.

Here are the original sources on which this book is based. In order of publication they are:
Bulkeley & Cummins, 1743; Campbell, 1747; Anson's *Voyage*, 1748; Young, 1751; Morris, 1751(?);
Bulkeley & Cummins's first American edition, 1757; Byron 1768.

There are several unofficial accounts of the voyage of Anson's squadron, some anonymous, some dubious, that appeared between 1744 and 1747. There are also many chap books (small, cheap and often fairly rough pirated editions) published at various dates. The last one here was printed in 1819.

All these books, from different perspectives and with varying degrees of competence, tell the same best-selling story. It was a story that fascinated the public, and influenced naval and political thinking for a generation.

PART 2

Mayhem and Mutiny

Chapter 3

SHIPWRECK

Byron is critical of the preparations made for the expedition, in particular of the clutter of stores which impedes the working of the ship. The Wager *is damaged in the vicinity of Cape Horn and separated from the other ships. Many men become ill with scurvy. The Captain pays little heed to doubts expressed about the course steered, and presses on to make a rendezvous with the rest of the squadron. In exceptionally foul weather* Wager *is driven onto a lee-shore and wrecked on an extremely inhospitable coast. One hundred and forty survivors get ashore in boats.*

From Midshipman Byron's narrative

It may be necessary for the better understanding the disastrous fate of the *Wager*, the subject of the following pages, to repeat the remark that "a strange infatuation seemed to prevail in the whole conduct of this embarkation." For though it was unaccountably detained till the season for its sailing was past, no proper use was made of that time, which should have been employed in providing a suitable force of sailors and soldiery; nor was there a due attention given to other requisites for so peculiar and extensive a destination.

This neglect not only rendered the expedition abortive in its principal object, but most materially affected the condition of each particular ship; and none so fatally as the *Wager*, who being an old Indiaman brought into the service upon this occasion, was now fitted out as a man-of-war, but, being made to serve as a store-ship, was deeply laden with all kinds of careening gear, military, and other stores, for the use of the other ships; and, what is more, crowded with bale goods, and encumbered with merchandise.[1] A ship of this quality and condition could not be expected to work with that readiness and ease which was necessary for her security and preservation in those heavy seas which she was to encounter.

Her crew consisted of men pressed from long voyages to be sent upon a distant and hazardous service; on the other hand, all her land forces were no more than a poor detachment of infirm and decrepit invalids from Chelsea Hospital, desponding under the apprehensions of a long voyage. It is not then to be wondered that Captain Kidd, under whose command this ship sailed out of the port, should in his last moments presage her ill success, though nothing very material happened during his command.

At his death he was succeeded by Captain Cheap, who, still without any accident, kept company with the squadron, till we had almost gained the southernmost mouth of the Straits le Maire; when being the sternmost ship we were, by the sudden shifting of the wind to the southward and the turn of the tide, very near being wrecked upon the rocks of Staten Island; which notwithstanding, having weathered, contrary to the expectation of the rest of the squadron, we endeavoured all in our power to make up our lost way and regain our station. This we effected, and proceeded in our voyage, keeping company with the rest of the ships for some time; when, by a great roll of a hollow sea, we carried away our mizzen-mast, all the chain-plates[2] to windward being broken. Soon after, hard gales at west

---

1. These were for trading with and befriending disaffected Indians in the Spanish colonies, should opportunity arise.
2. The chain-plates at the end of the shrouds take all the athwartships strain of the sail and mast. See Glossary.

coming on with a prodigious swell, there broke a heavy sea in upon the ship, which stove our boats, and filled us for some time.

These accidents were the more disheartening as our Carpenter was on board the *Gloucester*, and detained there by the incessant tempestuous weather and sea impracticable for boats. In a few days he returned, and supplied the loss of a mizzen-mast by a lower studding-sail boom; but this expedient, together with the patching up of our rigging, was a poor temporary relief to us. We were soon obliged to cut away our best bower anchor to ease the foremast,[3] the shrouds and chain-plates of which were all broken, and the ship in all parts in a most crazy condition.

Thus shattered and disabled, and a single ship (for we had now lost sight of our squadron), we had the additional mortification to find ourselves bearing for the land on a lee-shore, having thus far persevered in the course we held from an error in conjecture: for the weather was unfavourable

20th December 1740, Is. S. Caterina, Brazil.
The squadron arrives, and Commodore Anson salutes the Portuguese Governor with eleven guns.
Ships from left to right: *Anna* pink, *Wager*, *Gloucester* or *Severn*, *Severn* or *Gloucester*, *Centurion* firing the salute, *Pearl*, *Tryall*.
This engraving is after a drawing by Lieutenant Peircy Brett of the *Centurion*.

---

3. The best bower anchor would have been stowed in the vicinity of the foremast, but it is not clear why cutting it away would have relieved the situation.

A View of Streights LE MAIRE between TERRA DEL FUEGO and STATEN LAND.

7ᵗʰ *March 1741.*

The Squadron approaches the infamous Straits le Maire between Staten Island and Tierra del Fuego. Wager is on the left. Soon afterwards in worsening weather she nearly went aground on Staten Island. See chart on p47.

Anson's *Voyage* says: "We passed those memorable Streights, ignorant of the dreadful calamities which were then impending, and just ready to break upon us; ignorant that the time drew near, when the squadron would be separated never to unite again, and that this day of our passage was the last chearful day that the greatest part of us would ever live to enjoy."

After a drawing by Lieutenant Piercy Brett of the *Centurion*.

HMS *Wager* (centre) proceeds to her anchor berth off Cape Virgin Mary at the northern entrance to the Magellan Straits. On the left is *Centurion*; on the right probably *Pearl*. The sketch is by the First Lieutenant of *Centurion*, Lieutenant Peircy Brett. This was the last spell of fair weather the Squadron would enjoy for a long, miserable time, and for the *Wager* this was the last time in company.

Anson's route, adapted from his *A Voyage Round the World*, 1748.

for observation, and there are no charts of that part of the coast. When those officers who first perceived their mistake endeavoured to persuade the Captain to alter his course, and bear away for the greater surety to the westward, he persisted in making directly, as he thought, for the island of Socorro;[4] and to such as dared from time to time to deliver their doubts of being entangled with the land stretching to the eastward, he replied

4. See map p161.

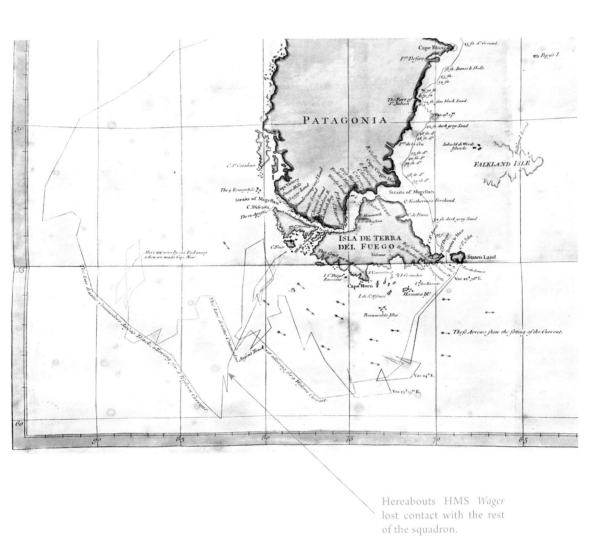

Hereabouts HMS *Wager* lost contact with the rest of the squadron.

This chart shows the difficulty of navigating round the Horn with no accurate means of determining longitude, scanty knowledge of a very strong current, and rudimentary charts. The dotted line shows Anson's estimated track; the solid line his actual track.

Note Pepys Island north of the Falkland Islands. Twenty-seven years later Byron, by then a Commodore, was sent out to find it, and was able to report that it did not exist.

that he thought himself in no case at liberty to deviate from his orders; and that the absence of his ship from the first place of rendezvous would entirely frustrate the whole squadron in the first object of their attack, and possibly decide upon the fortune of the whole expedition. For the better understanding the force of his reasoning, it is necessary to explain that the island of Socorro[5] is in the neighbourhood of Valdivia, the capture of which place could not be effected without the junction of that ship which carried the ordnance and military stores.

The knowledge of the great importance of giving so early and unexpected a blow to the Spaniards determined the Captain to make the shortest way to the point in view; and that rigid adherence to orders from which he thought himself in no case at liberty to depart, begot in him a stubborn defiance of all difficulties, and took away from him those apprehensions which so justly alarmed all such as, from ignorance of the orders, had nothing present to their minds but the dangers of a lee-shore.

We had for some time been sensible of our approach to the land, from no other tokens than those of weeds and birds, which are the usual indication of nearing the coast; but at length we had an imperfect view of an eminence, which we conjectured to be one of the mountains of the Cordilleras. This, however, was not so distinctly seen but that many conceived it to be the effect of imagination. But if the Captain was persuaded of the nearness of our danger it was now too late to remedy it; for at this time the straps of the fore jeer blocks breaking, the fore-yard came down; and the greatest part of the men being disabled through fatigue and sickness, it was some time before it could be got up again. The few hands who were employed in this business now plainly saw the land on the larboard beam bearing NW upon which the ship was driving bodily.[6]

---

5. Now Guamblin.

6. Byron is here slightly confusing. The ship would not be driving bodily on to the land they saw to the NW, which was Cabo Tres Montes, since the wind was W to WNW. But they were certainly embayed in a damaged ship, and the danger would have been obvious to all.

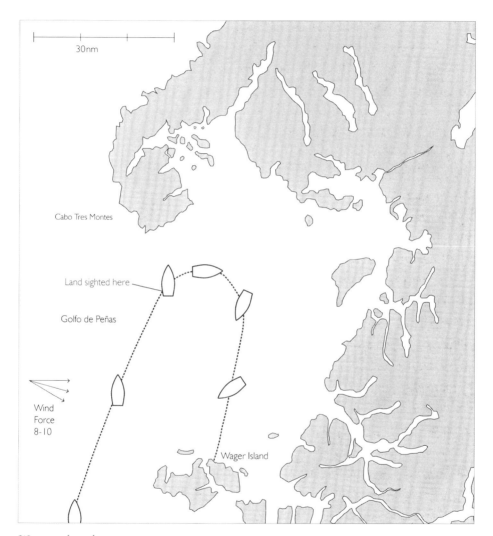

30nm

Cabo Tres Montes

Land sighted here

Golfo de Peñas

Wind
Force
8-10

Wager Island

Wager embayed.
This is the track of the ship estimated from survivors' reports. She tried desperately to claw off a lee-shore in a hurricane-force gale and escape from a perilous situation. The operation of wearing ship took three hours.

Orders were then given immediately by the Captain to sway the foreyard up, and set the foresail; which done, we wore ship[7] with her head to the southward, and endeavoured to crowd her off from the land. But the weather, from being exceedingly tempestuous blowing now a perfect hurricane and right in upon the shore, rendered our endeavours (for we were now only twelve hands fit for duty) entirely fruitless. The night came on, dreadful beyond description, in which, attempting to throw out our topsails to claw off the shore, they were immediately blown from the yards.

In the morning, about four o'clock, the ship struck. The shock we received upon this occasion, though very great, being not unlike a blow of a heavy sea, such as in the series of preceding storms we had often experienced, was taken for the same; but we were soon undeceived by her striking again more violently than before, which laid her upon her beam-ends, the sea making a fair breach over her. Every person that now could stir was presently upon the quarter-deck; and many even of those were alert upon this occasion that had not showed their faces upon deck for above two months before. Several poor wretches, who were in the last stage of the scurvy,[8] and who could not get out of their hammocks, were immediately drowned.

In this dreadful situation she lay for some little time, every soul on board looking upon the present minute as his last; for there was nothing to be seen but breakers all around us. However, a mountainous sea hove her off from thence; but she presently struck again and broke her tiller. In this terrifying and critical juncture, to have observed all the various modes of horror operating according to the several characters and complexions amongst us, it was necessary that the observer himself should have been free from all impressions of danger. Instances there

---

7. That is, turned away from the wind to put the wind through the stern and on to the other tack. It would have been difficult to do this without some sort of foresail.
8. Scurvy, the dreaded scourge of seamen of this era, is caused by lack of vitamin C. Symptoms are general debility of the body, extreme tenderness of the gums, foul breath, black eruptions on the skin, and severe pains in the limbs.

HMS Wager *in extremis, 13ᵗʰ May 1741.*
She lost her mizzen some weeks ago when rounding the Horn. Her foreyard and foretop came down last night, incapacitating the Captain in the process. She is now embayed in a hurricane-force wind and a vicious sea on a hostile coast – a seaman's worst nightmare. Painted by Charles Brooking, one of Britain's finest marine artists, probably about 1744, with information based on Bulkeley's published journal.

were, however, of behaviour so very remarkable, they could not escape the notice of any one who was not entirely bereaved of his senses; for some were in this condition to all intents and purposes, particularly one, in the ravings despair brought upon him, who was seen stalking about the deck, flourishing a cutlass over his head, and calling himself king of the country, and striking every body he came near, till his companions, seeing no other security against his tyranny, knocked him down. Some, reduced before by long sickness and the scurvy, became on this occasion as it were petrified and bereaved of all sense, like inanimate logs, and were bandied to and fro by the jerks and rolls of the ship, without exerting any efforts to help themselves.

So terrible was the scene of foaming breakers around us, that one of the bravest men we had could not help expressing his dismay at it, saying it was too shocking a sight to bear! And he would have thrown himself over the rails of the quarter-deck into the sea had he not been prevented. But at the same time there were not wanting those who preserved a presence of mind truly heroic. The man at the helm, though both rudder and tiller were gone, kept his station; and being asked by one of the officers if the ship would steer or not, first took his time to make trial by the wheel, and then answered with as much respect and coolness as if the ship had been in the greatest safety; and immediately after applied himself with his usual serenity to his duty, persuaded it did not become him to desert it as long as the ship kept together.

Mr Jones, Mate, who now survives not only this wreck, but that of the *Litchfield* man-of-war upon the coast of Barbary,[9] at the time when the ship was in the most imminent danger not only showed himself undaunted, but endeavoured to inspire the same resolution in the men, saying, "My friends, let us not be discouraged: did you never see a ship amongst breakers before? Let us endeavour to push her through them. Come, lend

---

9. Morocco or Algeria.

a hand; here is a sheet, and here is a brace;[10] lay hold; I don't doubt but we may stick her yet near enough to the land to save our lives." This had so good an effect that many who before were half dead seemed active again, and now went to work in earnest. This Mr Jones did purely to keep up the spirits of the people as long as possible; for he often said afterwards, he thought there was not the least chance of a single man's being saved.

We now ran in between an opening of the breakers, steering by the sheets and braces, when providentially we stuck fast between two great rocks; that to windward sheltering us in some measure from the violence of the sea. We immediately cut away the main and foremast, but the ship kept beating in such a manner that we imagined she could hold together but a very little while.

The day now broke, and the weather, that had been extremely thick, cleared away for a few moments and gave us a glimpse of the land not far from us. We now thought of nothing but saving our lives. To get the boats out, as our masts were gone, was a work of some time; which when accomplished, many were ready to jump into the first, by which means they narrowly escaped perishing before they reached the shore. I now went to Captain Cheap (who had the misfortune to dislocate his shoulder by a fall the day before, as he was going forward to get the foreyard swayed up) and asked him if he would not go on shore; but he told me, as he had done before, that he would be the last to leave the ship, and he ordered me to assist in getting the men out as soon as possible. I had been with him very often from the time the ship first struck, as he desired I would, to acquaint him with every thing that passed; and I particularly remarked that he gave his orders at that time with as much coolness as ever he had done during the former part of the voyage.

The scene was now greatly changed; for many who but a few minutes before had shown the strongest signs of despair, and were on their knees praying for mercy, imagining they were now not in that immediate danger

---

10. Sheets and braces control the set of the sails.

The wreck of HMS Wager, by Charles Brooking (1723-1759).

grew very riotous, broke open every chest and box that was at hand, stove in the heads of casks of brandy and wine, as they were borne up to the hatch-ways, and got so drunk that some of them were drowned on board, and lay floating about the decks for some days after.

Before I left the ship, I went down to my chest, which was at the bulkhead of the wardroom, in order to save some little matters if possible; but whilst I was there the ship thumped with such violence, and the water came in so fast, that I was forced to get upon the quarter-deck again, without saving a single rag but what was upon my back. The Boatswain, and some of the people, would not leave the ship so long as there was any liquor to be got at; upon which Captain Cheap suffered himself to be helped out of his bed, put into the boat, and carried on shore.

It is natural to think that, to men thus upon the point of perishing by shipwreck, the getting to land was the highest attainment of their wishes. Undoubtedly it was a desirable event; yet, all things considered, our condition was but little mended by the change. Whichever way we looked a scene of horror presented itself. On one side the wreck (in which was all we had in the world to support and subsist us), together with a boisterous sea, presented us with the most dreary prospect; on the other, the land did not wear a much more favourable appearance: desolate and barren, without sign of culture, we could hope to receive little other benefit from it than the preservation it afforded us from the sea. It must be confessed this was a great and merciful deliverance from immediate destruction; but then we had wet, cold, and hunger to struggle with, and no visible remedy against any of these evils.

Exerting ourselves, however, though faint, benumbed, and almost helpless, to find some wretched covert against the extreme inclemency of the weather, we discovered an Indian hut at a small distance from the beach within a wood, in which as many as possible without distinction crowded themselves, the night coming on exceedingly tempestuous and rainy. But here our situation was such as to exclude all rest and refreshment by sleep from most of us; for besides that we pressed upon one another extremely,

The original frontispiece of Byron's Narrative.
This is a fairly imaginative artist's impression of Cheap's Bay just after the shipwreck, with the
Wager breaking up in the background – but it is to be feared that the scene was not as orderly as this.

we were not without our alarms and apprehensions of being attacked by the Indians, from a discovery we made of some of their lances and other arms in our hut; and our uncertainty of their strength and disposition gave alarm to our imagination, and kept us in continual anxiety.

In this miserable hovel one of our company, a Lieutenant of Invalids, died this night; and of those who for want of room took shelter under a great tree, which stood them in very little stead, two more perished by the severity of that cold and rainy night.

In the morning the calls of hunger, which had been hitherto suppressed by our attention to more immediate dangers and difficulties, were now become too importunate to be resisted. We had most of us fasted eight and forty hours, some more; it was time, therefore, to make inquiry among ourselves what store of sustenance had been brought from the wreck by the providence of some, and what could be procured on the island by the industry of others. But the produce of the one amounted to no more than two or three pounds of biscuit dust reserved in a bag, and all the success of those who ventured abroad, the weather being still exceedingly bad, was to kill one seagull and pick some wild celery.[11] These, therefore, were immediately put into a pot with the addition of a large quantity of water, and made into a kind of soup, of which each partook as far as it would go; but we had no sooner thrown this down than we were seized with the most painful sickness at our stomachs, violent retchings, swoonings, and other symptoms of being poisoned. This was imputed to various causes, but in general to the herbs we made use of, in the nature and quality of which we fancied ourselves mistaken. But a little further inquiry let us into the real occasion of it, which was no other than this: the biscuit dust was the sweepings of the bread room, but the bag in which they were put had been a tobacco bag, the contents of which not being entirely taken out, what remained mixed with the biscuit dust, and proved a strong emetic.

---

11. However distasteful, the wild celery seems to have cured many who had been suffering from scurvy.

We were in all about a hundred and forty who had got to shore; but some few remained still on board, detained either by drunkenness or a view of pillaging the wreck, among which was the Boatswain. These were visited by an officer in the yawl, who was to endeavour to prevail upon them to join the rest; but finding them in the greatest disorder, and disposed to mutiny, he was obliged to desist from his purpose, and return without them.

Though we were very desirous, and our necessities required, that we should take some survey of the land we were upon, yet being strongly prepossessed that the savages were retired but some little distance from us, and waited to see us divided, our parties did not make this day any great excursions from the hut; but as far as we went, we found it very morassy and unpromising. The spot which we occupied was a bay formed by hilly promontories; that to the south so exceeding steep, that in order to ascend it (for there was no going round, the bottom being washed by the sea) we were at the labour of cutting steps. This, which we called Mount Misery, was of use to us in taking some observations afterwards, when the weather would permit; the other promontory was not so inaccessible. Beyond this I with some others, having reached another bay, found driven ashore some parts of the wreck, but no kind of provision, nor did we meet with any shellfish, which we were chiefly in search of. We therefore returned to the rest, and for that day made no other repast than what the wild celery afforded us.

Loss of the Wager, Man of War, on Wager Island, near Mount Misery.

This dramatic engraving comes from "*Loss of the* Wager *Man of War, one of Commodore Anson's Squadron... and the Embarrassments of the Crew, Separation, Mutinous Disposition, Narrow Escapes, Imprisonment and other Distresses.*" It was published in 1809, showing that even 60 years after the event interest in the story was still alive.

Chapter 4

THE CAPTAIN SHOOTS AN OFFICER

Wager Island, 15ᵗʰ April 1741. Shortage of food (but not liquor) makes the men turbulent, undisciplined and almost ungovernable. Some Indians appear in canoes and a little food is bartered for, but pilfering of stores is difficult to prevent. Eight men desert and are never heard of again. Midshipman Cozens becomes drunk and insubordinate, and the Captain shoots him as a mutineer, greatly increasing resentment and ill-will.

From Midshipman Byron's narrative.

The ensuing night proved exceedingly tempestuous; and the sea running very high threatened those on board with immediate destruction by the parting of the wreck. They then were as solicitous to get ashore, as they were before obstinate in refusing the assistance we sent them; and when they found the boat did not come to their relief at the instant they expected it, without considering how impracticable a thing it was to send it them in such a sea, they fired one of the quarter-deck guns at the hut, the ball of which did but just pass over the covering of it, and was plainly heard by the Captain and us who were within. Another attempt, therefore, was made to bring these madmen to land; which, however, by the violence of the sea, and other impediments occasioned by the mast that lay alongside, proved ineffectual.

This unavoidable delay made the people on board outrageous; they fell to beating everything to pieces that fell in the way; and, carrying their intemperance to the greatest excess, broke open chests and cabins for plunder that could be of no use to them. And so earnest were they in this wantonness of theft that one man had evidently been murdered on account of some division of the spoil, or for the sake of the share that fell to him, having all the marks of a strangled corpse. One thing in this outrage they seemed particularly attentive to was to provide themselves with arms and ammunition, in order to support them in putting their mutinous designs in execution, and asserting their claim to a lawless exemption from the authority of their officers, which they pretended must cease with the loss of the ship. But of these arms, which we stood in great need of, they were soon bereaved upon coming ashore, by the resolution of Captain Cheap and Lieutenant Hamilton of the marines.

Among these mutineers who had been left on board, as I observed before, was the Boatswain, who instead of exerting the authority he had over the rest, to keep them within bounds as much as possible, was himself a ringleader in their riot. Him, without respect to the figure he then made (for he was in laced clothes[1]), Captain Cheap, by a blow well laid on with his cane, felled to the ground. It was scarce possible to refrain from laughter at the whimsical appearance these fellows made, who, having rifled the chests of the officers' best suits, had put them on over their greasy trousers and dirty checked shirts. They were soon stripped of their finery, as they had before been obliged to resign their arms.

The incessant rains and exceeding cold weather in this climate rendered it impossible for us to subsist long without shelter; and the hut being much too little to receive us all, it was necessary to fall upon some expedient without delay which might serve our purpose. Accordingly the Gunner, the Carpenter, and some more, turning the cutter keel upwards, and fixing it upon props, made no despicable habitation.

---

1. Expensive clothes with lace and ruffles stolen from the officers' chests.

Having thus established some sort of settlement, we had the more leisure to look about us, and to make our researches with greater accuracy than we had before after such supplies as the most desolate coasts are seldom unfurnished with. Accordingly we soon provided ourselves with some sea-fowl, and found limpets, mussels, and other shellfish in tolerable abundance; but this rummaging of the shore was now becoming exceedingly irksome to those who had any feeling, by the bodies of our drowned people thrown among the rocks, some of which were hideous spectacles from the mangled condition they were in by the violent surf that drove in upon the coast. These horrors were overcome by the distresses of our people, who were even glad of the occasion of killing the gallinazo[2] (the carrion crow of that country) while preying on these carcasses, in order to make a meal of them. But a provision by no means proportional to the number of mouths to be fed could, by our utmost industry, be acquired from that part of the island we had hitherto traversed. Therefore till we were in a capacity of making more distant excursions, the wreck was to be applied to as often as possible for such supplies as could be got out of her.

But this was a very precarious fund in its present situation, and at best could not last us long, considering too that it was very uncertain how long we might be detained upon this island. The stores and provision we were so fortunate as to retrieve were not only to be dealt out with the most frugal economy, but a sufficient quantity if possible laid by to fit us out, whenever we could agree upon any method of transporting ourselves from this dreary spot. The difficulties we had to encounter in these visits to the wreck cannot be easily described; for no part of it being above water except the quarterdeck and part of the forecastle, we were usually obliged to purchase such things as were within reach by large hooks fastened to poles, in which business we were much incommoded by the dead bodies floating between decks.

In order to secure what we thus got in a manner to answer the ends

---

2. Turkey vulture.

and purposes above-mentioned, Captain Cheap ordered a store-tent to be erected near his hut as a repository, from which nothing was to be dealt out but in the measure and proportion agreed upon by the officers. And though it was very hard upon us petty officers,[3] who were fatigued with hunting all day in quest of food, to defend this tent from invasion by night, no other means could be devised for this purpose so effectual as the committing this charge to our care; and we were accordingly ordered to divide the task equally between us. Yet, notwithstanding our utmost vigilance and care, frequent robberies were committed upon our trust, the tent being accessible in more than one place. And one night when I had the watch, hearing a stir within, I came unawares upon the thief, and presenting a pistol to his breast obliged him to submit to be tied up to a post, till I had an opportunity of securing him more effectually.

Depredations continued to be made on our reserved stock, notwithstanding the great hazard attending such attempts; for our common safety made it necessary to punish them with the utmost rigour. This will not be wondered at when it is known how little the allowance which might consistently be dispensed from thence, was proportional to our common exigencies; so that our daily and nightly task of roving after food, was not in the least relaxed thereby; and all put together was so far from answering our necessities that many at this time perished with hunger. A boy, when no other eatables could be found, having picked up the liver of one of the drowned men (whose carcass had been torn to pieces by the force with which the sea drove it among the rocks) was with much difficulty withheld from making a meal of it. The men were so assiduous in their research after the few things which drove from the wreck, that in order to have no sharers of their good fortune, they examined the shore no less by night than by day; so that many of those who were less alert, or not so fortunate as their neighbours, perished with hunger or were driven to the last extremity.

---

3. Midshipmen were then classed as petty officers, and were subordinate to commissioned officers (e g. the Lieutenant), and also to warrant officers (e.g. the Gunner, Carpenter, Boatswain, and Purser).

It must be observed that on the 14th of May we were cast away, and it was not till the 25th of this month, that provision was served regularly from the store tent.

The land we were now settled upon was about 90 leagues[4] to the northward of the western mouth of the Straits of Magellan, in the latitude of between 47 and 48 degrees south, from whence we could plainly see the Cordilleras; and by two lagoons on the north and south of us, stretching towards those mountains, we conjectured it was an island. But as yet we had no means of informing ourselves perfectly whether it was an island or the main; for besides that the inland parts at little distance from us seemed impracticable, from the exceeding great thickness of the wood, we had hitherto been in such confusion and want (each finding full employment for his time in scraping together a wretched subsistence, and providing shelter against the cold and rain) that no party could be formed to go upon discoveries. The climate and season too were utterly unfavourable to adventures, and the coast as far as our eye could stretch seaward a scene of such dismal breakers as would discourage the most daring from making attempts in small boats. Nor were we assisted in our inquiries by any observation that could be made from that eminence we called Mount Misery toward land, our prospect that way being intercepted by still higher hills and lofty woods. We had therefore no other expedient by means of which to come at this knowledge but by fitting out one of our ship's boats[5] upon some discovery, to inform us of our situation. Our long-boat was still on board the wreck; therefore a number of hands were now dispatched to cut the gunwale[6] of the ship in order to get her out.

Whilst we were employed in this business there appeared three canoes of Indians paddling towards us; they had come round the point from the southern lagoons. It was some time before we could prevail upon them to lay aside their fears and approach us, which at length they were induced

4. A league is three nautical miles, or nearly three and a half land miles.
5. For a description of *Wager's* boats, see Appendix A.
6. The top edge of the ship's side.

to do by the signs of friendship we made them, and by showing some bale goods,[7] which they accepted, and suffered themselves to be conducted to the Captain, who made them likewise some presents. They were strangely affected with the novelty thereof, but chiefly when shown the looking-glass, in which the beholder could not conceive it to be his own face that was represented, but that of some other behind it, which he therefore went round to the back of the glass to find out.

These people were of a small stature, very swarthy, having long, black, coarse hair hanging over their faces. It was evident from their great surprise and every part of their behaviour, as well as their not having one thing in their possession which could be derived from white people, that they had never seen such. Their clothing was nothing but a bit of some beast's skin about their waists, and something woven from feathers over the shoulders; and as they uttered no word of any language we had ever heard, nor had any method of making themselves understood, we presumed they could have had no intercourse with Europeans.

These savages, who upon their departure left us a few mussels, returned in two days and surprised us by bringing three sheep. From whence they could procure these animals in a part of the world so distant from any Spanish settlement, cut off from all communication with the Spaniards by an inaccessible coast and unprofitable country, is difficult to conceive. Certain it is that we saw no such creatures, nor ever heard of any such, from the Straits of Magellan, till we got into the neighbourhood of Chiloé. It must be by some strange accident that these creatures came into their possession, but what that was we never could learn from them. At this interview we bartered with them for a dog or two, which we roasted and ate. In a few days after they made us another visit, and bringing their wives with them, took up their abode with us for some days, then again left us.

Whenever the weather permitted, which was now grown something drier but exceeding cold, we employed ourselves about the wreck, from

7. Merchandise, probably cloth, done up in bales.

which we had at sundry times recovered several articles of provision and liquor. These were deposited in the store tent.

Ill-humour and discontent, from the difficulties we laboured under in procuring subsistence, and the little prospect there was of any amendment in our condition, were now breaking out apace. In some it showed itself by a separation of settlement and habitation; in others, by a resolution of leaving the Captain entirely, and making a wild journey by themselves, without determining upon any plan whatever. For my own part, seeing it was the fashion, and liking none of their parties, I built a little hut just big enough for myself and a poor Indian dog I found in the woods, who could shift for himself along shore at low water by getting limpets. This creature grew so fond of me and faithful that he would suffer nobody to come near the hut without biting them.

Besides those seceders I mentioned, some laid a scheme of deserting us entirely; these were in number ten, the greatest part of them a most desperate and abandoned crew, who, to strike a notable stroke before they went off, placed half a barrel of gunpowder close to the Captain's hut, laid a train to it, and were just preparing to perpetrate their wicked design of blowing up their commander, when they were with difficulty dissuaded from it by one who had some bowels and remorse of conscience left in him. These wretches, after rambling some time in the woods and finding it impracticable to get off, for they were then convinced that we were not upon the mainland as they had imagined when they first left us, but upon an island within four or five leagues of it, returned and settled about a league from us. However they were still determined, as soon as they could procure craft fit for their purpose, to get to the main. But before they could effect this we found means to prevail upon the Armourer and one of the carpenter's crew, two very useful men to us, who had imprudently joined them, to come over again to their duty. The rest (one or two excepted) having built a punt, and converted the hull of one of the ship's masts into a canoe, went away up one of the lagoons and never were heard of more.

These being a desperate and factious set did not distress us much by their departure, but rather added to our future security. One in particular, James Mitchell by name, we had all the reason in the world to think had committed no less than two murders since the loss of our ship, one on the person found strangled on board, another on the body of a man whom we discovered among some bushes upon Mount Misery, stabbed in several places and shockingly mangled.

This diminution of our number was succeeded by an unfavourable accident much more affecting in its consequences: I mean the death of Mr Cozens, midshipman; in relating which, with the necessary impartiality and exactness, I think myself obliged to be more than ordinarily particular. Having one day among other things got a cask of pease out of the wreck, about which I was almost constantly employed, I brought it to shore in the yawl, when the Captain came down upon the beach and bid me to go up to some of the tents, and order hands to come down and roll it up; but finding none except Mr Cozens, I delivered him the orders, who immediately came down to the Captain, where I left them when I returned to the wreck. Upon my coming on shore again I found that Mr Cozens was put under confinement by the Captain for being drunk and giving him abusive language; however, he was soon after released. A day or two after, he had some dispute with the Surgeon, and came to blows. All these things incensed the Captain greatly against him. I believe this unfortunate man was kept warm with liquor, and set on by some ill-designed persons: for when sober I never knew a better natured man, or more inoffensive.

Some little time after, at the hour of serving provisions, Mr Cozens was at the store-tent; and having, it seems, lately had a quarrel with the Purser, and now some words arising between them, the latter told him he was come to mutiny; and without any further ceremony fired a pistol at his head, which narrowly missed him. The Captain, hearing the report of the pistol, and perhaps the Purser's words that Cozens was come to mutiny, ran out of his hut with a cocked pistol, and without asking any questions immediately shot him through the head. I was at this time in my hut, as the weather was extremely bad; but running out upon the alarm of this firing the first thing I saw was Mr Cozens on the ground weltering in his blood. He was sensible, and took me by the hand, as he did several others, shaking his head as if he meant to take leave of us.

A Representation of Cap.ᵗ Cheap, commander of the Wager, shooting M.ʳ Cozens his Midshipman; with the Crew building their Boat after the Ship was Cast away on a desolate Island on the Coast of PATAGONIA.

A critical moment.
This engraving of Captain Cheap shooting Midshipman Cozens comes from *A Voyage to the South Seas*, 1745, one of several anonymous accounts that were published before the authorised one came out in 1748. Cozens lingered on for 14 days before he died, with the ship's company becoming increasingly mutinous.

If Mr Cozens' behaviour to the Captain was indecent and provoking, the Captain's on the other hand was rash and hasty. If the first was wanting in that respect and observance which is due from a petty officer to his commander, the latter was still more inadvised in the method he took for the enforcement of his authority, of which indeed he was jealous to the last degree, and which he saw daily declining and ready to be trampled upon. His mistaken apprehension of a mutinous design in Mr Cozens, the sole motive of his rash action, was so far from answering the end he proposed by it, that the men, who before were much dissatisfied and uneasy, were by this unfortunate step thrown almost into open sedition and revolt. It was evident that the people, who ran out of their tents alarmed by the report of fire-arms, though they disguised their real sentiments for the present, were extremely affected with this catastrophe of Mr Cozens, for he was greatly beloved by them. Their minds were now exasperated, and it was to be apprehended that their resentment, which was smothered for the present, would shortly show itself in some desperate enterprise.

The unhappy victim, who lay weltering in his blood before them, seemed to absorb their whole attention. The eyes of all were fixed upon him, and visible marks of the deepest concern appeared in the countenances of the spectators. The persuasion the Captain was under at the time he shot Mr Cozens that his intentions were mutinous, together with a jealousy of the diminution of his authority, occasioned also his behaving with less compassion and tenderness towards him afterwards than was consistent with the unhappy condition of the poor sufferer. For when it was begged as a favour by his mess-mates that Mr Cozens might be removed to their tent, though a necessary thing in his dangerous situation, yet it was not permitted; but the poor wretch was suffered to languish on the ground some days, with no other covering than a bit of canvas thrown over some bushes, where he died.

"I even proceeded to extremities," the Captain had said. His action in shooting Mr Cozens was so controversial, and had such a disastrous effect on subsequent events, that it is worth scrutinising other versions of it. There are three of them, but the one that seems closest to the truth is that of the only eye-witness to the whole affair from the beginning, John Young, the Cooper.

His account follows.

Chapter 5

THE COOPER'S VERSION

Wager Island, 10th June 1741. John Young, the Cooper, gives a detailed and level-headed account of the actions of all participants in the Cozens affair, and hints at its consequences.

FROM THE ACCOUNT OF JOHN YOUNG, COOPER

On this day a quarrel happened between the Surgeon and Cozens. The former coming on some occasion to the tent where the other lodged, words arose between them. Cozens followed the Surgeon out, still provoking him with abusive language, till at length blows ensued, when Cozens was overpowered and his hands were tied behind him, in which condition he continued some hours, but not in the least mended by it. The very next day when provisions were serving, he somehow came to hear that one of the men's allowance was stopped. This concerned him no more than it did everyone else. However, as his delight was to fish in troubled waters, he officiously ran to demand the reason of it. The Purser, knowing his restless disposition, and having been in his turn very lately embroiled with him, swore he was come to a mutiny, and without more ado fired a pistol at his head; which would probably have ended him if it had not been diverted by the Cooper's[1] striking it aside just as it went off. It were to be wished his death had then immediately happened, for it would have been less misery to himself, and attended with far less mischief to others. But it was the will of Providence that our commander should be the instrument of his unlucky fate, and thereby bring upon his own head an almost insupportable load of vexation.

In few words, the Captain and the Lieutenant of Marines, hearing in their tent the discharge of the Purser's pistol, were both of them greatly alarmed. The latter ran out with a loaded piece in his hand, and seeing Cozens with the face and gesture of a mere fury, and the Purser raging at him with the titles Rogue, Incendiary, and the like, called eagerly to the Captain repeating the Purser's accusation. The Captain having a sufficient reason to apprehend everything of this sort from the fellow, and so taking it for certain that what the Lieutenant bawled out was the real case, he snatched up a loaded pistol which lay on his table ready cocked, and stepping hastily out cried, "Where is the villain?"

The unfortunate wretch, perhaps conscious of his innocence, and moreover inspired by his native insolence, advanced with an audacious bravado almost to the Captain's nose; who, thinking he intended some violence which it was necessary to prevent, let fly the pistol that was in his hand too precipitately, and shot him in the cheek. Cozens immediately dropped to the ground, where he lay a while bleeding and speechless, but sensible. The Captain ordered some who were by to carry him to the sick tent, where the Surgeon's Mate dressed him, and probing the wound felt a ball somewhat below the right eye. The Surgeon himself refused meddling with him, which some imputed to a revengeful ill-nature because there had been just before a bickering between them. But we may as justly ascribe it to the Surgeon's prudence, who thought if the patient should die under his hands it might be suggested that he, bearing him a grudge, had injured him

1. Young's account was written anonymously and in the third person, and possibly ghosted to some extent. His identity can only be deduced later from circumstantial evidence.

or at least not done what he might to save him. Besides, as he saw nothing in the case above his Mate's ability, there seemed to be no pressing cause of his interfering.

And, to speak plainly, the Captain's aversion to the fellow was so intense that as nobody supposed he was very solicitous for his preservation, so no one who desired to be on good terms above was over-forward to administer any relief to him. This was obvious; for the Mate being about to extract the ball (as he did very skilfully) was desirous some more experienced person might be at the operation, to direct or assist should any unforeseen difficulty occur. The Surgeon having declined being at all present, that favour was requested of Dr Oakley of the land forces, who answered as if he would be there. But when the hour came he refused going because, as he said, he perceived it was not agreeable to the Captain. This was the report of the Surgeon's Mate. The Carpenter gave out also that going the next morning on some business to the Captain's tent he saw the Surgeon by the way, who asked him how that unhappy creature Cozens did. The Carpenter answered that he had not seen him that day. The Surgeon then said he would have visited him but the Captain would not give him leave.

After the extraction of the ball the wound dressed kindly, and there was a likelihood of his recovering. Hereupon he expressed an inclination of being moved to the tent where he had lodged before this mischief befell him. The Gunner and Carpenter, whose tent that was, not presuming to act in this matter without the Captain's permission, waited on him for that purpose, earnestly praying him to indulge the sick man's desire. Here was an occasion offered for discovering that humanity of temper which is supposed to be in everyone towards enemies themselves in distress, and the want of which is a disreputation to a man's character, even in the eyes of the hard-hearted. The Captain had nothing to sacrifice but his revenge in granting the request of these petitioners; and his doing so might have been considered as some atonement for the cruelty he had exercised on the wretched object, in whose behalf they interceded. But so far was he from condescending to what they most reasonably asked, that he vehemently replied, "No. The scoundrel shan't be gratified."[2] These things, being reported among the crew, and according to the usual manner in such cases much aggravated, provoked them greatly and made the Captain to be excessively hated. The people propagated the disaffection from one to another in their cabals, muttering it would be more honourable of him to dispatch the prisoner at once than force him thus to languish out his miserable hours in a doleful cold wet place, dying as it were by piecemeal.

It is to be wished this gentleman had been of a disposition a little milder and more appeasable. Severity is sometimes necessary to answer the ends of government; but he who would rule over the hearts of men, and that surely is the most absolute and lasting dominion, must by all means shun the imputation of being inexorable. We find mercy ascribed even to the Almighty in scripture, as a ground or reason for his being feared. Yet it is but fair to say that the Captain's austerity, in respect of Cozens, might not proceed from inhumanity or mere resentment (for though warm and hasty, as aforesaid, he was of a generous forgiving nature) but from an apprehension of its being fitting at that time and in those circumstances to behave with intrepid steadiness, and to bewray no symptom of irresolution or weakness.

On Wednesday the 24th instant this unfortunate contentious fellow expired, after lingering fourteen days from the time of his being wounded. His shipmates buried him with all the decent formality their situation would then admit of. There were no tears shed at the funeral, for those distil but rarely from the eyes of sailors, but several resentful speeches dropped from envenomed tongues, and the obsequies were solemnised with volleys of scandal. It was among other like things said, that though the deceased was a conceited busy fellow, and would be always meddling, that was not a sufficient reason for killing him; that he had never appeared in arms on any occasion since they came ashore; and that to shoot a man

---

2. Bulkeley's version of the Captain's refusal is even stronger: "No – I am so far from it that if he lives I will carry him a prisoner to the Commodore, and hang him." But Campbell states that he had no knowledge of this alleged inhumanity until he read it in Bulkeley's published *Journal*.

through the head on a mere surmise, without any inquisition or process of law at all, was something worse than manslaughter, and what the Captain's commission would not bear him out in.[3] And that he should find if ever they returned to England.

---

3. That is, murder, which could not be justified by the Captain's legal authority as laid down in his commission.

Chapter 6

MURMURING AND DISAFFECTION

Wager Island, 17th June 1741. The long-boat is lengthened by 12 feet. Everyone suffers desperate hunger. Mutinous schemes by disaffected men begin to emerge.

FROM MIDSHIPMAN BYRON'S NARRATIVE

Now we had saved the long-boat from the wreck and got it in our possession, there was nothing that seemed so necessary towards the advancing our delivery from this desolate place, as the new modelling this vessel so as to have room for all those who were inclined to go off in her, and to put her in a condition to bear the stormy seas we must of course encounter. We therefore hauled her up, and having placed her upon blocks sawed her in two, in order to lengthen her about twelve feet by the keel. For this purpose all those who could be spared from the more immediate task of procuring subsistence were employed in fitting and shaping timber as the Carpenter directed them. I say, in procuring subsistence, because the weather lately having been very tempestuous, the wreck working much had disgorged a great part of her contents, which were every where dispersed about the shore. We now sent frequent parties up the lagoons, which sometimes succeeded in getting some sea-fowl for us.

The Indians appearing again in the offing, we put off our yawl in order to frustrate any design they might have of going up the lagoon towards the deserters, who would have availed themselves of some of their canoes to have got upon the main. Having conducted them in, we found that their intention was to settle among us, for they had brought their wives and children with them, in all about fifty persons, who immediately set about building themselves wigwams, and seemed much reconciled to our company. Could we have entertained them as we ought, they would have been of great assistance to us, who were extremely put to it to subsist ourselves, being a hundred in number; but the men, now subject to little or no control, endeavoured to seduce their wives, which gave the Indians such offence that in a short time they found means to depart, taking every thing along with them. And we, being sensible of the cause, never expected to see them return again.

The Carpenter having made some progress in his work upon the long-boat, in which he was enabled to proceed tolerably by the tools and other articles of his business retrieved from the wreck, the men began to think of the course they should take to get home; or rather, having borrowed Sir John Narborough's[1] *Voyage* from Captain Cheap, by the application of Mr Bulkeley, which book he saw me reading one day in my tent, they immediately upon perusing it concluded upon making their voyage home by the Straits of Magellan. This plan was proposed to the Captain, who by no means approved of it, his design being to go northwards with a view of seizing a ship of the enemy's, by which means he might join the Commodore. At present, therefore, here it rested. But the men were in high spirits from the prospect they had of getting off in the long-boat, overlooking all the difficulties and hazards of a voyage almost impracticable, and caressing the Carpenter, who indeed was an excellent workman, and deserved all the encouragement they could give him.

The Indians having left us, and the weather continuing tempestuous and

---

1. Sir John Narborough's voyage was in the years 1669-71, and his account of it was published in 1694.

rainy, the distresses of the people for want of food became insupportable. Our number, which was at first 145, was now reduced to 100, and chiefly by famine, which put the rest upon all shifts and devices to support themselves. One day when I was at home in my hut with my Indian dog, a party came to my door and told me their necessities were such, that they must eat the creature or starve. Though their plea was urgent, I could not help using some arguments to endeavour to dissuade them from killing him, as his faithful services and fondness deserved it at my hands. But without weighing any arguments they took him away by force and killed him; upon which, thinking that I had at least as good a right to a share as the rest, I sat down with them and partook of their repast. Three weeks after that I was glad to make a meal of his paws and skin, which, upon recollecting the spot where they had killed him, I found thrown aside and rotten.

The pressing calls of hunger drove our men to their wits' end, and put them upon a variety of devices to satisfy it. Among the ingenious this way, one Phipps, a Boatswain's Mate, having got a water puncheon, scuttled it. Then lashing two logs, one on each side, he set out in quest of adventures in this extraordinary and original piece of embarkation. By this means he would frequently, when all the rest were starving, provide himself with wild-fowl; and it must have been very bad weather indeed which could deter him from putting out to sea when his occasions required. Sometimes he would venture far out in the offing and be absent the whole day. At last it was his misfortune, at a great distance from shore, to be overset by a heavy sea; but being near a rock, though no swimmer, he managed so as to scramble to it, and with great difficulty ascended it. There he remained two days with very little hopes of any relief, for he was too far off to be seen from shore; but fortunately a boat, having put off and gone in quest of wild-fowl that way, discovered him making such signals as he was able, and brought him back to the island. But this accident did not so discourage him, but that soon after, having procured an ox's hide, used on board for sifting powder, and called a gunner's hide, by the assistance of some hoops he formed something like a canoe, in which he made several successful voyages.

When the weather would permit us we seldom failed of getting some wild-fowl, though never in any plenty, by putting off with our boats; but this most inhospitable climate is not only deprived of the sun for the most part by a thick, rainy atmosphere, but is also visited by almost incessant tempests. It must be confessed we reaped some benefit from these hard gales and overgrown seas, which drove several things ashore; but there was no dependence on such accidental relief and we were always alert to avail ourselves of every interval of fair weather, though so little to be depended on that we were often unexpectedly, and to our peril, overtaken by a sudden change. In one of our excursions I, with two more, in a wretched punt of our own making, had no sooner landed at our station upon a high rock, than the punt was driven loose by a sudden squall; and had not one of the men, at the risk of his life, jumped into the sea and swam on board her, we must in all probability have perished; for we were more than three leagues from the island at the time.

Among the birds we generally shot was the painted goose,[2] whose plumage is variegated with the most lively colours; and a bird much larger than a goose, which we called the race-horse, from the velocity with which it moved upon the face of the water, in a sort of half flying, half running motion.[3] But we were not so successful in our endeavours by land; for though we sometimes got pretty far into the woods we met with very few birds in all our walks. We never saw but three woodcocks,[4] two of which were killed by Mr Hamilton and one by myself. These, with some humming birds, and a large kind of robin red-breast,[5] were the only feathered inhabitants of this island, excepting a small bird, with two very long feathers in his tail, which was generally seen amongst the rocks, and

2. Possibly the Upland Goose.
3. The Flightless Steamer Duck.
4. Common Snipe.
5. The Long-tailed Meadow Lark or Military Starling.

was so tame that I have had them rest upon my shoulders whilst I have been gathering shellfish.[6] Indeed we were visited by many birds of prey, some very large, but these only occasionally; and, as we imagined, allured by some dead whale in the neighbourhood which was once seen. However if we were so fortunate as to kill one of them, we thought ourselves very well off.

In one of my walks, seeing a bird of this latter kind upon an eminence, I endeavoured to come upon it unperceived with my gun, by means of the woods which lay at the back of that eminence; but when I had proceeded so far in the wood as to think I was in a line with it, I heard a growling close by me, which made me think it advisable to retire as soon as possible. The woods were so gloomy I could see nothing; but as I retired, this noise followed me close till I had got out of them. Some of our men did assure me that they had seen a very large beast in the woods, but their description of it was too imperfect to be relied upon.[7]

The wood here is chiefly of the aromatic kind: the iron wood, a wood of a very deep red hue, and another of an exceeding bright yellow. All the low spots are very swampy; but what we thought strange, upon the summits of the highest hills were found beds of shells, a foot or two thick.[8]

The long-boat being near finished, some of our company were selected to go out in the barge in order to reconnoitre the coast to the southward, which might assist us in the navigation we were going upon. This party consisted of Mr Bulkeley, Mr Jones, the Purser, myself, and ten men. The first night we put into a good harbour, a few leagues to the southward of Wager Island; where finding a large bitch big with puppies, we regaled upon them.

In this expedition we had our usual bad weather and breaking seas, which were grown to such a height the third day that we were obliged,

6. The Thorn-tailed Rayadito.

7. Possibly this was a puma, although pumas tend to be secretive and not aggressive.

8. This part of Chile suffers from frequent earthquakes, which may be the reason for piles of shells on hilltops.

through distress, to push in at the first inlet we saw at hand. This we had no sooner entered than we were presented with a view of a fine bay, in which, having secured the barge, we went ashore. But the weather being very rainy, and finding nothing to subsist upon, we pitched a bell tent, which we had brought with us, in the wood opposite to where the barge lay. As this tent was not large enough to contain us all I proposed to four of the people to go to the end of the bay, about two miles distant from the bell tent, to occupy the skeleton of an old Indian wigwam, which I had discovered in a walk that way upon our first landing. This we covered to windward with seaweed, and lighting a fire laid ourselves down in hopes of finding a remedy for our hunger in sleep. But we had not long composed ourselves before one of our company was disturbed by the blowing of some animal at his face, and upon opening his eyes was not a little astonished to see, by the glimmering of the fire, a large beast standing over him.[9] He had presence of mind enough to snatch a brand from the fire, which was now very low, and thrust it at the nose of the animal, who thereupon made off. This done, the man awoke us, and related with horror in his countenance the narrow escape he had of being devoured. But though we were under no small apprehensions of another visit from this animal, yet our fatigue and heaviness was greater than our fears; and we once more composed ourselves to rest, and slept the remainder of the night without any further disturbance.

In the morning, we were not a little anxious to know how our companions had fared; and this anxiety was increased upon tracing the footsteps of the beast in the sand in a direction towards the bell tent. The impression was deep and plain, of a large round foot well furnished with claws. Upon our acquainting the people in the tent with the circumstances of our story, we found that they too had been visited by the same unwelcome guest, which they had driven away by much the same expedient. We now returned from this cruise, with a strong gale, to Wager Island, having found

9. Possibly a Huemul, a mid-sized deer, now very rare but then numerous and extremely tame.

it impracticable to make farther discoveries in the barge on so dangerous a coast and in such heavy seas.

Here we soon discovered, by the quarters of dogs hanging up, that the Indians had brought a fresh supply to our market. Upon inquiry, we found that there had been six canoes of them, who, among other methods of taking fish, had taught their dogs to drive the fish into a corner of some pond or lake, from whence they were easily taken out by the skill and address of these savages.

The old cabal during our absence had been frequently revived, the debates of which generally ended in riot and drunkenness. This cabal was chiefly held in a large tent, which the people belonging to it had taken some pains to make snug and convenient, and lined with bales of broad cloth driven from the wreck. Eighteen of the stoutest fellows of the ship's company had possession of this tent, from whence were dispatched committees to the Captain, with the resolutions they had taken with regard to their departure; but oftener for liquor. Their determination was to go in the long-boat to the southward by the Straits of Magellan; and the point they were labouring was to prevail upon the Captain to accompany them. But though he had fixed upon a quite different plan, which was to go to the northward, yet he thought it politic at present seemingly to acquiesce with them in order to keep them quiet. When they began to stipulate with him that he should be under some restrictions in point of command, and should do nothing without consulting his officers, he insisted upon the full exercise of his authority as before. This broke all measures between them, and they were from this time determined he should go with them, whether he would or no. A better pretence they could not have for effecting this design than the unfortunate affair of Mr Cozens, which they therefore made use of for seizing his person, and putting him under confinement, in order to bring him to his trial in England.

Chapter 7

MUTINY

Wager Island, 8th October 1741. The mutiny, led by the Gunner and the Captain of Marines, breaks out into the open. Captain Cheap is arrested and left behind as the long-boat, named the Speedwell, *sails for the south.*

FROM THE JOURNAL OF JOHN BULKELEY,[1] GUNNER

We imagined, if Captain Cheap was restored to the absolute command he had before the loss of the *Wager*, that he would proceed again upon the same principles, never on any exigence consult his officers, but act arbitrarily according to his humour and confidence of superior knowledge. While he acts with reason we will support his command with our lives, but some restriction is necessary for our own preservation. We think him a gentleman worthy to have a limited command, but too dangerous a person to be trusted with an absolute one.

Today I overhauled the powder, and told the Lieutenant that I had twenty-three half barrels in store, and that we could not carry off in the long-boat above six half barrels; therefore I proposed to start the overplus

---

1. As published this journal was by John Bulkeley, Gunner and John Cummins, Carpenter, but there is good reason to think that Cummins had little to do with the writing of it. I have therefore referred to it throughout as Bulkeley's, as he frequently does himself.

into the sea, and make water-casks of the half barrels, they being very proper for that purpose. I desired him to acquaint the Captain with my intention; that since he had no regard for the public good, or to anything that tended to promoting it, the Carpenter and I had determined never to go near him again. The Lieutenant declined going, fearing the Captain would murder him; but he sent the Master to him, to let him know the necessity of starting the powder. The Captain's answer to the Master was, I desire you will not destroy any one thing without my orders.

We now are convinced the Captain has no intention of going to the southward, notwithstanding he had lately given his word and honour that he would; therefore Captain Pemberton,[2] in order to put an end to all future obstructions, demanded our assistance to make him a prisoner for the shooting of Mr Cozens, intending to carry him as such to England; at the same time to confine Lieutenant Hamilton with him; which was readily agreed to by the whole body. It was reckoned dangerous to suffer the Captain any longer to enjoy liberty; therefore the Lieutenant, Gunner, Carpenter, and Mr Jones the Mate, resolved next morning to surprise him in his bed.

Friday the 9th, this morning went in a body and surprised the Captain in bed, disarmed him, and took every thing out of his tent. The Captain said to the seamen, what are you about? Where are my officers? At which the Master, Gunner, Carpenter and Boatswain went in. The Captain said, gentlemen, do you know what you have done, or are about? He was answered, yes, sir; our assistance was demanded by Captain Pemberton, to secure you as a prisoner for the death of Mr Cozens; and as we are subjects of Great Britain, we are obliged to take you as such to England. The Captain said, gentlemen, Captain Pemberton has nothing to do with me; I am your commander still; I will show you my instructions; which he did to the people. On this we came out. He then called his officers a second

---

2. The Captain of Marines, who were at this stage under the jurisdiction of the War Office, not the Admiralty.

time and said, what is this for? He was answered, as before, that assistance was demanded by Captain Pemberton to take him prisoner for the death of Mr Cozens. He still insisted, Captain Pemberton has no business with me; I could not think you would serve me so. It was told him, sir, it is your own fault; you have given yourself no manner of concern for the public good, on our going from hence; but have acted quite the reverse, or else been so careless and indifferent about it, as if we had no commander; and if other persons had given themselves no more trouble and concern than you have, we should not be ready to go from hence as long as provisions lasted.

The Captain said, very well, gentlemen, you have caught me napping; I do not see any of you in liquor; you are a parcel of brave fellows, but my officers are scoundrels. Then turning himself to me, he said, Gunner, where's my Lieutenant? Did not he head you? I told him, no, sir; but was here to see it executed, and is here now. One of you (says the Captain) call Mr Baynes. When Mr Baynes came, he said, what is all this for, sir? Sir, it is Captain Pemberton's order. Captain Pemberton has no business with me, and you will answer for it hereafter; if I do not live to see England, I hope some of my friends will. On this the Lieutenant left him.

The Captain then addressed himself to the seamen saying, my lads, I do not blame you; but it is the villainy of my officers, which they will answer for hereafter. He then called Mr Baynes again and said, well, sir, what do you design to do by me? The Lieutenant answered, sir, your officers have designed the Purser's tent for you. Hum! I should be obliged to the gentlemen, if they would let me stay in my own tent. The Lieutenant came to acquaint the officers of the Captain's request; but they judged it inconvenient; as Mr Hamilton's tent joined the Purser's, one guard might serve them both. Accordingly all his things were moved to the Purser's tent.

As he was coming along he said, gentlemen, you must excuse my not pulling my hat off, my hands are confined. Well, *Captain* Baynes! you will be called to an account for this hereafter.

The Boatswain, after the Captain's confinement, most barbarously insulted him, reproaching him with striking him, saying, then it was your time; but now, God damn you, it is mine. The Captain made no reply but this, you are a scoundrel for using a gentleman ill when he is a prisoner.

When the Captain was a prisoner, he declared he never intended to go to the southward, having more honour than to turn his back on his enemies; and farther, he said, gentlemen, I do not want to go off in any of your craft; for I never designed to go for England, and would rather choose to be shot by you. There is not a single man on the beach dare engage me; but this is what I feared.

It is very odd, that Captain Cheap should now declare he never intended to go to the southward, when he publicly gave his word and honour he would go that way, or any way where the spirit of the people led; but he afterwards told his officers he knew he had a severe trial to go through, if ever he came to England; and as for those who lived to return to their country, the only favour he requested from them was to declare the truth, without favour or prejudice; and this we promised faithfully to do. His words in this respect were as much regarded by us as the words of a dying man, and have been most punctually observed.

Saturday the 10th, little wind at N and NW. Getting all ready for going off this afternoon, the Captain sent for the Lieutenant and me, desiring us both to go to Captain Pemberton, to know what he intended to do with him. We accordingly came, and both promised to go directly and bring him his answer. When we came out, we went to the Lieutenant's tent; from thence I expected, and made no doubt, but he would go to Captain Pemberton's: but when I asked him he refused, which very much surprised me. I thought it very ungenerous to trifle with Captain Cheap, or any gentleman in his unhappy situation; therefore I went alone to Captain Pemberton. When I delivered him Captain Cheap's message, the answer was, I design and must carry him prisoner to England.

I returned and acquainted Captain Cheap with Captain Pemberton's answer. He asked me then, if the Lieutenant was with me. I told him, no, and I believe did not design it. He said, Mr Bulkeley, I am very much obliged to you, and could not think the Lieutenant would use me thus. In the evening the Lieutenant and I were sent for again. The Captain said to the Lieutenant, sir, have you been with Captain Pemberton? He answered, no, sir. I thought, sir, you promised me you would; however, I have his answer from Mr Bulkeley. I am to be carried a prisoner to England. Gentlemen, I shall never live to see England, but die by inches in the voyage; and it is surprising to me to think what you can expect by going to the southward, where there are ten thousand difficulties to be encountered with. I am sorry so many brave fellows should be led to go where they are not acquainted, when by going to the northward there is the island of Chiloé, not above ninety leagues, where we need not fear taking prizes, and may have a chance to see the Commodore.

I made answer, sir, you have said that we shall be called to an account for this in England. I must tell you, for my part, had I been guilty of any crime and was sure of being hanged for it in England, I would make it my choice to go there sooner than to the northward; have not you given your word and honour to go to the southward? It is true there is a chance in going to the northward, by delivering us from this unhappy situation of life to a worse, viz. a Spanish prison. The Captain said no more but this, gentlemen, I wish you well and safe to England.

Sunday the 11th, this morning the Captain sent for me, and told me, he had rather be shot than carried off a prisoner, and that he would not go off with us. Therefore he desired me to ask the people to suffer him to remain on the island. The people readily agreed to his request, and also consented to leave him all things needful for his support, as much as could be spared. Lieutenant Hamilton and the Surgeon chose to stay with him. We offered him also the barge and yawl, if he could procure men to go with him. The question was proposed before the whole body; but they all cried aloud for England, and let him stay and be d—ned; does he want to carry us to a prison? There is not a man will go.

The Captain being deprived of his command in the manner above-mentioned, and for the reasons already given, it was resolved to draw some articles to be signed for the good of the community, and to give the Lieutenant a limited command. The paper was drawn up in this manner:

> Whereas Captain David Cheap, our commander in His Majesty's ship the *Wager*, never consulted any of his officers for the safety and preservation of the said ship, and His Majesty's subjects thereto belonging; but several times, since the unhappy loss of the said ship, he has been solicited in the most dutiful manner, promising him at the same time to support his command with our lives, desiring no more than to go off heart in hand from this place to the southward, which he gave his word and honour to do; and being almost ready for sailing, did apply to him some few days past, to draw up some proper articles, in order to suppress mutiny, and other material things, which we thought necessary to be agreed to before we went off; but he in the most scornful manner hath rejected everything proposed for the public good; and he is now a prisoner, and the command given to the Lieutenant…

There follow a number of rules for the coming voyage, dealing with the apportionment of food and the maintenance of discipline, which were signed by most of the men about to leave.

Tuesday 13th October. I went and took my leave of the Captain: he repeated his injunction that at my return to England I would impartially relate all proceedings. He spoke to me in the most tender and affectionate manner; and as a token of his friendship and regard for me, desired me to accept of a suit of his best wearing apparel. At parting, he gave me his hand with a great deal of cheerfulness, wishing me well and safe to

England[3]. This was the last time I ever saw the unfortunate Captain Cheap.[4] However, we hope to see him again in England, that Mr Cummins and myself may be freed from some heavy imputations to our prejudice laid on us by the gentleman who succeeded him in command, and who, having an opportunity of arriving before us in England, not only in the places he touched at abroad but at home, has blackened us with the greatest calumnies; and by an imperfect narrative has not only traduced us, but made the whole affair so dark and mystical that till the Captain's arrival the Lords of the Admiralty will not decide for or against us.

But if that unfortunate Captain never returns to his country, let us do so much justice to his character to declare that he was a gentleman possessed of many virtues; he was an excellent seaman himself, and loved a seaman; as for personal bravery, no man had a larger share of it. Even when a prisoner he preserved the dignity of a commander; no misfortunes could dispirit or deject him, and fear was a weakness he was entirely a stranger to. The loss of the ship was the loss of him; he knew how to govern while he was a commander on board; but when things were brought to confusion and disorder, he thought to establish his command ashore by his courage, and to suppress the least insult on his authority on the first occasion. An instance of this was seen on the Boatswain's first appearing ashore. Shooting Mr Cozens, and treating him in the manner he did after his confinement, was highly resented by the people, who soon got the power in their own hands, the officers only had the name, and they were often compelled, for the preservation of their lives, to comply sometimes with

---

3. The Cooper's account of this scene is somewhat different: "Just as we were going off Bulkeley would run to take a final adieu of the Captain, and give him a friendly embrace. He returned seemingly much affected with the tender reception he had found, and the melting farewell at parting. Some of the circumstances we fancied were of his own invention, as they were quite unsuitable with the gallant spirit of that haughty officer, whose genius and disposition were formed to command, but never could descend to cringe or wheedle. To hear Bulkeley's moving account you would have thought he was painting the last separation of David and Jonathan."
4. This was written before Captain Cheap had arrived home. Bulkeley did indeed meet Cheap face-to-face at the court-martial four and a half years later.

the most unreasonable demands. And it is a miracle, amidst the wildness and distraction of the people, that there was no more bloodshed.

At eleven in the forenoon the whole body of people embarked, to the number of eighty-one souls: fifty-nine on board the long-boat, on board the cutter twelve, and in the barge ten. At noon we got under sail, the wind at NW by W. The Captain, Surgeon, and Mr Hamilton being on the shore-side we gave them three cheers, which they returned.

In spite of this allegedly cheerful parting, the Gunner was extremely concerned about how his behaviour would be seen back home. Whatever the circumstances, the inescapable facts were that the Captain had been tied up and his command removed from him under the direction of his own officers and petty officers, and then abandoned on one of the most inhospitable places on earth. There was no defence to be had from the fact that the ship was a wreck. While the ship's company could perhaps claim that, because their pay ceased when a ship was lost, they were no longer subject to naval discipline, no such flimsy justification was available to an officer or a petty officer. The Gunner, a sea-lawyer if ever there was one, would be acutely aware of this. He therefore wrote a clever defence of their actions in his journal, and most of the officers signed it:

These are to certify the Right Honourable the Lords Commissioners for executing the office of Lord High Admiral of Great Britain, &c. that we, whose names are under-mentioned do beg leave to acquaint your Lordships, that Captain David Cheap, our late commander in His Majesty's ship *Wager*, having publicly declared that he will never go off this spot, at his own request desires to be left behind. But Captain Pemberton of His Majesty's land forces, having confined him a prisoner for the death of Mr Henry Cozens midshipman, with Lieutenant Hamilton for breaking his confinement, did insist on delivering them up on the beach to the charge of Lieutenant Baynes; but he, with his officers and people, consulting the ill consequences that might attend carrying two prisoners off in so small a vessel, and for so long and tedious a passage as we are likely to have, and that they might have opportunities of acting such things in secret as may prove destructive to the whole body; and also in regard to the chief article of life, as the greatest part of the people must be obliged, at every place we stop, to go on shore in search of provisions, and there being now no less than eighty-one souls in this small vessel, which we hope to be delivered in; we therefore, to prevent any difficulties to be added to the unforeseen we have to encounter with, think proper to agree, and in order to prevent murder, to comply with Captain David Cheap's request: the Surgeon also begs leave to be left with him. Dated on board the *Speedwell*[5] long-boat in Cheap's Bay, this 14th day of October, 1741.

> *(Signed)*
> *Robert Baynes,* Lieutenant
> *Thomas Clark,* Master
> *John King,* Boatswain
> *John Bulkeley,* Gunner
> *John Cummins,* Carpenter
> *Robert Elliot,* Surgeon's Mate
> *John Jones,* Master's Mate
> *John Snow,* ditto
> *Captain Pemberton,* of His Majesty's land forces
> *Vincent Oakley,* Surgeon of ditto

---

5. There is a certain irony in the choice of this name. The *Speedwell*, Captain Shelvocke, had been wrecked on the island of Juan Fernandez in 1720. Captain Shelvocke built a schooner out of her timbers, and after cruising off the coast for a while captured a Spanish ship. This is of course was what Captain Cheap had been planning to do.

Chapter 8

EXTREME HUNGER IN THE LONG-BOAT

Long-boat Speedwell, *at sea, October 1741. The company in the long-boat sets off for the Straits of Magellan. They encounter many difficulties, above all extreme hunger. Eleven men are put ashore at their request, never to be heard of again. Nine men starve to death on board.*

FROM THE ACCOUNT OF JOHN YOUNG, COOPER

For several days we encountered everything that was most terrible. The furious waves frequently threatened to overwhelm us; the rocks often menaced immediate destruction; and the prospect of that horridest tormentor, Famine, was continually before our eyes. All these impending evils were still enhanced by the indolent listless temper of some among us, who were through fatigue and despair become regardless of life, and could scarcely be moved to do anything towards even their own preservation; or by the inquietude and turbulence of others who were ready to mutiny, though they had hardly room to breathe, if their brutal demands were not instantly satisfied. Add to this, that being so closely penned up, the steams of our bodies and filthy wet apparel infected the air about us to such a degree that it was almost intolerable, and enough to cause a pestilence.

We made very little progress in our voyage for several days. Our opportunities of getting at all out to sea were but rare. We were generally in the evenings obliged to shelter in some bay or creek, where now and then the intemperateness of the weather confined us many hours beyond our inclination. And we were oftentimes delayed by the necessity of going on shore in quest of food, such as shellfish, wild fowl, and the like.

On Tuesday 3rd November 1741 the cutter was parted from us. This disagreeable incident was in great measure owing to the obstinacy of those on board her. She had the misfortune of splitting her square sail in the morning, on which we offered to take her in tow, but those in her refused it. They would in no respect follow direction or conduct themselves according to our advice. Notwithstanding this obstinacy, whereby they justly forfeited any concern of ours for their safety, yet we followed them, desiring to afford them all the succour and assistance in our power, till we thereby ran ourselves into the utmost peril. Indeed we gave not over till they disappeared. Our losing them after all this was extremely vexatious; partly through an apprehension of so many of our companions perishing, when we had undergone such pains and hazards for their preservation; and partly because our own condition was thereby rendered much worse, having nothing left us now to go ashore in, though the most urgent occasion required.

On Friday the 6th instant we got sight of the cutter again. This was an event that gave us in the *Speedwell* abundance of joy. But our pleasure, alas, was of very short duration; for having when the night came on made her fast astern of us, with only two men in her (one of which left her at 11 o'clock and came into the long-boat), about two in the morning she broke loose, having one James Stewart in her, and was soon out of our sight for ever. The poor fellow that was on board cried out to us when she loosened, and we did all we could to recover the boat and save him. But our efforts were ineffectual, so that most probably she was staved among the rocks, and he went to the bottom.

On Sunday following the people were importunate for a distribution of provisions, though it was four days before the appointed time. No representation of the unhappy effect that might attend such a proceeding could prevail with them to forbear. No sooner was this unreasonable demand satisfied (for they would be refused nothing they set on) but several of them offered another, far more surprising. That was, to be put ashore, with the allowance only of a few necessaries that we could spare them, and which would be their share in case a partition was to be now made. When some of us enquired the cause of this odd motion, those who started it answered, "that they were not without hopes of meeting with the cutter, in which, if that happened, they would go back northward. Or if they were not so fortunate as to find her, they should have means for some way of making a canoe that might serve their intention. And upon the whole, they thought they could not run a greater risk or be in a worse situation anyhow, than at present." We did all we could by arguing to divert their purpose, but they were not to be dissuaded. So, as they persisted, we hauled close on shore and landed them. They were eleven who thus left us. We furnished them with all they could in conscience ask, and they on their part signed an instrument that we drew up, certifying the Lords of the Admiralty, "that their parting from us and staying behind was absolutely their own choice, and that we had done the most which could be fairly required in their behalf."

Indeed the conduct of these folks, all things considered, was not so unaccountable as it seemed to us at first sight. Our condition in the *Speedwell* was the miserablest imaginable, as I have already described. We could scarcely breathe for want of space, and were perishing through scarcity of food. So that if their attempts failed they would hardly be accommodated worse in any situation than that wherein they left us; whereas if they succeeded anyhow in their hopes they had a probability of mending their circumstances; and who, that may be better and cannot be worse, is blameable for taking a course leading to such an issue?

Four days after this separation the Gunner and a few others went ashore in hope of getting some provisions. Here they met two of the native savages, whose sole attendant was a mangy dog. You know it is a proverb, that *hunger will break through stone walls*; no wonder then if it prevailed on Mr Bulkeley and his comrades to violate a commandment, as it did on this occasion. For they could not refrain from coveting somewhat of these poor Indians; and what think you that was, but the nasty scabby animal I have now mentioned, their faithful dog that bore them company.

In short, their eyes and their appetites were so moved with this sweet creature that they forced it, in a manner, from its owners; who did not quit their dear domestic without great reluctance, notwithstanding one of the sailors presented one of them with a pair of trousers in exchange for it. No sooner had our folks gotten it into their hands, than it was slain, dressed, and sacrificed to Comus, the god of good cheer. It was greedily devoured as a delicious feast; and it might well be relished, when it was accompanied with a full measure of the very best sauce – as hunger is accounted.

But I must give these adventurers due praise. They were not satisfied with regaling themselves only in this little expedition, for they brought off shore with them an abundance of fine mussels, which were distributed among us to our great relief and pleasure.

Next morning being Friday 13th November most of us went ashore fishing. One of us killed a large seal, which we thought excellent food, though in a time of less necessity it would have been too coarse for our stomachs.

Such hits as these were but rare, and very far from affording supplies sufficiently extensive. They were neither frequent enough, nor when they happened did they answer in any competent measure the cravings of such a number. All we could anyhow get was too little to prevent several of us being famished. Hunger had by degrees got such an ascendance as obliged many to part with everything they had for the appeasing it. On Sunday the 15th a sort of traffic in this way was carried on among us: those who were in greatest distress bartering their silver buckles, or anything that would pass, for flour. This precious commodity was rated early in the day at twelve shillings the pound only, but soon rose to a guinea.

In the afternoon of the next day George Bateman, a youth of 16 years old, died, a mere skeleton, purely for want of victuals. Two days after Thomas Capel, son of the late Lieutenant Capel, aged but 12 years, underwent the same miserable fate. The guardian of this poor child was aboard, who had of his money above 20 guineas, besides a watch and a silver cup. The poor hapless creature, with prayers and tears, beseeched him to deliver up this small inheritance that he might purchase somewhat to save his life; but the vile savage told him that he must keep what he had of his in hand to buy clothes and other pretty things for him in Brazil. Alas, replied the dying victim (for he was in truth sacrificed to the cruelty and avarice of this vulture), "I shall never see Brazil. I am even now starving, starved almost to death. Therefore for Christ's sake have compassion on me and give me only the silver cup, to procure me a little food, that I may be relieved from my insufferable torture. A morsel of victuals is of more worth to me than all the apparel in the world." But his tears and solicitations to that obdurate man were in vain. Heaven only heard, and succoured him by putting a period to his breath.

Those who have never witnessed these dismal scenes can hardly imagine how anyone should be so inhuman as to see their fellow creatures languishing in the most doleful manner, and administer them no relief. But hunger is destitute of all compassion. Each man's calamity is so great that it absorbs all his pity and concern, which cannot but centre in himself. Such was our miserable case at that time, when every one of us was on the verge of this wretched orphan's condition, and so could not part with a morsel to prolong his life without the utmost danger of finishing his own. Nay, we may even believe the fellow who was possessed of his effects withheld them merely through a principle of self-preservation and as a resource for his own extreme necessities.

Beside the afore-mentioned, there perished by famine within the compass of a few days Peter Delroy, our barber; Thomas Thorpe, Thomas Woodhead, John Turner, Marines; and Sergeant Ringall.

It was remarkable of these people that some hours before they expired they became delirious. In this state they would joke, laugh immoderately, and play ridiculous pranks, as if they were really merry; in which temper they died. Those of us that survived had almost ground to envy the deceased, who were thereby freed from the horrid circumstances under which we groaned, tortured with hunger and thirst, catching at the most nauseous things that could any way appease the rage of these cruel appetites, and an abhorrence even to ourselves by reason of stench and vermin. Was not death in such a case a release or deliverance?

Chapter 9

THROUGH THE STRAITS OF MAGELLAN

Long-boat Speedwell, *at sea, 24th November 1741. They continue the voyage, trying to find the entrance to the Straits of Magellan. There are doubts about their position, and 18 days are lost as they back-track – but find they were correct. There is some trading with the Indians, but food is extremely scarce and further deaths by starvation occur. They clear the Straits at last.*

FROM THE JOURNAL OF JOHN BULKELEY, GUNNER

This morning, it being calm, rowed out; at eight o'clock had the supposed right Straits open, having a breeze at WNW, SE by E through the first reach, and SSE through the second. Then saw three islands, the largest of which lies on the north shore; and there is a passage about two miles broad between that and the islands to the southward. There is also another passage between that island and the north shore, of a mile and a half broad. Before you come to those islands there is a sound lying on the south shore. You can see no sea-passage until you come close up with the island, and then the imaginary Straits are not above two miles broad.

Steered away for the island SE about two leagues; then came into a narrow passage, not above a cable's length[1] over, which put us all to a stand, doubting of any farther passage. The wind took us ahead, and the tide being spent, we put into a small cove and made fast. At seven in the evening, being calm, cast loose, being willing to see if there was any opening; but to our great misfortune found none; which very much surprised us. The Lieutenant is of opinion that we are in a lagoon to the northward of the Straits. This I cannot believe, and am positive, if ever there was such a place in the world as the Straits of Magellan, we are now in them and above thirty leagues up.[2] If he or any of the officers had given themselves the trouble of coming upon deck to have made proper remarks,[3] we had been free from all this perplexity, and by this time out of the Straits to the northward. There is not an officer aboard, except the Carpenter and myself, who will keep the deck a moment longer than his watch, or has any regard to a reckoning or anything else. It is agreed to go back again.

Thursday the 26th, little wind; rowed out, got about five leagues down. This day we were in such want of provisions, that we were forced to cut up the seal-skin and broil it, notwithstanding it has lain about the deck for this fortnight.

Sunday 29th November. Hard gales from NW to SW with heavy rains. Great uneasiness among the people, many of them despairing of a deliverance, and crying aloud to serve provisions four days before the time. Finding no way to pacify them, we were obliged to serve them. We endeavoured to encourage and comfort them as much as lay in our power, and at length they seemed tolerably easy.

---

1. 200 yards.
2. Bulkeley has been following Sir John Narborough's Journal, which is very clear about approaching the Straits from the west: "The best landfall in my opinion, is to make the face of Cape Deseada for to come out of the South Sea to go into the Streights of Magellan; they lie in East and West at the first, till you come abreast of Cape Pillar; then the course is South East and by East nearest. Be careful to keep the South shore in fair view, for the North shore is broken islands and sounds, that a man may mistake the right Channel or Streight, and steer up into one of them, as he comes out of the South Sea, if he lose sight of the South shore."
3. Navigational observations.

Tuesday 1st December 1741. Little wind, and fair weather; which is a kind of prodigy in those parts. In the morning put out of the cove, and got four leagues down. Then the wind took us ahead, and we put into another cove, where we got mussels and limpets. At four this afternoon saw an Indian canoe coming over from the north shore; they landed two of their men to leeward of the cove; they came opposite to us and viewed us; then went back, and came with the canoe within a cable's length of our boat, but no nearer; so that we had no opportunity to truck with them.

Wednesday 2nd December. Little wind, with rain. At nine this morning rowed out, and got about a league farther down. The wind beginning to blow fresh, we put into another cove, and found plenty of shellfish, which kept up our spirits greatly; for it is enough to deject any thinking man, to see that the boat will not turn to windward; being of such length, and swimming so buoyant upon the water, that the wind, when close hauled, throws her quite to leeward. We have been seventeen days going seven or eight leagues to windward, which must make our passage very long and uncomfortable.

Friday the 4th. Little wind at S and fair. This morning rowed out; at ten got down, where we saw a smoke but no people. We saw a dog running along shore, and keeping company with the boat for above a mile. We then put in with a design to shoot him, but he soon disappointed us by taking into the woods. We put off again with a fine breeze, steering NW by W down the Straits. The Carpenter gave a guinea this day for a pound of flour, which he made into cakes and ate instantly. At six in the evening abreast of Cape Munday; at eight abreast of Cape Upright, being fair weather. Intend to keep under sail all night.

Saturday the 5th. Little wind, and fair. At four this morning I saw Cape Pillar, bearing W by N distant eight leagues; saw a smoke on the south shore, and at noon we saw a smoke on the north shore, but we did not care to lose time. At three o'clock saw Cape Deseada, bearing from Cape Pillar SW distant four leagues.

At four o'clock wore the boat, and steered ESE. The Lieutenant was now fully convinced we have been all along in the right Straits, and had we run but one league further on Monday November 17th we had escaped all this trouble and anxiety. As for my own part, I was very well assured from the first entrance that we were right, but the Lieutenant would not believe that it was Cape Pillar on the south shore coming into the Straits, but thought we were in a lagoon to the northward. So that we have been above a fortnight coming back to rectify mistakes, and to look at Cape Pillar a second time. At eight o'clock came abreast of the smoke seen in the morning. The people, being well assured that we are actually in the Straits of Magellan, are all alive. Wind at WSW.

Sunday, little wind at W with rain. At three this morning abreast of Cape Munday; at six abreast of Cape de Quad opposite to which on the south shore saw a smoke, on which we went ashore to the Indians, who came out on a point of land at the entrance of a cove, hallooing and crying, Bona! Bona! endeavouring to make us understand that they were our friends. When ashore we traded with them for two dogs, three Brent geese, and some seal, which supply was very acceptable to us. We supped on the dogs, and thought them equal in goodness to the best mutton in England. We took from the Indians a canoe, made of the bark of trees, but soon towed her under water, and were obliged to cut her loose. Steered NE by E. At eight o'clock abreast of St Jerome's Sound; at twelve, abreast of Royal Island.

Tuesday the 8th, at four this morning, being calm, weighed, and rowed towards Elizabeth's Island, it bearing WNW. At four in the afternoon anchored off the northernmost point in eight fathom water, fine sand, about half a cable's length from the shore. Put the vessel in and landed some people to seek for wood and water. In the evening the people came aboard, having been all over the island in search of wood and water, but found none. Here indeed we found shags and seagulls in great numbers, it being breeding time. We got a vast quantity of their eggs, most of them having young ones in the shell; however we beat them up all together with a little flour, and made a very rich pudding. Elizabeth's Island is a beautiful spot of ground to appearance, with very good pasture, but it is entirely barren of anything for the support of man. This day John Turner, Marine, perished for want of food.

Wednesday the 9th, at four this morning weighed, and steered ENE for the narrows, with the wind at SSW. When abreast of the Sweepstakes Foreland steered SSE on purpose to look for water. After going along shore about six leagues into a deep bay, we saw a fine delightful country. Here we saw guanacos in great numbers, ten or twelve in a drove. They are to be seen in such droves all along the shore for several leagues.

The guanaco is as large as any English deer, with a long neck, his head, mouth, and ears resembling a sheep. He has very long slender legs, and is cloven-footed like a deer, with a short bushy tail of a reddish colour. His back is covered with red wool, pretty long; but down his sides and all the belly part is white wool. Those guanacos, though at a distance very much resembling the female deer, are probably the sheep of this country; they are exceeding nimble, of an exquisite quick sight, very shy, and difficult to be shot.

At noon, finding neither wood nor water, wore to the northward. At three got abreast of the foreland, hauled in for Fish Cove, which lies just round the eastern point. Here we expected to land, and shoot some of those guanacos; but when abreast of the cove, the wind blew so hard right out, that we were obliged to bear away for the first narrows, it being impossible to get in. At eight this evening entered the first narrows, meeting the flood, which runs here very strong. At twelve came to an anchor in five fathom about a mile off shore. The tide flows on the western shore seven hours, and ebbs five. This day Robert Vicars, Marine, perished with want.

Thursday the 10th, at four this morning weighed, and came to sail. At six got out of the first narrows, hauled in for a deep bay on the N shore to seek for water. The Boatswain swam ashore, and in half an hour afterwards came down on the beach and brought us the news of finding fresh water. It being rocky ground and ebbing water, the vessel struck. We were obliged, in this exigence, to slip the cable, time not permitting us to haul up the anchor. We stood off and on the shore till half flood, then went in and took the cable on board. After landing some people with casks to fill, hauled the anchor up and went about two miles farther out.

Friday the 11th, at three this morning the boat struck upon the tide of ebb. It ebbing so fast, we could not get her off. In a quarter of an hour's time the boat was dry. We were favoured with little wind and smooth water, otherwise she must have stove to pieces, the ground being very foul. It ebbs dry above a league off, and there is shoal water a great deal further out, so that it is dangerous for a ship to haul into this bay. While the boat was dry, we got all the water-casks out of the hold, and put them ashore to be filled. At six hauled the boat off, having received no damage. At eight, it being four feet flood, ran the boat close in shore and took off our water, the whole quantity being four tons, out of which we were obliged to leave two puncheons, one quarter-cask, with three muskets, a funnel, and some other necessaries; and were very much concerned, lest we should also leave some of the people ashore. The wind blowing hard and the sea tumbling in, we were under a necessity of hauling off and putting to sea, for fear of losing the boat.

Since we left the island where the *Wager* was lost, we have several times very narrowly escaped being made a wreck, and sometimes have been preserved when we have seen our fate before our eyes, and every moment expected it, and when all the conduct and ability of men could have availed nothing. Any one, who has been a witness of those providential deliverances, and doubts the being of a supreme power, disqualifies himself from any title to all future mercy, and justly deserves the wrath of an incensed deity.

This day at noon, being well out of the bay and nigh mid-channel over, steered ENE for Cape Virgin Mary, with a fine gale at SW. At one we saw the cape bearing NE by E distant nine leagues. At seven in the evening saw a low point of flat land, stretching away from the cape SSE two leagues. At eight, little or no wind, steered E by S. At twelve at night doubled the point, the wind at W right in the middle of the bay, where we filled the water. Inland lie two peaks, exactly like asses' ears. We would advise all vessels from hauling into this bay, it being shoal water and foul ground. As for every other part of the Straits of Magellan, from Cape Victory to Cape Virgin Mary, we recommend Sir John Narborough,[4] who in his account is so just and exact that we think it is impossible for any man living to mend his works. We have been a month in those Straits, from our first sight of Cape Pillar to Cape Virgin Mary. The whole length of the Straits, the reaches and turnings included, is reckoned one hundred and sixteen leagues.

---

4. It seems possible that Bulkeley had made off with the Captain's copy of this vital book, Sir John Narborough's *Voyage*. Perhaps, to be generous, he had copied out the relevant directions, but he never states this although it would be somewhat to his credit as a prudent seaman.

Chapter 10

SURVIVORS ARRIVE AT RIO GRANDE

Long-boat Speedwell, *16th December 1741. They make the uninhabited harbour of Port Desire; seals and water are available, but little else. There is dissent and disaffection in the boat, and all are in a miserable condition. More deaths by starvation and some accidents occur; and while foraging for provisions ashore the wind and surf increase, and eight men, including Midshipman Morris, are left to their fate. Landings are made on the north side of the River Plate estuary, and some unofficial help obtained from Spaniards. Finally, after an epic voyage of 2500 miles in an open boat, they arrive at Portuguese Rio Grande, 107 days after leaving Wager Island. The 30 survivors are hospitably received by an incredulous Governor and population.*

FROM THE JOURNAL OF JOHN BULKELEY, GUNNER

We steered NW by N for the harbour of Port Desire.[1] The going into this harbour is very remarkable: on the south side lies, one mile in the land, a high peaked-up rock much like a tower, looking as though it was a work of art set up for a landmark to steer into this harbour; this rock is forty feet high. At five o'clock got into the harbour and ran up to Seal Island which

---

1. See chart p112.

lies about a league up. Here we killed more seal in half an hour than we could carry off, being obliged to leave the greatest part of what we killed behind. The people eating greedily of the seal were seized with violent fevers and pains in their heads.

While we were at Port Desire we had seal and fowl in abundance. The Carpenter found here a parcel of bricks, some of them with letters cut in them. On one of those bricks these words were very plain and legible, "Captain Straiton, 16 cannons, 1687." Those we imagine have been laid here from a wreck.[2]

The Carpenter with six men went in search of water; a mile up the water's side they found Peckett's Well, mentioned in Sir John Narborough's book. The spring is so small that it does not give above thirty gallons per day; but the well being full, supplied us.

The people grow very turbulent and uneasy, requiring flour to be served out, which in our present circumstances is a most unreasonable request. We have but one cask of flour on board, and a great distance to run to Brazil, and no other provision in the boat but the seal we have killed here. Nay, they carry their demands much higher, insisting that the marine officers, and such people as cannot be assisting in working the boat, shall have but half the allowance of the rest; accordingly they have pitched upon twenty to be served half a pound of flour each man, and themselves a pound. This distinction the half-pounders complain of, and that twenty are selected to be starved.

Monday 28th December 1741. Moderate gales, and fair. This day served out all the flour in the boat, at three pound and a half to each man. We have now nothing to live on but seal, and what Providence throws in our way.

Friday, January 1st 1742. Fresh gales, and fair weather, with a great sea. At ten last night, shifting the man at helm, brought her by the lee,[3] broke the boom, and lost a seaman overboard. The greatest part of our seal taken

---

2. Probably of a Privateer.

3. Turned down wind to spill the wind from the sail. Normally this would be an easy manoeuvre, but clearly something went disastrously wrong.

in at Port Desire, for want of salt to cure it, now stinks very much; but having nothing else we are obliged to eat it. We are now miserable beyond description, having nothing to feed on ourselves, and at the same time almost eaten up with vermin.

Wednesday 6th, departed this life Mr Thomas Harvey, the Purser; he died a skeleton for want of food. This gentleman probably was the first Purser belonging to His Majesty's service that ever perished with hunger. We see daily a great number of whales.

Sunday 10th. This day at noon, in working the bearings and distance to Cape St Andrew, do find myself not above thirteen leagues distant from the land; therefore hauled in NW to make it before night. We saw today abundance of insects, particularly butterflies and horse-stingers. We have nothing to eat but some stinking seal, and not above twenty out of the forty-three which are now alive have even that, and such has been our condition for this week past. Nor are we better off in regard to water, there not being above eighty gallons aboard. Never were beheld a parcel of more miserable objects; there are not above fifteen of us healthy (if people may be called healthy that are scarce able to crawl). I am reckoned at present one of the strongest men in the boat, yet can hardly stand on my legs ten minutes together, nor even that short space of time without holding. Every man of us has had a new coat of skin from head to foot. We that are in the best state of health do all we can to encourage the rest.

At four this afternoon we were almost transported with joy at the sight of land (having seen no land for fourteen days before) the extremes of which bore NW about seven leagues. We ran in with it, and at eight anchored in eight fathom; fine sand about a league from the shore; the northern point bore about NE, the southern point about SW by S.

Monday 11th, at four this morning weighed, and came to sail, steering along shore NE by E. This is a pleasant and delightful country to sail by; we kept within a mile of the shore. We saw horses and large dogs in great numbers, the shore being perfectly covered with them. At noon I had a good observation in the latitude of 38:40 S. At the same time saw ahead land, which I take for Cape St Andrew's; it is a long sandy point, very low, where a shoal runs off SE about three leagues. Sounded and had but two fathom and a half at high water. When we got clear of this we steered NE into a sandy bay, and anchored there in three fathom and a half, fine sand. Here is a great swell, and shoal water. This bay we call Shoalwater Bay.

Tuesday 12th. Lying in Shoalwater Bay, the wind at SE and fair weather. Having nothing on board the vessel to eat and but one cask of water to drink, we put her in as nigh as we could venture; so that any person who had the least skill in swimming might get ashore. Here runs a pretty large surf, which may endanger our vessel. This puts us to a stand: to go from hence without meat or drink is certain death. A few of the healthiest were resolved to swim on shore to get water and provisions. The officers, viz. the Boatswain, Carpenter, and Lieutenant Ewers, to animate the rest first leaped into the water; eleven of the people followed them. In this attempt one of the marines was unfortunately drowned. We tossed overboard four quarter-casks to fill with water, with ammunition for shooting.

When the officers and people got on shore they saw thousands of horses and dogs; the dogs are of a mongrel breed and very large. They also saw abundance of parrots and seals on the rocks, but not a bush growing on the place. They made a fire with horse-dung, and shot a great many seal, which they cut up in quarters to bring aboard. One of the water-casks being leaky, they cut it up and converted it into fuel to dress the seal. They caught four armadillos; they are much larger than our hedgehogs, and very like them; their bodies are cased all over with shells, shutting under one another like shells of armour. In this country thirteen of His Majesty's British subjects put to flight a thousand Spanish horse. Horses are more numerous here than sheep are on the plains in Dorset and Wiltshire.

We on board see abundance of seal lying on the shore cut up in pieces, but the wind blows so hard we can by no means get at it. We think ourselves now worse off than ever, for we are actually starving in the sight of plenty. We have but two people on board that can swim; to give them all the assistance we can, the Lieutenant and myself, with the rest of the people, proposed to haul the long-boat nearer in, and make a raft for one of the two to swim ashore on, and to carry a line to haul some of the seal aboard. With much entreaty these two swimmers were prevailed on to cast lots. The lot falling on the weakest of them, who was a young lad about fifteen years of age and scarce able to stand, we would not suffer him to go. While our brethren were regaling in the fullness of plenty ashore, we aboard were obliged to strip the hatches of a seal-skin, which has been for some time nailed on, and made use of for a tarpaulin. We burnt the hair off the skin, and for want of anything else fell to chewing the seal-skin.

Wednesday 13th, fine weather, and calm. At six this morning the Boatswain shot a horse, and the people a wild dog. The horse was branded on the left buttock with the letters AR. By this we conjecture there are inhabitants not far off. At nine veered the boat in, lashed the oars to the hatches, and made a stage to haul up the seal. The people swam off three casks of water. Sent on shore one quarter-cask more, and two breakers. Came aboard the Boatswain, Carpenter, and Lieutenant Ewers; and four men more are getting the seal and the horse on board, which was no sooner in the vessel than a sea-breeze came on, and blew so hard that we were obliged to weigh, leaving ashore one quarter-cask, two breakers, and eight of the people. The wind at ESE and a tumbling sea, came to an anchor about a league off the shore. We shared all the provisions among the company. We still see the people ashore, but can't get them off.

Thursday 14th, hard gales at ESE and fair weather. Last night the sea was so great that it broke the rudder-head off. We were doubtful every moment of the vessel's parting, which if she had we must have been all of us inevitably lost. We were obliged to put to sea, not being able to get the people off.[4] We sent ashore in a scuttled puncheon some wearing apparel, four muskets, with balls, powder, flints, candles, and several necessaries; and also a letter to acquaint them of the danger we were in, and of the impossibility of our riding it out till they could get off.

---

4. For Midshipman Morris's version of why he and seven others were abandoned, see p127.

In Freshwater Bay, dated on board the *Speedwell*, on the coast of South America, in the latitude of 37:25 S, longitude from the meridian of London, 65:00 W, this 14th day of January 1742.

These are to certify the Right Honourable the Lords Commissioners for executing the office of Lord High Admiral of Great Britain, &c. that we, whose names are under-mentioned, having nothing left on board the vessel but one quarter-cask of water, were obliged to put into the first place we could for subsistence, which was in Freshwater Bay; where we came to an anchor, as near the shore as we could without endangering the vessel, having no boat aboard and a large surf on the shore; therefore Mr King the Boatswain, Mr Cummins the Carpenter, and Lieutenant Ewers, with eleven of the people, jumped overboard, in order to swim ashore, with three casks for water; in which attempt James Greenham was drowned in the surf off the shore: the sea breeze coming on prevented the people getting on board the same night; therefore on Wednesday morning, it being then calm, they brought to the beach the casks filled with water, with seal and other provisions in great quantities, which we hauled on board. The Boatswain, Carpenter, Lieutenant Ewers, and three of the people swam off, but the sea breeze coming in, and the surf rising, the rest were discouraged from coming off; we hauled a good berth off the shore, where we lay the remainder of the day and all the night. The greatness of the sea broke off our rudder-head, and we expected every minute the vessel would founder at her anchor. Thursday morning we saw no probability of the people coming aboard; and the wind coming out of the sea, and not one stick of firewood in the vessel to dress our victuals, and it being every man's opinion that we must put to sea or perish, we got up a scuttled cask, and put into it all manner of necessaries, with four small arms lashed to the cask, and a letter to acquaint them of our danger; which cask we saw them receive, as also the letter that was in it; they then fell on their knees, and made signals wishing us well; at which we got under sail, and left our brethren, whose names are under-mentioned.

Signed by
  Robert Baynes, Lieutenant
  John Cummins, Carpenter
  John King, Boatswain
  Robert Elliot, Surgeon's Mate
  John Bulkeley, Gunner
  Thomas Clark, Master
  John Jones, Master's Mate
  John Snow, ditto
The names of the people left on shore in lat. 37:25 S, long 65:00 W.
  Guy Broadwater, born Blackwall
  John Duck   London
  Samuel Cooper   Ipswich
  Benjamin Smith   Southwark
  Joseph Clinch   ditto
  John Allen   Gosport
  John Andrews   Manchester
  Isaac Morris   Topsham

Those people had a good prospect of getting provisions, and we believe inhabitants are not far off. They have all necessaries for shooting; we hope to see them again, but at present we leave them to the care of Providence and the wide world.

Tuesday 19th January, little wind at S and clear weather. At four this morning saw breakers right ahead; sounded, and found five fathom; saw the land making like an island, bearing NE by E distant twelve leagues; steered N for about a mile or two; shoaled the water from two fathom to nine feet; then steered NNE and deepened the water to five fathom. By the appearance of the land we are well up the River Plate, and do take the breakers for the English bank. Steered and sailed all day ENE along shore; in the evening anchored in a fine sandy bay; saw two men coming down on horseback; the Boatswain swam ashore, and got up behind one of them, and rode away to their caravans. When we made the land, we had not one drop of water on board. Several people swam ashore to fill water; one of them when ashore drank very plentifully of water, and in attempting to come off was so weak that he could not reach the vessel, but was unfortunately drowned. Got one cask of water aboard, which revived us exceedingly.

Wednesday 20th, Mr Cummins and myself went ashore. Four of the inhabitants came down to us on horseback. As I could talk Portuguese, I fell into discourse with them. They told me the English were still at war with the Spaniards; that they[5] had two fifty-gun ships up the River Plate, and one sixty-gun ship cruising off Cape St Mary's; and not above six weeks ago a seventy-gun ship lying at anchor parted from her anchors and drove on shore;[6] that the ship was lost, and every man perished. They also told me they were Spaniards, Castilians, and fishermen; that they came here a-fishing; the fish they took they salted and dried, then sold them at Buenos Aires. The town they belonged to they called Montevideo, two days journey from hence.

I asked them how they came to live in the King of Portugal's land. They said there were a great many Spanish settlements on this side, and gave us an invitation to their caravan. We got up behind them, and rode about a mile to it, where they entertained us with good jerk-beef, roasted and boiled, with good white bread. We sought to buy some provision of them, but they had none but twenty-six loaves, about as big as twopenny loaves in England, which they would not part with under four guineas. We being in a weak condition, scarce able to stand on our legs, and without bread for a long time, gave them their price. Their patroon[7] told us at the same time, if it should be known that they had supplied us, they should be all hanged. He promised, if we would give him a firelock,[8] he would get us

5. The Spaniards.
6. This was the Spanish ship *Guipuscoa*, 74, of Pizarro's squadron. In fact her ship's company had mutinied and driven the ship ashore. See footnote on p153.
7. Chief.
8. Musket.

some wild fowl and as many ducks in an hour or two as would serve all
the people aboard. Mr Cummins sent for his firelock and gave it him with
some powder and slugs. On our coming away, finding one of their company
missing with a horse, we were apprehensive of his being gone to betray us;
therefore immediately went on board, got our water in, and made all ready
for sailing to the Rio Grande.

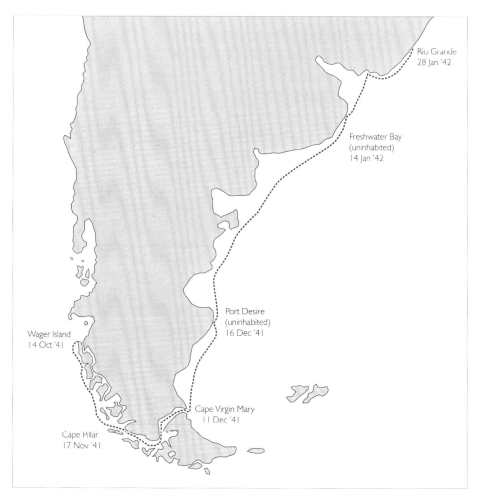

Bulkeley's epic 2500 nautical-mile voyage from Wager Island to Rio Grande in an open boat through
the world's worst seas without a chart, perhaps the greatest feat of castaway navigation of all time
(see Appendix D).

Saturday 23ʳᵈ January, little wind and calm. This day departed this life Mr Thomas Clark, the Master; as did also his son the day following.

Wednesday 27ᵗʰ January 1742, moderate gales at W. At noon had an observation, latitude in 32:40 S. I reckon myself 18 leagues from the Rio Grande, and hope to see it in the morning.

Thursday 28ᵗʰ, kept the shore close aboard, and sounded every half hour, not caring to go within three fathom, nor keep without five, sailing along by the lead all night. At six in the morning saw the opening of the River Grande; kept within the breakers of the bar, having at some times not above seven feet water at half flood; steered NE by E until the river's mouth was fairly open; then steered N and NNW until abreast of the town; anchored on the east shore in two fathom water. There presently came a boat from the shore, with a sergeant of the army and one soldier. The Lieutenant, myself, and Mr Cummins, with Captain Pemberton of the land forces, went on shore with them. The Commandant, the officers, and people of the place, received us in a most tender and friendly manner. They instantly sent on board to the people four quarters of beef, and two bags of farine bread. We were conducted to the surgeon's house, the handsomest habitation in the place, where we were most hospitably entertained.

At four in the afternoon the Governor came to town. After a strict enquiry into our misfortunes and the reasons of our coming into this port, being somewhat doubtful that we might be inspectors[9] of their coast, he began to examine me, the Lieutenant having reported me to him as pilot. He asked me if there was a chart of the coast on board, and if not how it was possible we could hit the bar, and venture into so hazardous a place as this is? I told him, as for a chart, we had none of any kind; but I had a good observation the day before, that our vessel drew but a small draught of water; that we kept the lead always going, and in the necessity we were in, we were obliged at all events to venture; and if we had not seen the opening of the river before night, we must have been compelled to run the vessel ashore.

9. Spies.

He examined me also concerning the places we stopped at, from Cape Virgin Mary to this port, and more particularly relating to the River Plate. He was very nice in his enquiry of our putting in at Cape St Mary's, and of the bearings and distance along shore from thence to this port.

When he had thoroughly satisfied himself, he embraced us and blest himself to think of our deliverance, which he termed a miracle. He offered everything the country could afford to our relief; the sick were ordered to be taken care of in the hospital;[10] he took the Lieutenant and the land officers home with him; and desired the Commandant to see that the rest of the officers and people wanted for nothing.

Before he went he informed us, that His Majesty's ships the *Severn* and *Pearl* were at Rio Janeiro in great distress; that they had sent to England for men, and could not sail from thence until the arrival of the Flota,[11] which would be in May or June. He also told us that we should be dispatched in the first vessel which arrived in this port; for he did not think we could with safety go any farther on our own; and that there could not be found twelve seamen in the Brazils that would venture over the bar in her to sail to Rio Janeiro. Therefore he ordered our little *Speedwell* ashore. This wonder the people are continually flocking to see.

It is now about nine months since we were cast away in the *Wager*; in which time, I believe, no mortals have experienced more difficulties and miseries than we have. This day may be justly styled the day of our deliverance, and ought to be remembered accordingly.

10. One of them soon after died in hospital, making the number of *Speedwell* survivors 29.
11. Annual convoy with supplies.

Chapter 11

MUTINEERS RETURN
TO A DOUBTFUL FUTURE

Rio Grande, 28th January 1742. The Governor looks after them well, but disharmony breaks out among the survivors. Bulkeley, Cummins and Young take passage in a Portuguese ship for Bahia, Brazil, where the Governor is hostile and refuses to help them with money or provisions. After four months' delay they sail again, and narrowly escape shipwreck off Lisbon. Ashore at Lisbon they hear that Lieutenant Baynes has been there before them and blackened their characters; Bulkeley asserts that his journal will bear him out. They take passage in HMS Stirling Castle to Spithead, but find themselves confined on board on arrival. They are released after a fortnight, but the charge of mutiny is in everyone's mind. Bulkeley still puts his faith in his journal which he submits for Admiralty inspection. An official Board of Inquiry into all the circumstances is deferred until Captain Cheap should return home.

FROM THE JOURNAL OF JOHN BULKELEY, GUNNER

This afternoon the Governor, Commandant and Commissary came on board to see our little *Speedwell*. They were surprised that thirty souls, the number of people now living, could be stowed in so small a vessel; but that she could contain the number which first embarked with us[1] was to them amazing and beyond all belief. They could not conceive how the man at the helm could steer without falling overboard, there not being above four inches rise from the deck.[2] I told them he sat down and clapped his feet against the rise; and showed them in what manner we secured ourselves.

The Governor, after viewing the vessel over, told us we were more welcome to him in the miserable condition we arrived than if we had brought all the wealth in the world with us. At the same time he fully assured us that he would dispatch us the first opportunity to Rio Janeiro; and whenever we stood in need of anything, he ordered us to acquaint the Commandant, and our wants should be instantly supplied. He then took leave of us, and wished us well. All the deference and dutiful respect we could show him to express a grateful sense of his favour was by manning the vessel,[3] and giving him three cheers.

The next day arrived at this place the Brigadier-governor of the island of St Catharine. He came close by our vessel, and we manned her and gave him three cheers. The soldiers of the garrison, having twenty months' arrears due to them, expected the Brigadier was come to pay them; but when they found themselves disappointed, they made a great disturbance among themselves.

I applied to the Commandant for a house, the vessel in rainy weather not being fit to lie in. He ordered me one joining to his own, and gave me the key. I took with me Mr Cummins, Mr Jones, Mr Snow, Mr Oakley, and the Cooper. We brought our trifling necessaries on shore, and removed to our new habitation. Here we were dry and warm; and though we had no bedding we lodged very comfortably. Since the loss of the *Wager* we have been used to lie hard; at present we think ourselves very happily fixed, and heartily wish that all the persons who survived the loss of the ship were in so good a situation as ourselves.

---

1. Fifty-nine originally, and 72 after the cutter was lost.
2. That is, with four inches of gunnel.
3. That is, lining up standing along the side of the boat.

But disagreements, sometimes amounting to blows, arise among the survivors. Bulkeley is at odds with Baynes about raising money by selling the long-boat, how to get away, and who goes first; and the Boatswain's violent and abusive temper makes trouble with everyone, and particularly with the Cooper. Eventually they get to Rio Janeiro, and from there obtain leave to take passage in the St Tubas, *a Portuguese vessel bound for Bahia and Lisbon. Bulkeley, Cummins and Young go aboard.*

21st April 1742, early this morning the Captain of the *St Tubas* came on board. On seeing us he asked us how we came on board without his leave. Notwithstanding he gave leave to the Consul for our passage, we ought to have waited on him ashore. There was on board the ship a Spanish don, a passenger, who told the Captain no Englishman should go in the same ship with him; therefore he desired we might be turned ashore. But the Captain insisted upon doing what he pleased aboard his own ship, and would not comply with his request.

The Spanish don, when we came to converse with him, was very much moved with the relation of our misfortunes; and said to us, though our royal masters, the Kings of England and Spain, were at war, it was not our fault; that we were now on board a neutral ship belonging to a King who was a friend to both nations; that he would not look upon us as enemies, but do us all the service he could. He extolled the conduct and bravery of Admiral Vernon at Portobello; but above all applauded him for his humanity and generous treatment of his enemies. He made great encomiums on the magnificence of the British fleet, and the boldness and intrepidity of the sailors, styling the English "the Soldiers of the Sea." He supplied us in our passage not only with provisions from his table, but also with wine and brandy; and during the whole voyage appeared so different from an enemy that he took all opportunities of giving us proofs of his generosity and goodness.[4]

Friday 7th May 1742, this morning anchored before the city of Bahia,[5] went on shore to the Viceroy, and showed him the pass we had from the Governor of Rio Janeiro. He told us the pass was to dispatch us to Lisbon, and that the first ship which sailed from hence would be the ship we came in. We petitioned him for provisions, acquainting him of our reception at Rio Grande and Rio Janeiro, that we had hitherto been supplied at the rate of eight vintems[6] each day. He refused supplying us with anything; upon which I told him we had better been prisoners to the King of Spain, who would allow us bread and water, than in a friend's country to be starved.

The Captain of the ship we came in, hearing the Viceroy would not supply us, was so kind as to go with us to him, acquainting him how we were provided for at Rio Janeiro, and that he would supply us himself, if he would sign an account to satisfy the Consul General at Lisbon, so that he might be reimbursed. The Viceroy answered he had no orders concerning the English, that he had letters from the King of Portugal his master to supply the French but had no orders about any other nation, and if he gave us anything, it must be out of his own pocket; therefore he would not supply us. The Captain then told him that we were officers and subjects to the King of England, and in distress; that we did not want great matters, only barely enough to support life, and begged that he would allow but four vintems per day, being but half the sum hitherto allowed us. The Captain's entreaties availed nothing, the Viceroy continuing fixed in his resolution of giving us no relief.

I don't believe there ever was a worse representative of royalty upon the face of the earth than this Viceroy. His royal master the King of Portugal is very well known to have a grateful affection for the British nation, nor can

---

4. Young writes of this gentleman: "All this was agreeable to the noble disposition of the Spanish nation, which, though with a full measure of pride, yields to no other on earth for magnanimity or generosity of temper."

5. Now Salvador, Brazil.

6. A coin of small value.

we believe he is so Frenchified as this Viceroy makes him. He has given a proof of his aversion to the English. We think persons in the distress we were represented in to him could in no part of the world be treated with more barbarity than we were here. At this place we must have starved if I had not by me some money and a watch of my own, which I was obliged to turn into money to support us.

Since our being here we have been informed of one of His Majesty's ships[7] with three store-ships being arrived at Rio Janeiro, supplied with stores and men for the relief and assistance of the *Severn* and *Pearl* (which were sailed before in January last for Barbados), and that our people were gone on board of them, and bound for the West Indies.[8]

After living here above four months without any relief from the Governor or the inhabitants, who behaved to us as if they were under a combination to starve us, we embarked on board the *St Tubas* with our good friend the Captain who brought us from Rio Janeiro. We sailed from Bahia 11th September for Lisbon, in company with one of the King of Portugal's ships of war and two East-India ships; but the *St Tubas* not being able to sail so well as the other ships lost sight of them the first night. About 70 leagues to the west of Madeira we bent on a new foresail; within two or three days afterwards we had a very hard gale of wind, scudding under the foresail, and no danger happening to the ship during this gale. Then the wind ceased and we had fair weather.

On Monday 23rd November, in the latitude 39:17 N and longitude 6:00 W, at noon the Rock of Lisbon bearing S by W distant sixteen leagues, we steered ESE to make the Rock before night. At four o'clock it blew a very hard gale and right on the shore. The ship lay to under a foresail with her head to the southward. At six it blew a storm; the foresail splitting, it obliged us to keep her before the wind, which was running her right on the shore.

---

7. HMS *Advice*.
8. If Bulkeley and the others had waited a little longer in Rio Janeiro they would have got home sooner.

The ship was now given over for lost. The people all fell to prayers and cried out to their saints for deliverance, offering all they had in the world for their lives. And yet at the same time they neglected all means to save themselves: they left off pumping the ship, though she was exceeding leaky. This sort of proceeding in time of extremity is a thing unknown to our English seamen; in those emergencies all hands are employed for the preservation of the ship and people, and if any of them fall upon their knees it is after the danger is over. The Carpenter and myself could by no means relish this behaviour. We begged the people for God's sake to go to the pumps, telling them we had a chance to save our lives while we kept the ship above water, and that we ought not to suffer the ship to sink while we could keep her free. The Captain and officers, hearing us pressing them so earnestly, left off prayers and entreated the men to keep the pumps going; accordingly we went to pumping, and preserved ourselves and the ship.

In half an hour afterwards the wind shifted to the WNW, then the ship lay south, which would clear the course along shore. Had the wind not shifted we must in an hour's time have run the ship ashore. This deliverance, as well as the former, was owing to the intercession of Nuestra Senhora Boa Mortua.[9] On this occasion they collected fifty moidores[10] more, and made this pious resolution, that when the ship arrived safe at Lisbon the foresail, which was split in the last gale of wind, should be carried in procession to the church of this grand saint, and the Captain should there make an offering equal in value to the foresail, which was reckoned worth eighteen moidores.

On Saturday 28th November, we arrived at Lisbon, and on the next morning every person who came in the ship (excepting the Carpenter, myself, and the Cooper), officers, passengers, the Spanish don himself, and all the people, men and boys, walked barefooted, with the foresail in procession, to the Church of Nuestra Senhora Boa Mortua; the weather

---

9. Our Lady of a Peaceful Death. Young writes: "Our deliverances were by the Captain and the whole crew most devoutly ascribed to a she-saint whose name I have forgotten."
10. Gold coins, valued then at 27s.

at that time being very cold, and the church a good mile distant from the landing-place.

We Englishmen, when we came ashore, went immediately on the Change.[11] I was pretty well known to some gentlemen of the English factory. When I informed them that we were three of the unfortunate people that were cast away in the *Wager*, and that we came here in one of the Brazil ships, and wanted to embrace the first opportunity of going for England, they told me that the Lieutenant had been before us; that he was gone home in the packet-boat, and left us a very indifferent character. I answered that I believed the Lieutenant could give but a very bad account of himself, having kept no journal, nor made any remarks[12] since the loss of the ship, nor perhaps before; that we doubted not but to acquit ourselves of any false accusations, having with us a journal which gave an impartial relation of all our proceedings. The journal was read by several gentlemen of the factory, who treated us, during our stay at Lisbon, with exceeding kindness and benevolence.

On the 20th December we embarked on board His Majesty's ship *Stirling Castle* for England. Here we had again the happiness of experiencing the difference between a British and a foreign ship, particularly in regard to cleanliness, accommodation, diet, and discipline. We met with nothing material in our passage, and arrived at Spithead, on the 1st January 1743.

Here we thought of nothing but going ashore immediately to our families; but were told by the Captain, we must not stir out of the ship till he knew the pleasure of the Lords of the Admiralty, having already wrote to them concerning us. This was a very great affliction to us; and the more so, because we thought our troubles at an end. The Carpenter and myself were in view of our habitations; our families had long given us over for lost; and on the news of our safety our relatives looked upon us as sons, husbands, and fathers restored to them in a miraculous manner. Our being

---

11. Meeting-place for the conduct of business.
12. Navigational observations.

detained on board gave them great anxiety; we endeavoured to console them as well as we could, being assured that we had done nothing to offend Their Lordships; that if things had not been carried on with that order and regularity which is strictly observed in the navy, necessity drove us out of the common road.

Our case was singular: since the loss of the ship, our chiefest concern was for the preservation of our lives and liberties; to accomplish which, we acted according to the dictates of nature and the best of our understanding.

In a fortnight's time Their Lordships ordered us at liberty, and we instantly went ashore to our respective habitations, having been absent from thence about two years and six months.

After we had stayed a few days with our families we came to London to pay our duties to the Lords of the Admiralty. We sent in our journal for Their Lordships' inspection; they had before received a narrative from the Lieutenant; which narrative he confesses to be a relation of such things as occurred to his memory; therefore of consequence could not be so satisfactory as a journal regularly kept. This journal lay for some time in the Admiralty Office; when we were ordered to make an abstract by way of narrative, that it might not be too tedious for Their Lordships' perusal. After the narrative was examined into, Their Lordships, upon our petition, were pleased to fix a day for examining all the officers lately belonging to the *Wager*. The gentlemen appointed to make enquiry into the whole affair were three commanders of ships, persons of distinguished merit and honour. However, it was afterwards thought proper not to admit us to any examination till the arrival of the Commodore, or else Captain Cheap.

It was also resolved that not a person of us should receive any wages, or be employed in His Majesty's service,[13] till everything relating to the *Wager* was more plain and conspicuous. There was no favour shown in this case to one more than another; so that everybody seemed easy with Their Lordships' resolution.

---

13. The Admiralty relented on this later.

All that we have to wish for now is the safe arrival of the Commodore and Captain Cheap. We are in expectation of soon seeing the former; but of the Captain we have as yet no account. However, we hope, when the Commodore shall arrive, that the character he will give of us will be of service to us. He was very well acquainted with the behaviour of every officer in his squadron, and will certainly give an account of them accordingly.

Bulkeley cannot have been feeling as confident as he is here trying to appear in his journal. Whatever the reasons, he and the others had surprised the Captain in his sleep, and forcibly deprived him of his command. They had then abandoned him to an unknown fate – albeit at his own request. If Bulkeley was going to argue that the circumstances were extenuating, his case would have to be very strong indeed to convince a court-martial that this affair was not a very serious mutiny, for which the ringleaders deserved to swing.

Lieutenant Baynes's narrative (which regrettably has not survived) had caused a great stir in the Admiralty a few weeks before Bulkeley's return, and Their Lordships had convened a Board of Inquiry. The Board directed that the Admiralty's copy of the Wager's *muster list should be annotated from the Lieutenant's narrative, and that he should provide such details as he could of the fate of the ship's company. This document survives. There is a note at the top: "Memorandum. The deaths and discharges, with the other notations set off on this book, were taken from an account of Lieutenant Baynes's, at the direction of the Board. E.B."[14] Alongside Midshipman Henry Cozens the same hand has written, "Shot by the Captain about the end of June 1741." There is a page devoted to the names of marines embarked: one is marked "R" (run, deserted), two "Come Home", and of the remainder almost all have the melancholy notation "DD" – discharged dead.*

The overarching question of mutiny must have been in everyone's mind, but as far as the Board of Inquiry was concerned enough witnesses and supporting

---

14. "E.B." has not been identified, but it is not Baynes.

evidence were not yet available for the necessary court-martial. The Board therefore made the decision to defer matters until more survivors should return. We can now follow those survivors in their continuing hardships.

Way back in time and space, off the uninhabited coast of Argentina just south of what is now Mar del Plata, the long-boat had been under the nominal command of Lieutenant Baynes, but with Gunner Bulkeley effectively in charge. They had abandoned eight of their shipmates on shore, with Bulkeley claiming in his journal, "those people had a good prospect of getting provisions, and we believe inhabitants are not far off; they have all necessaries for shooting." Such a claim seems to ring somewhat hollow when his motive for moving on, rather than waiting a day or two for the sea to moderate, was allegedly an inability to procure food. The fate of these eight castaways is now told by one of their number.

This document was compiled by Lieutenant Baynes, who had been ordered by the Navy Board to attempt to recreate the Ship's Muster Book, which had of course been lost with the wreck.

The notation DD stands for Discharged Dead, and here we have the record of many *Wager* deaths, not in action but by scurvy, starvation, hypothermia, and in some cases violence. DD, a terse and seemingly callous notation, is still in use on official documents in the Royal Navy, perhaps with a hint of black humour.

PART 3
Isaac Morris's Story

Chapter 12

THE MISFORTUNES OF
EIGHT CASTAWAYS

Argentine Patagonia, 10ᵗʰ January 1742. Midshipman Morris from Topsham in Devon describes with bitterness being one of eight men of the long-boat's company to be cast away on an uninhabited coast south of Buenos Aires. They make ingenious efforts to subsist. Two attempts to reach the River Plate fail; and winter approaches. His account starts while he is still in the long-boat.

FROM MIDSHIPMAN MORRIS'S ACCOUNT

After having being fourteen days without sight of land and almost destitute of provisions, we were blessed with the agreeable prospect of it distant about seven leagues. We stood in directly for it, and came to an anchor in eight fathom water. At five next morning we weighed, and steered NE by E about a mile from the shore, where we saw a great many wild horses and some dogs. At noon we had a good observation and found ourselves in 38:40 S. We sounded and had but two fathom and a half at high water, a shoal of sand running out to the SE four or five leagues, which when we got clear of we steered NE into a large sandy bay, and anchored in three fathom and a half.

On 12ᵗʰ January our provisions being quite done, and only one cask of water remaining, we ran as near in to the shore as we could with safety, and fourteen of the healthiest of us agreed to swim ashore in order to try for provisions. I was of the number, and we all landed safe except one of the marines, who became quite spent and was drowned within three fathom of the beach, and none of us near enough to assist him. We had four casks thrown overboard after us in order to be filled with fresh water, if we should be so happy as to find any; and to them were lashed some muskets with ammunition. After we had walked about a mile in from the beach we saw a great number of wild horses and dogs; the horses were of a small size, but the dogs a large mongrel breed. There were flocks of parrots about the rocks, and near the water-side a few seal. We likewise met with a good spring of fresh water, rising from a trench not far from the shore. We shot a wild horse and some seal, and filled three casks with fresh water, which were next morning towed aboard by five of those who swam ashore. Soon after this, the sea-breeze blowing strong, the long-boat stood farther off to sea.

On the 14th January the wind blew fresh at ESE, and we saw our vessel stretching farther off. Soon afterwards we received, in a scuttled cask, a few necessaries, with ammunition, and a letter to acquaint us of the risk which they should run in lying near the shore, and that they were obliged to stand farther off for their own safety, till the weather should be more favourable.

Next morning we had the wind at NNW with fair weather, when we expected the long-boat would have stretched in for the land; but to our great surprise we saw her, with her ensign hoisted at the topping lift, and under sail from us. The moderate weather with the wind off-shore gave them a good opportunity of standing in again, if they had thought fit. Why they did not is best known to themselves: but the most probable reason we could give for such inhuman treatment was, that by lessening the number of their crew they might be better accommodated with room and provisions. Possibly they might apprehend some inhabitants to be near us; but if so, they could be none but Indians. And we could not help looking on it as an act of the greatest cruelty, thus to maroon us under a false pretence of an utter impossibility of taking us on board with them.

The dismal apprehensions we were under at such an unexpected stroke appeared plainly in our countenances, and can be much easier imagined than described. We found ourselves on a wild desolate part of the world, fatigued, sickly, and destitute of provisions. It is true we had arms and ammunition; and whilst these lasted we made a tolerable shift for a livelihood. The nearest inhabited place we knew of was Buenos Aires, about three hundred miles to the north-west; but at present we were in a very poor condition to undertake so hazardous a journey, being so miserably reduced by our tedious passage through the Straits of Magellan. Nothing remained but to commit ourselves to kind Providence, and make the best of our melancholy situation until we had recruited ourselves.

We were in number eight who were thus abandoned by our comrades, for whose preservation we had risked our lives in swimming ashore for provisions. Our names were Guy Broadwater, Samuel Cooper, Benjamin Smith, John Duck, Joseph Clinch, John Andrews, John Allen, and myself.

After deliberating upon our unhappy circumstances, and comforting each other with imaginary hopes, we came to a resolution of taking up our quarters on the beach where we landed, till we should grow strong enough to undergo the fatigue of a journey to Buenos Aires. The weather being very favourable, we took up our lodging in a trench near the sea-side, quite exposed, without any covering but the heavens. Here we stayed about a month, and during that time we lived upon seal, which were very plentiful, and which we knocked down with stones after we had cut off their retreat by getting between them and the sea. Here was likewise plenty of fresh water from a small spring which rose out of the trench, so that at the month's end we had pretty well recovered ourselves, and concluded upon laying in a stock of provisions for our journey to Buenos Aires.

Having provided ourselves each with a knapsack of seal-skin, made in the best manner possible, we put into it as much dried flesh of the seal as we could carry; and the bladders of these animals, filled with fresh water, served us for bottles. We took our muskets and ammunition with us, and thus accoutred we set out on our journey about the middle of February;

and that we might proceed with the more certainty, we were determined to keep close to the sea-side, until reaching the mouth of the River Plate.

The first two days we travelled about sixty miles, but could meet with no fresh water besides what we carried along with us, the country being scorched with drought and the rains not yet set in. Our water being near expended, we were afraid to proceed lest we should perish for want of more, so after a few debates, we agreed to return to our old quarters, and wait till the rainy season.

We were two days and a half on our return, after which we employed ourselves in building a sort of hut under a cliff adjoining the sea-side, to secure us from the inclemencies of the weather. Here we tarried three months, during which time our food was seals and armadillos, which was the only provision to be met with here except sea-weed, which we sometimes made use of with our meat instead of bread.

The seal here differ from those which I have seen in other parts, both in size and make. The males are of the bigness of a good calf, their neck shaggy, and the head and face somewhat like a lion's. Before, the females are like lionesses, but their hair is smooth all over like that of a horse, whereas only the hinder parts of the male are smooth. Two large fins like feet grow out from behind, and two more out of the breast, by means of which they can climb rocks and precipices, though they chiefly delight to lie asleep near the shore. Some are fourteen feet long, and very fat, but in general they are about eight feet. The flesh of the young ones is almost as white as lamb, and tolerably good eating. From their shoulders to the tail they taper like a fish, and the females sit on the fins growing out behind when they give suck to their young. Their hair is of different colours, looking very sleek when they first come out of the sea.

The armadillo is as big nearly as a small sucking-pig, the body of it pretty long. It is enclosed in thick shell which guards all its back and, meeting under the belly, leaving room for the four legs. The head is small, with a nose like a hedgehog. It thrusts out its head before it as it walks, but on any danger withdraws it into the shell, and then lies quite still like a land-turtle, and though you kick her about she will not move herself. With strong claws it digs holes, and burrows in the ground like a rabbit. Its flesh, which tastes much like a turtle, is very good eating.

Nothing remarkable happened to us in these three months. Our provisions, such as they were, were not very difficult to be procured, and we were supplied with firewood enough from a small coppice about seven miles from us. We seldom failed of bringing home something every night, and generally had a hot supper. We passed our time as cheerful as poor fellows in our circumstances could. But we knew that we could not take up this place for our settled abode; and there was no likelihood of any inhabitants near us, nor for many miles around could we perceive the least traces of any having ever been there. It was to no purpose to expect the sight of any vessel at sea, it being a deep bay and shoal water, and no ship could ever put in there unless forced by stress of weather, and then they must be wrecked. Nothing remained for us but to make a second attempt for the River Plate; because, if we marched to the inland country in quest of inhabitants, possibly we should meet with insuperable difficulties in finding the way back again to what I may call our home, whereas if we kept our course along the sea-shore we could not err. For these reasons we resolved upon making another attempt by the same route; and having laid in our stock of seal, armadillos, and fresh water, towards the latter end of May we set forward once more.

In three days we travelled about seventy miles, when towards night there came on a violent storm with rain, thunder, and lightning, which continued the whole night. We had a plain open country, and no place of shelter could be found; we had nothing to cover us but a seal-skin jacket, were half-dead with cold, and afraid whether our provisions would hold out, for we met with no supplies of any kind by the way. To proceed farther was only lengthening our journey back again, which we feared would be the consequence at last, even though we should still push on.

There had been the strictest harmony and good-nature between us till now, but now we were like to have disagreed, even to parting. Some were for pushing forward, be the event what it might, and it was with much difficulty they were persuaded not to divide. However, on a representation of the great distance which we were as yet from the mouth of the river, and the improbability of meeting with supplies on the journey, our debates ended. We jointly concluded on making the best of our way back to our hut, having been a second time disappointed in our attempt.

Arriving at our old quarters, we began to consult what measures to take for our security from the inclemencies of the weather, and to provide for our subsistence till it should please God, one way or other, to deliver us out of this melancholy situation. In order to avoid disputes about the laborious part of getting provisions, we agreed to divide ourselves into two parties, who should alternately provide for the whole. Four were appointed to scour the country one day, and the other four the next. And we bound ourselves by an oath never to quit each other unless obliged by a superior force; for, though we had yet seen no footsteps of inhabitants, we could not be certain that there were none on this part of the globe.

We had killed such a number of seal that they now became very shy of us, and had lived upon them so long that we were almost surfeited, yet there was hardly anything else to be met with. We saw a great number of wild dogs, but could never come near enough for us to kill any, though now and then we chanced to shoot a puppy, which, as it was a change of diet, we thought delicious fare. We saw also some deer, but could contrive no method of taking them.

One day, in our rambles, we found a litter of young puppies; they were but three, and seemed to be about two months old, and had taken shelter in a hole of one of the sand-hills. We took them out, and brought them home to our hut. Having discovered that these puppies were whelped in holes like those of rabbits, but larger, we went out all next day in quest of more. We had the good luck to find three litters, in number thirteen, which we carried home with us, designing if possible to bring them up tame. We fed them with broth made of seal, and sometimes with the flesh minced small; and they afterwards became very serviceable to us. Each of us had his brace of dogs, which were brought up under as much command as an English spaniel, nor would they leave us to associate with the wild ones. They often supplied us with armadillos, and once they killed a deer for us.

Being one day hunting we saw some wild hogs with their young. Our dogs pursued them, took two of the young which we saved alive, and we shot one of the old ones, which afforded us many dainty suppers. The two young proved to be a boar and a sow, which was very fortunate, and we designed to rear them for breeding, lest we should be obliged to make a long residence in this desolate country. We brought them up very tame, insomuch that they followed our dogs whenever we went a-hunting, and at night both dogs and pigs took up their lodging with us in our hut.

For the present our condition seemed tolerable; nay, we thought ourselves in very comfortable circumstances; we wanted for nothing, and, if we could have confined our thoughts to present enjoyments, our situation was very agreeable. But our views went farther, and the fears of what might happen frequently struck a damp on our pleasures. Winter was now approaching: we had the inclemencies of the season to guard against, and, if possible, a stock of provisions to be laid up against future exigencies. But we could not be much beforehand with provisions, having no salt to cure them, and at present not sun enough to dry them; for with winter came on continual storms, insomuch that some days we could not stir out of our hut.

Chapter 13

FOUR MURDERS

Argentine Patagonia, August 1742. Morris and his companions encounter wild beasts. Four of the party are murdered or abducted by Indians, the hut plundered, and their firearms stolen. The remainder immediately resolve to make a third desperate attempt to reach Buenos Aires, but find the swamps completely impassable, and return with foreboding to their old hut. They start trying to make a canoe out of a fallen tree, but suddenly Indians appear menacingly on horseback.

FROM MIDSHIPMAN MORRIS'S ACCOUNT

It was now more than seven months since the long-boat left us. Winter came on very fast, and we were but badly secured from the severity of the weather. We resolved immediately to put our habitation in order, and to secure our hut in the best manner we could. Accordingly it was agreed that six should stay at home next day to prepare materials, and only two go out after provisions. The lot fell on myself and John Duck to go abroad, but though we travelled many miles, all the game we could meet was three armadillos. It was so dark before we returned that we despaired of finding our hut, and were like to have taken up our lodging in the open plain if our comrades had not come out in quest of us, and by making a fire directed us towards them. After we had broiled our game and fed heartily, about 12 we went to sleep. But about two in the morning a violent storm, with rain, thunder, and lightning, threw down upon us part of the cliff under which we had built our hut, which was very near proving fatal to all of us. Through Providence none were hurt.

With daylight came on tolerable weather, and now the first thing we had to do was to rebuild our hut. We immediately went to the coppice where we used to fetch our firewood in order to fell some poles. As we had but one hatchet betwixt us only one could fell them, and the rest of us brought them out and bundled them. We had cut several, and were bundling them, when we saw Joseph Clinch running out of the wood, and crying, "Lord have mercy on us, here's a great tiger!"[1] We were in the utmost consternation; for having frequently been there before and never once seeing any footsteps of wild beasts, we came without our arms, suspecting no danger from that quarter. We all took to our heels, and soon saw the tiger running out of the wood in pursuit of us. When he was come within twenty yards of us, finding it impossible to escape, we all turned towards him, clapping our hands and making a loud halloo in order to frighten him, which had the desired effect, for he immediately sat back on his tail gazing at us. What to do we knew not, whether it was best to fly or to wait for his turning; but fear prevailed, and we walked gently off, without his pursuing us. Next day we all went in chase of the brute with our muskets, but could not meet with him. Therefore we brought home our poles, and fitted up the hut in the best manner we could, sufficient to guard us from the rain.

About three weeks after, when we were hunting on the plain about four miles from home, we saw a lion[2] couched on the ground watching his prey, as we imagined, it being close by a wild cat's hole. We joined close together in a body, with our muskets ready, and Joseph Clinch, resting his

---

1. This was probably a jaguar, now extinct in this area.
2. Presumably a puma.

piece on my shoulder, fired a ball at twenty yards, but missed him. The lion took no notice of the report of the gun, nor stirred from his position. Then Clinch loaded a second time, those of the others being kept in readiness in case the animal should advance towards us. He fired, and shot him in the right shoulder. He fell on his back, and we ran to him and knocked him on the head with the bones of a dead horse which lay near him. We carried him to our hut, dressed the heart and part of the ribs, but it was very indifferent eating.

Finding ourselves beginning to be surrounded by wild beasts, and every day and night in continual danger (for we now seldom went abroad without meeting some beast of prey, this being I suppose the time of year when they take their haunts towards the sea-coast), we determined to make another push for our deliverance, and try our fortune once more in an expedition to Buenos Aires. So we provided ourselves shoes and jackets of seal-skin, and also knapsacks to carry our provender. The weather was set in fair, and we fully determined to lay in such a stock of provisions as should last to the end of our journey, if we should be a month in performing it. We divided ourselves into two parties, four of us were to go to the rocks for seal, and the other four to hunt on the plain.

Accordingly we set out early in the morning; and it was my lot, with Samuel Cooper, John Andrews, and John Duck, to go to the rocks. Our usual way of killing seal being with stones or clubs, we never carried our muskets with us. We had been out all day, and killed three; and in the dusk of the evening having got within a stone's-cast of our hut, I perceived our dogs very busy at a small distance wagging their tails in a very fondling manner. Being ahead of my companions I passed on without much regarding it, thinking they had lighted on a dead colt; but when I came to the hut I was quite confounded: the hut was rifled, and all our necessaries taken away. In the utmost consternation I ran back to my comrades, whom I saw standing where I had left the dogs; seeing me running eagerly towards them, they cried out, "What's the matter, Isaac?" I told them our hut was pulled down, and everything taken away.

"Aye," said they, "and something worse has happened, for yonder lie poor Guy Broadwater and Benjamin Smith murdered." It was a most shocking sight: one had his throat cut, and the other was stabbed in the breast. They were hardly cold, so that we thought the murderers could not be far off; and were under no small apprehensions of sharing a like fate. We went to inspect the hut more narrowly, and we found everything taken away, our powder, ball, and muskets gone, the fire extinguished, and not the least utensil left. Where to go, or what to do, we knew not. We durst not trust ourselves another night on this fatal spot, and yet were afraid to venture farther. At last we came to the resolution of proceeding to the next sandy bay, about a mile off, and taking up our quarters there for that night. But when there we could find no shelter, not so much as a cliff to lie under, so were obliged to return to our old place, and pass the night there, happen what would.

Next morning, the dogs that belonged to our comrades stood on the top of the cliff barking at us, and would not come down, though we called them by their names; and it was with difficulty that we enticed them down in the evening. What became of Joseph Clinch and John Allen we knew not, nor could we afterwards learn any account of them. What seemed most probable to us was that the Indians had carried them off and murdered the other two, who possibly might make some resistance, as we had all agreed to do in case we should be attacked. But if so, we might probably have expected to have found some or other of their enemies killed, as our people had firearms with them. And it was impossible, too, it could be the result of a quarrel among themselves from the manner of their death; for the one was stabbed, and the other had his throat cut, both very plainly done with a knife, an instrument none of us had possession of. We buried them in the best manner we could, by scraping away the light sand with our hands two feet deep, and raising a bed of sand over the corpses.

This was the most afflicting stroke of any we had received since our residence in this unhappy country. I will not attempt to describe the horror we felt; the compassionate reader will paint our distress in his imagination in stronger colours than can be described by words. To see four of our companions snatched suddenly from us, we knew not how, ourselves deprived of our arms and utensils, left without fire or any method of procuring it, expecting every moment to share their fate, or to be starved to death, filled us with unspeakable terrors.

In this melancholy state, the only thing that remained to be done was immediately to quit this unhappy place, and make one attempt more for Buenos Aires. We had no time to lose, but instantly set about tearing up the seal in small pieces, raw as it was, with which we filled our knapsacks, and their bladders we filled with water. Having furnished ourselves with as much provision as we could carry, we set forward on our journey with our sixteen dogs and two pigs, praying the Almighty to be our guide.

We kept close along the sea-coast as before, by which means we could not miss the mouth of the River Plate, designing, when we reached it, to travel along the side of that river until coming to some inhabited place; a scheme easy enough in imagination, but in practice attended, as we found, with insuperable difficulties. The whole sea-coast is a plain sandy beach. On the land side are here and there very high sand-hills, in the valleys of which we reposed ourselves at night. On the beach we sometimes found a few cockles which the sea had washed in, and these were a great dainty to us. We met with part of the wreck of a large ship which was drove upon the beach, particularly a man-of-war's gang-board, and a piece of plank marked fifteen foot. In the valleys of the sand-hills was plenty of water which had ponded up after the rains, and we frequently discovered dead fish thrown in upon the beach, so that we had a variety of raw meat to feed upon. We also found a very large dead whale by the sea-side, which was a feast for our dogs and pigs, and at a little distance a parcel of fine whalebone.

At the end of ten days we made the cape of the river, having travelled very hard every day with tolerable weather, but there found a multitude of small streams and muddy swamps to obstruct us. We swam over several of them with our knapsacks across our shoulders; and when night came on we covered ourselves with the rushes, but were almost devoured by mosquitoes. Next day we made several attempts to proceed further, but found it was impossible to accomplish our journey: the farther we went, the greater the difficulties we met with. We were in danger of being suffocated several times, the bogs often sinking us to the shoulders, so that after many fruitless attempts to proceed we found that we had no remedy left but to tread back the melancholy path, and return to our old place of rendezvous. This we performed in less than ten days.

At our return we were afraid to ramble far abroad, having neither arms nor ammunition to defend ourselves from the wild beasts. Our two pigs maintained us near a fortnight, and afterwards we were obliged to live on some of our trusty dogs. But this raw way of feeding, which continued three months longer, brought us into an ill state of health. About a quarter of a mile from the hut we found a dead horse, of which we now and then took a morsel, by way of change; and could we have got fire to dress it the variety would have been agreeable enough. Notwithstanding our fears, necessity compelled us to go abroad in search of other kind of provisions; and sometimes we had the good fortune to bring home an armadillo.

One morning we found the trunk of a large tree, and imagined it was not impossible, with the help of the skins of seals and horses, to make a sort of boat with it, which might serve to convey us along shore to the River Plate. But we had no kind of tool to use. John Duck recollected that about eleven months before, at the end of our first attempt for Buenos Aires, he had thrown away his musket, it being a very indifferent one and not worth the trouble of carrying home, and we had enough besides. We proposed going in search of it, which if we could find might serve to make a hatchet. Accordingly, having furnished ourselves with some raw seal and water, we went and found the musket, though above sixty miles distant. On our return home we discovered several ostrich[3] eggs (though we never met with any of the birds themselves) about half-buried in the sand, and they proved a refreshing meal to us.

---

3. Rhea.

When we brought the musket home, we beat half the length of the barrel flat with stones, and whetted an edge to it against a rock; the other half served for the handle. And it made a tolerable hatchet, at least what would have served instead of one, if Providence had not soon after put an end to our design in the following manner.

Two days after we had finished our hatchet, it being my turn to stay in the hut, my three comrades went to a place which we called the Long Point in quest of provisions. Towards evening I walked out to see if they were returning when, to my astonishment, I discovered about a dozen horses galloping down the sandy bay towards our hut; and as they came nearer I plainly saw men on their backs, and that they were Indians. It was vain to fly. I imagined nothing but death approaching, and prepared to meet it with all the resolution I could muster up.

Chapter 14

ENSLAVED

Argentine Patagonia, February 1743. The four remaining survivors are captured by Indians, and bought and sold among them as slaves. They undergo a long journey of a thousand miles or so to the interior to meet the Indian chief, who claims them as his property, treats them humanely, and promises them each a Spanish slave-wife. Morris describes the habits of the Indians, and how they eventually managed to persuade the chief that they had English friends in Buenos Aires who would pay a handsome price for them. They set out for Buenos Aires, but John Duck, being dark-skinned, is left behind; the Indians would not part with him.

FROM MIDSHIPMAN MORRIS'S ACCOUNT

I ran towards the Indians and fell on my knees, begging my life with all the signs of humility I could make, when I heard a voice saying, "Don't be afraid, Isaac, we are all here." This revived me.

The Indians alighted; and whilst some were intent on examining the hut, others stood with drawn knives ready to dispatch us in case we made any resistance. When they had satisfied their curiosity they gave three confused shouts, and immediately made us get behind them, carried us away a few miles in from the sea-shore to the south-west, where there were about a dozen more of their companions with upwards of four hundred horses which they had taken in hunting. They treated us with great humanity: killed a horse for us, kindled a fire, and roasted a part of it; which to us, who had for three months been eating raw flesh, was most delicious entertainment. They also gave each of us a piece of an old blanket to cover our nakedness.

I had been in great danger, it seems, of being left alone; for when the Indians met with my three comrades they were immediately hurrying them away to their place of rendezvous, till they were with difficulty made to understand by signs that there was one more belonging to them a little way off; and then my comrades guided them to the hut, where I had the happiness of being taken prisoner with them.

Next morning we decamped from this place, driving a troop of horses before us. We travelled nineteen days before we reached their next place of rendezvous, which I imagine was about two hundred miles from our hut to the south-west, in a valley between two very high mountains, where was fine pasture for their horses and several small rivers of fresh water, but with very little wood to be seen for many miles round. In this valley were about a dozen Indian huts built with poles and the skins of horses, inhabited by another party of Indians, with their wives and children, who gazed very earnestly on us as though they had never seen any white people before.

Here we were bought and sold four different times – for a pair of spurs, a brass pan, ostrich feathers, and suchlike trifles, which was the low price generally set on each of us; and sometimes we were played away at dice, so that we changed masters several times in a day. In this place we remained nearly a month, by which time the several parties of Indians had returned from their hunting and joined us, each party bringing the horses they had taken in hunting and mixing them in the common stock, which were examined and told over by one of the Indians, who seemed to be a sort of captain over the rest; and they amounted to the number of fifteen hundred and upwards, some of which were in no way inferior to the best of our European breed.

After one day's grand feasting we set out in a body for their chief town, where the king or captain lived, with fifteen hundred string of horses in our cavalcade. We were four months in performing our journey, and by the method of our travelling I believe it must be a thousand miles from the sea-coast where our hut stood. In the daytime we travelled, and at night reposed ourselves in their movable huts, which sheltered us from the weather. Our constant food was horseflesh, which some chose to eat raw, and others broiled or roasted; and as for drink we never failed of water, for I found they were well acquainted with every small rivulet; of which there are numbers in the route they took, though a stranger would hardly have found them.

At length we arrived at the end of our journey in the chief town where their king lives. But our masters who had made the purchase of us were carrying us with them to their own home (which we learnt afterwards was about two hundred miles beyond the town where the king resided), and had actually conducted us some miles on the way when a party of horse came after us, and brought us back to the capital, the king claiming us as his property.

This town consists of about thirty huts, built in a low, irregular manner with poles and horse-skins, surrounded with palisades about three foot distant from each other. The inhabitants, men, women, and children, were about fourscore.

We were soon summoned to appear before His Majesty, who received us sitting on the ground in his hut, with a javelin on one side of him, and a bow and arrows on the other. A loose mantle was round his waist, a sort of turret of ostrich feathers on his head, and a long reed pipe in his mouth, smoking. After we had paid our obeisance to him, he began to ask several questions in Spanish, of which they can all speak a little, and which we soon let him know we understood a little of. He enquired what countrymen we were, and how we came hither. We told him we were Englishmen; that we were lost in an English man-of-war in the South Sea, as we were going to fight against our enemies, the Spaniards; that we were eight in number, who were left on a desolate part of the continent; and that one evening, on our return from procuring provisions, we found two of our companions murdered and two carried off, on the same spot of ground where we were taken, our hut pulled down and everything taken from us, which we supposed must have been done by some of his countrymen.

The king then called three or four of his men, and talked very earnestly to them in their own language. But it seems they knew nothing of the affair, as he told us, though he was pleased to assure us that strict inquiry should be made of the other parties which were out at the same time. For I found by him that he sends out different parties every spring from every different town under his government, who take different routes, and sometimes join one another accidentally on their return. But more of this hereafter. When he found that we were at war with the Spaniards he expressed a great deal of joy, and asked if we were great men in our own country. We told him "Yes"; and he said the Spaniards were great enemies to his people, had taken away their country from them, and drove them to the mountains.

When the king had done examining us he ordered a horse to be killed immediately and dressed for us, and lodged us in his own hut for that night, till we had one built for us, which was the next day. Here we stayed eight months and wintered, during which time we frequently had snow five or six feet deep. Our work was chiefly to fetch wood and water, and skin all the horses which they killed; and although we were their slaves we were treated very humanely, and they would suffer no one to use us ill. There were four Spanish women in the town, whom they had taken captive in a skirmish near Buenos Aires, and the king told us with a smile that he would give each of us a wife.[1]

The country where these Indians resided is very fruitful in pasture, as indeed is the whole coast of Patagonia. It abounds with great plenty of wild horses and has a few black cattle, which last are entirely neglected by the Indians, horse-flesh being preferred by them for eating before any

---

1. Morris is a little coy about this. Campbell says that the survivors told him later that they had fathered several children.

other kind of flesh and what they constantly feed upon. The people, at least those in that part of the country where we resided, are tall and well made, being in general from five to six feet high, good-natured and obliging to one another, and never seeing each other want. Though they have what they call a king, yet he seems to be only a chief or captain of a party, as they have no settled abode but live scattered throughout that part of the world in little towns or parties, and each party seems to have a chief who presides over them like a petty king. I never could observe any rules of government among them, but at a drinking bout king and subjects are all alike. Their king is distinguished from the rest by being the biggest man, and by wearing a kind of sash around his waist. It is true he has a deference paid him by his subjects, and whatever he orders to be done is immediately performed, he being exempted from any kind of work. But I never saw any punishments inflicted by him, nor any quarrels among themselves, except when they get at a drinking feast, and then their wives always took care that no ill consequence should follow by putting every weapon out of their way, and especially taking care of their knives. For which reason, I imagine that they are always quarrelsome in liquor; one or two instances of that kind happened while we were among them.

Their method of feasting is this: they have in the summer a plenty of small sweet berries, growing like our whortleberries,[2] and when they have secured a sufficient quantity of them they dig a pit in the ground, about four feet square, the bottom and sides of which they line with horses' hides. This cask, if I may so call it, they half fill with these berries and then fill it up with water, which they stir well with sticks and leave to ferment about forty-eight hours. They all sit round, smoking and drinking, for a whole night together, women as well as men, singing in their way, but more like shrieking cries, and when drunk frequently proceed to blows.

These Indians seldom live long in one place, for when their horses have eaten up the pasture in one place, they remove their town and all their

---

2. Blaeberries, blueberries, or bilberries.

goods a few miles, which is soon done; and this several times in a year, so that they have no settled abode. They have habitations scattered all over the country, and but a few huts together, and the town where the chief resides has three times the number of dwellings to any of the rest that I saw. They seem to have some notion of the devil, and at least are afraid of apparitions, for none of them will stir out of his hut when dark without company. And one night in particular we heard a great noise in the town like several drums beating, which next day we found had been some of the Indians beating the sides of their houses, which are made of horses' skins, to frighten away the devil.

Each Indian has but one wife, and they live together in a very loving manner. A new-born child is wrapped up in a sheep's skin, and instead of a bed or cradle is laid on a machine somewhat like our hand-barrow, the bottom of which is likewise covered with a sheep's skin. This is hung up by the four corners, and the child swings backwards and forwards instead of being rocked in a cradle, its arms and legs being fastened to this engine by a lash of horse's skin to prevent its falling over. Every morning they take all their children, young and old, and carry them to the next brook or rivulet and plunge them naked under water, even when the ground is covered with snow, by which means they are hardened to run about naked, even in the midst of winter.

And now their time for making the hunting voyage approaching, which they do every spring, and generally spend a whole summer in taking their wild horses, we made great intercession to go with them. But we were given to understand that we must be sent further into the country, to remain with other Indians till their return. But at last we prevailed, by assuring the chief that we had English friends at Buenos Aires, who would make him a very handsome satisfaction for us, and who would redeem us at any price he should put upon us. This seemed to please him, and he then consented.

We were at present about a thousand miles from Buenos Aires; and their route extends to the eastern coast of Patagonia, quite to the sea, about a hundred miles to the southward of Buenos Aires. When they set out, they carry with them everything belonging to them: women, children, houses, and all. These last are slung across the horses, and at night taken down for sheltering themselves from the weather. They take with them a few horses more than they ride, which serve for maintaining them till their hunting begins, which seldom happens before they have travelled seven or eight days.

And now the wished-for time was come, when we all set out in a body, except John Duck, whose misfortune it was to be too near of a complexion with those Indians, for he was a mulatto born in London; for which reason he was sold by the chief to a master farther up the country, where I believe he will end his days, there being no prospect of his ever returning to England.

We had travelled ten or twelve days before we had seen any wild horses, but soon after several stragglers fell victim to their ingenuity. They have two different methods of taking them, each of which I have seen them perform with incredible dexterity. The first is with a lash made of horses' skins, about fifty feet long and two inches broad, with a running noose at the end of it. This noose they hold in their right hand, and the other end in the left, till they come within a few yards of the beast, when they throw the noose over its head, even at full speed, and hold the other end fast in their left hand. The beast is soon stopped and taken.

The other method is with a narrow strap of horse skin, about twelve feet long, to each end of which is fastened a round ball of iron about two pounds weight. When within distance of their game they hurl one of the balls several times round their head, till they have got the proper swing, and then throw it at the horse's legs, parting with the ball in their left hand at the same time, which seldom fails of entangling the legs and throwing the horse to the ground. Horses thus taken are secured by some of the company, whose business is chiefly to tie these horses together in a string, and guard them. In a few days they become very tame.

They are likewise very dextrous in killing birds with these balls, and will throw them to a prodigious height in the air. This is what they are trained up to in their infancy, and are very expert at even in their youth. These iron balls, fastened in the above manner, are likewise their chief warlike weapons, next to their bows and arrows.

Being now arrived within a hundred miles of Buenos Aires, we begged of the chief to despatch one of his men to the Governor, to acquaint him of three English prisoners he had with him and to ask if he would redeem us. The chief did so, and the messenger on his return brought a certain pledge of fulfilling his promise, which was a gold-laced waistcoat. Next day we were told to get ourselves ready to go to Buenos Aires, and that he and some of his men would go with us. The hopes of once more seeing our fellow-Christians filled us with joy.

Chapter 15

RANSOMED, BUT FAR FROM SAFE

Buenos Aires, May 1744. The survivors, now reduced to three, are brought in to the city and ransomed from the Indians by an English agent. They are confined aboard the Asia, Admiral Pizarro's flagship, as prisoners of war, and make an unsuccessful attempt to escape. Midshipman Campbell joins the prisoners, having come from Santiago across the Andes with Admiral Pizarro, and the Asia sails for Spain. There is a dramatic attempt by eleven Indian slaves to take over the ship, which is very nearly successful. Campbell describes the same event.

FROM MIDSHIPMAN MORRIS'S ACCOUNT

We were brought immediately before the Governor of Buenos Aires, who satisfied our Indian prince and paid him his ransom, which was ninety dollars and a few trifles, and then dismissed him. We returned him our hearty thanks for his kindness towards us during our abode with him, in which time we were treated with greater humanity than we afterwards met in our long confinement on board of the flagship of the Spanish Admiral Pizarro.

After we had passed examination by the Governor and had given him a full account of our past misfortunes, we were dismissed for a short space upon parole. And here I should be very ungrateful if I did not do justice to the president of the English Assiento[1] house, Mr. Grey, by acknowledging that it was entirely owing to his compassion and kind intercession with the Governor that we were thus redeemed from the hands of the Indians, he offering to do it at his own charge. We were sent for several times before the Governor, and earnestly pressed to turn Catholics and serve the King of Spain; but our answer was that we were Protestants and true Englishmen, and hoped to die so. Many tempting offers were made to seduce us, but thank God we resisted them all.

When the Governor found all his efforts were of no effect, we were sent as prisoners of war on board the *Asia*, which lay then at Montevideo, about thirty leagues down the river, waiting for orders, and had lain there upwards of two years. This was the Spanish Admiral Pizarro's ship, which, after an unsuccessful attempt to pass Cape Horn in order to be in the South Seas with her squadron before ours, was driven back by tempestuous weather, and obliged to put into the River Plate, having lost nearly half her crew. The Admiral had quitted her and gone overland to Chile.

We were confined on board the *Asia* above a year, with sixteen other English, in which time we were treated more like slaves than prisoners of war. Our business was to do all their nasty work: to swab and clean the decks fore and aft every morning; and after the work was done we were confined between decks, with a sentinel over us as if we had been criminals, with a poor allowance of victuals.

Our usage was so bad that we agreed, with the rest of the English prisoners, to attempt our liberty, though at the risk of our lives. Accordingly one night we escaped from our guard, intending to swim ashore, and travel to a Portuguese settlement on the north side of the river, as the ship lay within a quarter of a mile of the shore. Myself and one other got safe to land in safety, the rest were discovered before they got into the water. I was quite naked, and my comrade had a shirt wrapped round his head;

1. The Assiento was a contract between Spain, Britain and some other nations for the procurement of slaves for the Spanish in South America. It functioned even in wartime.

but before we got half-way to the shore a gun was fired from the ship to alarm the town. We travelled until two in the morning, and then lay down among the rushes. The weather being very frosty, our feet swelled and full of thorns, we could travel no further. Soon after daylight we met with some men on horseback belonging to the plantations, to whom we surrendered ourselves, and they took us behind them to their house. The next day we were carried from thence by some soldiers who were in pursuit of us, and carried on board the ship, where we were put in the stocks, neck and heels, four hours every day for a fortnight.

At length we were informed of the Admiral's arrival at Buenos Aires; who soon after came on board, and gave orders for refitting the ship in the best manner they could, being determined to carry her to Old Spain. But there was a great deficiency of hands, for which reason orders were given to impress what men they could at Montevideo. These, with eleven Indians whom the Spaniards had four months before taken prisoners in a skirmish and now designed for their row-galleys, were sent on board; and soon afterwards I had the pleasure of seeing my brother midshipman, Mr. Campbell,[2] who was lost in the *Wager* with us, but choosing to follow the fortune of Captain Cheap, arrived with him at Chile. He came by land from thence with some officers belonging to the Spanish Admiral, and arrived in March at Buenos Aires. In the latter end of October 1745 we sailed from Montevideo in the *Asia*, bound for Spain.

Three days after we sailed an affair happened on board, which was like to have proved fatal to the whole crew. About nine at night we were alarmed with the cry of a mutiny, and so indeed it proved; but such a one as would never have been suspected by any of the ship's crew, or perhaps credited by posterity, if such a number of persons were still not living to attest the fact.[3] The Indians above mentioned were a chief named Orellana and ten of his followers, who belonged to a very powerful tribe which had

2. It is astonishing that these two midshipmen from the *Wager* should meet here after four and a half years of almost unbelievable perils and hardships on different sides of the continent.
3. For a discussion of the authorship of this passage describing the Indian insurrection, see Appendix B.

committed great ravages in the neighbourhood of Buenos Aires. Now on board the *Asia*, they were treated with much insolence and barbarity by the Spaniards, the meanest officers among whom were accustomed to beat them on the slightest pretences, and sometimes only to show their superiority.

Orellana and his followers, though in appearance sufficiently patient and submissive, meditated a severe revenge for all these inhumanities. As he conversed very well in Spanish (these Indians having, in time of peace, a good intercourse with Buenos Aires), he affected to talk with such of the English as understood that language, and seemed very desirous of being informed how many Englishmen were on board, and which they were. As he knew that the English were as much enemies to the Spaniards as himself, he had doubtless an intention of disclosing his purpose to them, and making them partners in the scheme he had projected for revenging his wrongs and recovering his liberty. But having sounded them at a distance, and not finding them so precipitate and vindictive as he expected, he proceeded no further with them; but resolved to trust alone to the resolution of his ten faithful followers. These, it should seem, readily engaged to observe his directions, and to execute whatever commands he gave them.

Having agreed on the measures necessary to be taken, they first furnished themselves with Dutch knives, sharp at the point, which being the common knives used in the ship, they found no difficulty in procuring. Besides this, they employed their leisure in secretly cutting out thongs from raw hides, of which there were great numbers on board, and in fixing to each end of these thongs the double-headed shot of the small quarterdeck guns. This, when swung around their heads according to the practice of their country, was a most mischievous weapon, in the use of which the Indians are trained from their infancy, and consequently are extremely expert. These particulars being in good forwardness, the execution of their scheme was perhaps precipitated by a particular outrage committed on Orellana himself. For one of the officers, who was a very brutal fellow, ordered Orellana aloft, which he was incapable of performing, and under pretence of his disobedience beat him with such violence that he left him bleeding on the deck, and stupefied for some time with his bruises and wounds. This usage undoubtedly heightened his thirst for revenge, and made him eager and impatient till the means of executing it were in his power; so that within a day or two after this incident he and his followers opened their desperate resolves in the ensuing manner.

It was about nine in the evening, when many of the principal officers were on the quarterdeck, indulging in the freshness of the night air. The waist of the ship was filled with live cattle, and the forecastle was manned with its customary watch. Orellana and his companions under cover of the night, having prepared their weapons and thrown off their trousers and the more cumbrous part of their dress, came altogether on the quarterdeck and drew towards the door of the great cabin. The Boatswain immediately reprimanded them, and ordered them to be gone. On this Orellana spoke to his followers in his native language, and four of them drew off, two towards each gangway, and the chief and the six remaining Indians seemed to be slowly quitting the quarterdeck. When the detached Indians had taken possession of the gangway, Orellana placed his hands hollow to his mouth, and bellowed out the war cry used by these savages, which is the harshest and most terrifying sound known in nature. This hideous yell was the signal for beginning the massacre; for on this they all drew their knives, and brandished their prepared double-headed shot; and the six with their chief who remained on the quarterdeck immediately fell on the Spaniards, who were intermingled with them, and laid near 40 of them at their feet; of which about 20 were killed on the spot, and the rest disabled.

Many of the officers in the beginning of the tumult pushed into the great cabin, where they put out the lights, and barricaded the door; and of the others, who had avoided the first fury of the Indians, some endeavoured to escape along the gangways into the forecastle; but the Indians, placed there on purpose, stabbed the greatest part of them as they attempted to pass by, or forced them off the gangways into the waist. Others threw themselves voluntarily over the barricades into the waist and thought themselves happy to lie concealed among the cattle. But the greatest part escaped up the main shrouds and sheltered themselves either in tops or rigging. And though the Indians attacked only the quarterdeck, yet the watch in the forecastle, finding their communication cast off and being terrified by the wounds of the few who, not being killed on the spot, had strength sufficient to force their passage along the gangways, and not knowing either who their enemies were, or what were their numbers, they likewise gave all over for lost, and in great confusion ran up into the rigging of the foremast and bowsprit.

Thus these eleven Indians, with a resolution perhaps without example, possessed themselves almost in an instant of the quarterdeck of a ship mounting 66 guns, with a crew of near 500 men, and continued in peaceable possession of this post a considerable time. As for supporting the officers in the great cabin (among whom were Pizarro and Mindinuetta[4]) the crew between decks and those who had escaped into the tops and rigging were only anxious for their own safety, and were for a long time incapable of forming any project for suppressing the insurrection and recovering the possession of the ship. It is true, the yells of the Indians, the groans of the wounded, and the confused clamours of the crew, all heightened by the obscurity of the night, had at first greatly magnified their danger and had filled them with the imaginary terrors which darkness, disorder, and an ignorance of the real strength of an enemy, never fail to produce. For as the Spaniards were sensible of the disaffection of their pressed hands, and were also conscious of their barbarity to their prisoners, they imagined the conspiracy was general, and considered their own destruction as certain. It was said that some of them had taken the resolution of leaping into the sea, but were prevented by their companions.

However, when the Indians had entirely cleared the quarterdeck, the

---

4. Don Joseph Mindinuetta (other sources call him Pedro de Mendinueta) was captain of the *Guipuscoa*, 74, the most powerful ship in Pizarro's squadron. Her ship's company mutinied and ran the ship on to the coast of Brazil, where she became a total wreck. Subsequently Mindinuetta took command of the *Esperanza*, 50, and finally got round the Horn in early 1743 – but Anson had gone.

tumult in a great measure subsided; for those who had escaped were kept silent by their fears and the Indians were incapable of pursuing them to renew the disorder. Orellana, when he saw himself master of the quarterdeck, broke open the arms chest, which on a slight suspicion of mutiny had been ordered there a few days before, as to a place of the greatest security. Here he took it for granted that he should find cutlasses sufficient for himself and his companions, in the use of which they were all extremely skilful; and with these it was imagined they purposed to force the great cabin. But on opening the chest there appeared nothing but firearms, which to them were of no use. There were indeed cutlasses in the chest but they were hidden by the firearms being laid over them. This was a sensible disappointment to them.

By this time Pizarro and his companions in the great cabin were capable of conversing aloud through the cabin windows and portholes with those in the gunroom and between decks; and from hence they learnt that the English (whom they principally suspected) were all safe below, and had not meddled in this mutiny. By other particulars they at last discovered that none were concerned in it but Orellana and his people. On this Pizarro and the officers resolved to attack them on the quarterdeck before any of the discontented on board should so far recover their first surprise as to reflect on the facility and certainty of seizing the ship by a junction with the Indians in the present emergency.

With this in view Pizarro got together what arms were in the cabin, and distributed them to those who were with him; but there were no other firearms to be met with but pistols, and for these they had neither powder nor ball. However having now settled a correspondence with the gunroom, they lowered down a bucket out of the cabin window, into which the Gunner put a quantity of pistol cartridges. When they had thus procured ammunition and had loaded their pistols, they set the cabin door partly open, and fired some shot among the Indians on the quarterdeck, at first without effect; but at last Mindinuetta, whom we have mentioned, had the good fortune to shoot Orellana dead on the spot. On which his faithful companions, abandoning all thoughts of further resistance, instantly leapt into the sea, and every man perished. Thus was this insurrection quelled and the possession of the quarterdeck regained, after it had been full two hours in the power of this great and daring chief, and his gallant and unhappy countrymen.

Midshipman Campbell has also left an account of this dramatic incident, and his version, in which he gives himself a starring role, is questionable in that his heroics have not been mentioned by Morris at all.

From Midshipman Campbell's account

17th October 1745, being got out of sight of land, about 9 o'clock at night as I was going to bed, something fell down upon the quarterdeck, which as the ship was in a very bad condition I imagined was one of her masts or yards carried away, of which I had all along been apprehensive. But the noise being repeated and growing louder, I got up to see what was the matter. As I was going up the after ladder, I was saluted with a blow on the head which knocked me down. Soon after I saw a soldier drop down dead. All the ship's company were now in an uproar, crying out, "A mutiny! A mutiny." Hereupon I went to my berth, and sat down awaiting the issue.

At last seeing several officers and men wounded, while others were killed outright, I inquired the cause of so much bloodshed, and was informed that twelve Indians from the plains of Buenos Aires, whom the Spaniards had taken prisoners and were carrying to Spain for galley slaves, had risen upon their captors, and seemed as if resolved to be cut to pieces rather than be carried into slavery. Hearing this I went on the forecastle, where I found the Irish and Scots captains with most of the Spanish officers, all in confusion. By this time the twelve Indians had made themselves masters of the quarterdeck, and not a Spaniard dared attack them. Fearing they would set fire to the ship, which they might easily have done, all the nettings on the quarterdeck being full of hay for the cattle which were on board, I therefore proposed to go on the quarterdeck, and attack them sword in hand. I was bravely seconded by one of the Irish officers, who though an old man had as much courage as the youngest aboard. Followed by a few others, we attacked both gangways at once, pressed the Indians hard, and killed their Captain and one other.

Their Captain (whom they called a king, and whose name was Gallidana) was a very brave fellow; during the whole action he continually encouraged his men by putting his hand to his mouth and making the noise they called the war-whoop; and crying out, "We are brave Indians but the Spaniards are poltroons," or words to that effect. As long as he spoke, his men stood their ground, though attacked two ways at once; but when he fell, as soon as his voice ceased they all got on the rails of the quarterdeck and jumped overboard crying out, "Though you have killed our king you shan't have the pleasure of killing us."

The enemy having thus fled the field, the Spaniards began to look after their dead and wounded. They found eleven men slain outright, among whom were the master of the ship and two mates. Thirty eight were wounded, five of whom died of their wounds.[5] A Jesuit also had his arm broken, and was other ways very much hurt. All this havoc did twelve Indians make (armed with nothing but knives, and some of the double-headed shot slung in the middle with which they knocked down the Spaniards) among 444 men that were aboard, among whom were 32 commissioned officers, most of them formerly belonging to other ships of Pizarro's squadron which had been lost.

5. Spanish sources give the number of casualties as 60, being 20 killed and 40 injured.

Chapter 16

CAMPBELL'S DUBIOUS BEHAVIOUR

They reach Spain, and Morris is treated very roughly by the Spaniards, but eventually returns home under a prisoner of war agreement. Very different is Campbell's experience: he is sent for by the authorities in Madrid, and interviewed. He is given a passport home, and returns via Portugal to England, where he has to defend himself against the charge of having volunteered to join the Spanish navy.

FROM THE ACCOUNTS OF MIDSHIPMEN MORRIS AND CAMPBELL

Morris writes:

Towards the latter end of February 1746 we arrived at Corcubion, a harbour about five leagues south of Cape Finisterre, where we requested to be sent on shore as prisoners of war, but were told that we must all go in the ship to the Groyne.[1] Whereupon we went on the quarter-deck in a body, and told the Admiral that we would no longer be slaves on board. Next day we were sent ashore and confined fifteen days in a prison, with an allowance only of bread and water, chained together as criminals, till

---

1. Old seafaring term for the Spanish port of Corunna or La Coruña.

the ship sailed for the Groyne, when we were released from our dungeon and guarded to the Groyne by land with a file of musketeers. As soon as we arrived we were put into the guard-house for two days, and from thence sent to St Antonio's Castle, which is on an island at the entrance of the harbour, a prison for thieves and felons. In this dismal place we were kept fourteen weeks among the worst of malefactors, till an order came from the court of Spain to send us to Portugal, allowing us a guide and a real per day.

In eight days we got to Oporto, and made application to the English consul, who after hearing the hardships we had gone through, gave us each three days' maintenance, and a quarter of a moidore.

On 28th April 1746 we embarked on board the *Charlotta* snow, Captain Henry Miller, bound for London, under convoy of the *York* and *Folkestone* men-of-war, and arrived at London on the 8th July following; three only of the eight left on the Patagonian coast, Samuel Cooper, John Andrews, and myself, being so happy as to see once more their native country.

Campbell writes:

After this unlucky affair (the near-successful mutiny by the Indians) nothing occurred to us but what is common at sea till we arrived on the coast of Portugal, when the appearance of some ships put the Spaniards into a great fright, and they immediately confined me and the other prisoners. They were under arms three days and three nights, and it is certain they had good reason for their fears. For in the first place the ship was very rich, having upwards of five millions of dollars on board, though not all registered. Secondly she was in great want of hands, and those that were on board were very weak and sickly.

20th January 1746, we arrived at the port of Corcubion, near Cape Finisterre, where I waited twenty days while the ship went round. Coming to Ferrol, I was ordered to Madrid, where on the day after my arrival I was introduced to one of the Ministry, who after asking me some questions ordered me to a room till further notice. Two days after I was called for again, and he inquired of me the particulars of Mr Anson's voyage, to which I answered in general that I was only a petty officer in the fleet, and that all my business was to do as I was ordered by my superiors. When they made me offers of entry into their service I plainly refused, telling them that I would rather be a common sailor in the service of my own King than an officer under another. When I begged to be set at liberty and to go home by the way of Portugal, the minister said he would acquaint His Majesty with my demand, and that I should soon have an answer.

Next day I waited on the same minister, and he ordered me to go to the Secretary of War's office, where I should have a passport to Lisbon. I went directly and got the passport with fifteen dollars for my travelling charges; then I would have set out immediately, but the weather being bad was obliged to stay at Madrid five days longer. When I did set out I found it almost impossible to travel, the heavy rains had so spoiled the roads. But the most disagreeable circumstance was the lightness of my purse, which rendered my journey very uncomfortable indeed.

At last it pleased God that I got safe to Lisbon, where I no sooner arrived than I waited on the English consul, who told me that the *Edinburgh*, Commodore Coats, was going from thence to England. Hereupon I waited on the Commodore, and desired my passage home, which he readily granted. After staying at Lisbon only three days, I embarked for England, and in six more arrived at Plymouth, thus happily surmounting, through the mercy of the Almighty, a long and unfortunate voyage of five years and eight months.

From Plymouth I went to Portsmouth in the same ship, and proceeded directly to London, where I arrived at the beginning of May 1746; and informed the Lords of the Admiralty of my arrival by a petition to their Lordships. Speaking at the same time with Mr Corbett, Secretary to the Admiralty, I found to my great surprise that Their Lordships had been told by Captain Cheap that I was in the Spanish Service! That this was a false assertion the public will hardly require any other proof than the reading of the foregoing narrative. If I had been in the Spanish service, how could I have acquired a passport (which I sent enclosed in a letter to Mr Secretary Corbett) from a minister of Spain, and how could I likewise arrive here in England so soon after the Captain? Upon the whole I hope that what I have here written will be sufficient to satisfy the public of my innocence, and clear me of what is so wrongfully laid to my charge.[2]

To summarise this complex and interlocking story, we have followed the 29 long-boat survivors home, and we can leave for the present Lieutenant Baynes and Gunner Bulkeley in England awaiting an uncertain future, and no doubt hoping their Captain will never return to bring charges of mutiny.

Midshipman Morris and two others have also come home after an absence of five years spent mostly as Indian slaves and prisoners of the Spanish. Midshipman Campbell too has now returned, protesting his innocence against the suspicion of treason in having joined the Spanish navy. And back on Wager Island, long before Campbell was to leave his compatriots in dubious circumstances, Captain Cheap and a small party are assessing their chances of survival in dire conditions on a deserted shore. John Byron, who is just setting off in the long-boat, takes up the tale.

2. For an assessment of this, see p267-268.

The red track is that of the *Speedwell*. The blue track is that followed by Cheap, Byron, Campbell and eventually Hamilton. The green route is how Campbell then reached the *Asia* in Montevideo in company with some Spanish officers.

161

PART 4
The Captain and his Few

Chapter 17

PREPARATIONS TO STRUGGLE NORTH

Back to Wager Island, 13ᵗʰ October 1741. The long-boat, cutter and barge are about to depart with Lieutenant Baynes, Gunner Bulkeley and 79 men. The Captain has been arrested and deprived of his command, ostensibly for the shooting of Midshipman Cozens, but in reality because he has insisted on a plan of going north to capture a Spanish ship and rejoin the Commodore, whereas the popular opinion is that going south offers the only chance of survival. The Captain is at the last minute left behind with Mr Hamilton of the marines and Mr Elliot the Surgeon, both of whom refuse to leave him. Byron, who had thought the Captain was being taken in custody with the company in the long-boat, takes the opportunity to slip away in the barge to rejoin his Captain, and eight men including Campbell agree to go with him. Plans are made to go to the north.

FROM MIDSHIPMAN BYRON'S NARRATIVE

The long-boat was now launched and ready for sailing, and all the men embarked except Captain Pemberton with a party of marines, who drew them up upon the beach with intent to conduct Captain Cheap on board; but he was at length persuaded to desist from this resolution by Mr Bulkeley. The men too, finding they were straitened for room, and that their stock of provision would not admit of taking supernumeraries aboard, were now no

164

less strenuous for his enlargement[1], and being left to his option of staying behind. Therefore, after having distributed their share in the reserved stock of provision, which was very small, we departed, leaving Captain Cheap, Mr Hamilton of the marines, and the Surgeon upon the island.

I had all along been in the dark as to the turn this matter would take; and not in the least suspecting but that it was determined Captain Cheap should be taken with us, readily embarked under that persuasion. But when I found that this design, which was so seriously carried on to the last, was suddenly dropped, I was determined upon the first opportunity to leave them, which was at that instant impossible for me to do, the long-boat lying some distance offshore at anchor. We were in all eighty-one when we left the island, distributed into the long-boat, cutter, and barge; fifty-nine on board the first, twelve in the second, in the last ten.

It was our purpose to put into some harbour, if possible, every evening, as we were in no condition to keep those terrible seas long; for without other assistance our stock of provisions was no more than might have been consumed in a few days. Our water was chiefly contained in a few powder-barrels. Our flour was to be lengthened out by a mixture of seaweed; and our other supplies depended upon the success of our guns and industry among the rocks.

Captain Pemberton having brought on board his men, we weighed. A sudden squall of wind having split our foresail, we with difficulty cleared the rocks by means of our oars, bore away for a sandy bay on the south side of the lagoon, and anchored in ten fathom. The next morning we got under way; but it blowing hard at W by N with a great swell put into a small bay again, well sheltered by a ledge of rocks without us.

At this time it was thought necessary to send the barge away back to Cheap's Bay for some spare canvas, which was imagined would be soon wanted. I thought this a good opportunity of returning, and therefore made one with those who went upon this business in the barge.

---

1. Release.

We were no sooner clear of the long-boat than all those in the barge with me declared they had the same intention. When we arrived at the island we were extremely welcome to Captain Cheap.

The next day I asked him leave to try if I could prevail upon those in the long-boat to give us our share of provision. This he granted, but said if we went in the barge they would certainly take her from us. I told him my design was to walk it, and only desired the barge might land me upon the main, and wait for me till I came back. I had the most dreadful journey of it imaginable, through thick woods and swamps all the way; but I might as well have spared myself that trouble, as it was to no manner of purpose. They would not give me, nor any one of us that left them, a single ounce of provisions of any kind. I therefore returned, and after that made a second attempt; but all in vain. They even threatened that if we did not return with the barge they would fetch her by force.

It is impossible to conceive the distressed situation we were now in, at the time of the long-boat's departure. I don't mention this event as the occasion of it; by which, if we who were left on the island experienced any alteration at all, it was for the better; and which in all probability had it been deferred might have been fatal to the greatest part of us. But at this time the subsistence on which we had hitherto depended chiefly, which was the shellfish, were everywhere along shore eaten up; and as to stock saved from the wreck, it may be guessed what the amount of that might be, when the share allotted to the Captain, Lieutenant Hamilton, and the Surgeon was no more than six pieces of beef, as many of pork, and ninety pounds of flour. As to myself and those that left the long-boat, it was the least revenge they thought they could take of us to withhold our provision from us, though at the same time it was hard and unjust.

For a day or two after our return there was some little pittance dealt out to us, yet it was upon the foot of favour; and we were soon left to our usual industry for a farther supply. This was now exerted to very little purpose for the reason before assigned; to which may be added, the wreck was now blown up, all her upper works gone, and no hopes of any valuable driftage from her for the future. A weed, called slaugh, fried in the tallow of some candles we had saved, and wild celery, were our only fare; by which our strength was so much impaired that we could scarcely crawl. It was my misfortune too to labour under a severe flux, by which I was reduced to a very feeble state; so that in attempting to traverse the rocks in search of shellfish, I fell from one into very deep water, and with difficulty saved my life by swimming.

As the Captain was now freed by the departure of the long-boat from the riotous applications, menaces, and disturbance of an unruly crew, and left at liberty to follow the plan he had resolved upon of going northward, he began to think seriously of putting it in execution; in order to effect which, a message was sent to the deserters[2] who had seated themselves on the other side of the neighbouring lagoon, to sound them whether they were inclined to join the Captain in his undertaking; and if they were, to bring them over to him. For this set, the party gone off in the long-boat had left a half allowance proportion of the common stock of provision. These men upon the proposal readily agreed to join their commander; and being conducted to him, increased our number to twenty.

The boats which remained in our possession to carry off all these people were only the barge and yawl, two very crazy bottoms; the broadside of the last was entirely out, and the first had suffered much in a variety of bad weather she had gone through, and was much out of repair. And now as our Carpenter was gone from us, we had no remedy for these misfortunes but the little skill we had gained from him. However, we made tolerable shifts to patch up the boats for our purpose. In the height of our distresses, when hunger, which seems to include and absorb all others, was most prevailing, we were cheered with the appearance once more of our friendly Indians, as we thought, from whom we hoped for some relief; but as the consideration was wanting, for which alone they would part with their commodities,

---

2. These were the men who had deserted the main party some months before and set up a camp on their own.

we were not at all benefited by their stay, which was very short.

The little reserve too of flour made by the Captain for our sea-stock when we should leave the island was now diminished by theft. The thieves, who were three of our men, were however soon discovered, and two of them apprehended; but the third made his escape to the woods. Considering the pressing state of our necessities, this theft was looked upon as a most heinous crime, and therefore required an extraordinary punishment; accordingly the Captain ordered these delinquents to be severely whipped, and then to be banished to an island at some distance from us. Before this latter part of the sentence could be put in execution, one of them fled; but the other was put alone upon a barren island, which afforded not the least shelter. However we, in compassion, and contrary to order, patched him up a bit of a hut and kindled him a fire, and then left the poor wretch to shift for himself. In two or three days after, going to the island in our boat with some little refreshment, such as our miserable circumstances would admit of, and with an intent of bringing him back, we found him dead and stiff.

I was now reduced to the lowest condition by my illness, which was increased by the vile stuff I ate. When we were favoured by a fair day, a thing very extraordinary in this climate, we instantly took the advantage of it, and once more visited the last remains of the wreck. Here our pains were repaid with the great good fortune of hooking up three casks of beef, which were brought safe to shore. This providential supply could not have happened at a more seasonable time than now, when we were afflicted with the greatest dearth we had ever experienced, and the little strength we had remaining was to be exerted in our endeavours to leave the island. Accordingly we soon found a remedy for our sickness, which was nothing but the effects of famine, and were greatly restored by food. The provision was equally distributed among us all, and served us for the remainder of our stay here. We began to grow extremely impatient to leave the island, as the days were now nearly at their longest, and about mid-summer in these parts; but as to the weather, there seems to be little difference of seasons.

Chapter 18

FOUL WEATHER DEFEATS THEM

Wager Island, 15th December 1741. The 17 survivors set out in the two small boats to attempt the perilous crossing of the bay. Foul weather defeats them again and again, and they suffer desperate hunger and cold. The yawl is overturned and lost with one man drowned. There being insufficient room for all in the barge, four marines are left ashore.

FROM MIDSHIPMAN BYRON'S NARRATIVE

The day being tolerable, we told Captain Cheap we thought it a fine opportunity to run across the bay. But he most desired two or three of us to accompany him to our place of observation, the top of Mount Misery, when looking through his perspective,[1] he observed to us that the sea ran very high without. However this had no weight with the people, who were desirous at all events to be gone. I should here observe that Captain Cheap's plan was if possible to get to the island of Chiloé; and if we found any vessel there to board her immediately, and cut her out.[2] This he certainly might have done with ease had it been his good fortune

---

1. Telescope.
2. Capture and make away with her.

to get round with the boats.

We now launched both boats and got everything on board of them as quick as possible. Captain Cheap, the Surgeon, and myself, were in the barge with nine men, and Lieutenant Hamilton and Mr Campbell in the yawl with six. I steered the barge, and Mr Campbell the yawl; but we had not been two hours at sea before the wind shifted more to the westward, and began to blow very hard and the sea run extremely high, so that we could no longer keep our heads towards the cape or headland we had designed for. This Cape[3] we had had a view of in one of the intervals of fair weather, during our abode on the island, from Mount Misery; and it seemed to be distant between twenty and thirty leagues from us. We were now obliged to bear away right before the wind. Though the yawl was not far from us, we could see nothing of her, except now and then upon the top of a mountainous sea. In both the boats the men were obliged to sit as close as possible, to receive the seas on their backs, to prevent their filling us, which was what we every moment expected. We were obliged to throw everything overboard to lighten the boats, all our beef and even the grapnel, to prevent sinking.

Night was coming on and we were running on a lee-shore fast, where the sea broke in a frightful manner. Not one amongst us imagined it possible for boats to live in such a sea. In this situation, as we neared the shore, expecting to be beaten to pieces by the first breaker, we perceived a small opening between the rocks, which we stood for, and found a very narrow passage between them, which brought us into a harbour for the boats as calm and smooth as a millpond.

The yawl had got in before us, and our joy was great at meeting again after so unexpected a deliverance. Here we secured the boats, and ascended a rock. It rained excessively hard all the first part of the night, and was extremely cold; and though we had not a dry thread about us, and no wood could be found for firing, we were obliged to pass the night in

---

3. Cabo Tres Montes. See chart on p186.

that uncomfortable situation, without any covering, shivering in our wet clothes. The frost coming on with the morning, it was impossible for any of us to get a moment's sleep; and having flung overboard our provision the day before, there being no prospect of finding anything to eat on this coast, in the morning we pulled out of the cove. But we found so great a sea without that we could make but little of it.

After tugging all day, towards night we put in among some small islands, landed upon one of them, and found it a mere swamp. As the weather was the same, we passed this night much as we had done the preceding. Sea-tangle was all we could get to eat at first, but the next day we had better luck: the Surgeon got a goose, and we found materials for a good fire. We were confined here three or four days, the weather all that time proving so bad that we could not put out.

As soon as it grew moderate we left this place, and shaped our course to the northward; and perceiving a large opening between very high land and a low point we steered for it, and found a large bay down which we rowed, flattering ourselves there might be a passage that way. But towards night we came to the bottom of the bay, and finding no outlet, we were obliged to return the same way we came, having found nothing the whole day to alleviate our hunger.

Next night we put into a little cove, which, from the great quantity of red wood found there, we called Redwood Cove. Leaving this place in the morning, we had the wind southerly, blowing fresh, by which we made much way that day, to the northward. Towards evening we were in with a pretty large island. Putting ashore on it, we found it clothed with the finest trees we had ever seen, their stems running up to a prodigious height, without knot or branch and as straight as cedars. The leaf of these trees resembled the myrtle leaf, only somewhat larger. I have seen trees larger than these in circumference on the coast of Guinea, and there only; but for length of stem, which gradually tapered, I have nowhere met with any to compare to them. The wood was of a hard substance, and if not too heavy, would have made good masts, the dimension of some of these trees being equal to the main-mast of a first-rate man-of-war. The shore was covered with driftwood of a very large size, most of it cedar, which makes a brisk fire; but is so subject to snap and fly, that when we waked in the morning after a sound sleep, we found our clothes singed in many places with the sparks, and covered with splinters.

The next morning being calm, we rowed out; but as soon as clear of the island, we found a great swell from the westward. We rowed to the bottom of a very large bay, which was to the northward of us, the land very low, and we were in hopes of finding some inlet through, but did not; so kept along shore to the westward. This part, which I take to be above fifty leagues from Wager's Island, is the very bottom of the large bay it lies in. Here was the only passage to be found, which (if we could by any means have got information of it) would have saved us much fruitless labour. Of this passage I shall have occasion to say more hereafter. [4]

We were so pinched with hunger that we ate the shoes off our feet, which consisted of raw seal skin. In the morning we got out of the bay; but the incessant foul weather had overcome us, and we began to be indifferent as to what befell us, and the boats in the night making into a bay, we nearly lost the yawl, a breaker having filled her and driven her ashore upon the beach. (This, by some of our accounts, was Christmas Day; but our accounts had so often been interrupted by our distresses, that there was no depending upon them.) Upon seeing the yawl in this imminent danger, the barge stood off, and went into another bay to the northward of it where it was smoother lying, but there was no possibility of getting on shore. In the night the yawl joined us again.

The next day was so bad, that we despaired of reaching the headland, so rowed down the bay in hopes of getting some seal, as that animal had been seen the day before, but met with no success. So we returned to the same bay we had been in the night before, where the surf having abated somewhat we went ashore, and picked up a few shellfish. In the morning

---

4. See p193.

we got on board early, and ran along shore to the westward for about three leagues in order to get round the Cape, which was the westernmost land we could see. It blew very hard, and there ran such a sea that we heartily wished ourselves back again, and accordingly made the best of our way for that bay which we had left in the morning. But before we could reach it night came on, and we passed a most dismal one, lying upon our oars.

The weather continuing very bad, we put in for the shore in the morning, where we found nothing but tangle[5] and seaweed. We now passed some days roving about for provisions, as the weather was too bad to make another attempt to get round the Cape as yet. We found some fine lagoons towards the head of the bay; and in them killed some seal, and got a good quantity of shellfish, which was a great relief to us. We now made a second attempt to double the Cape; but when we got the length of it and passed the first headland (for it consists of three of an equal height), we got into a sea that was horrid; for it ran all in heaps, like the Race of Portland, but much worse. We were happy to put back to the old place, with little hopes of ever getting round this Cape.

Next day, the weather proving very bad, all hands went ashore to procure some sustenance, except two in each boat, which were left as boat-keepers. This office we took by turns, and it was now my lot to be upon this duty with another man. The yawl lay within us at a grapnel. In the night it blew very hard, and a great sea tumbled in upon the shore; but being extremely fatigued, we in the boats went to sleep. Notwithstanding, however, I was at last awakened by the uncommon motion of the boat, and the roaring of the breakers everywhere about us. At the same time I heard a shrieking, like to that of persons in distress. I looked out, and saw the yawl canted bottom upwards by a sea, and soon afterwards she disappeared. One of our men, whose name was William Rose, a quartermaster, was drowned; the other was thrown ashore by the surf, with his head buried in the sand; but by the immediate assistance of the people on shore was saved. As for us in the

5. Kelp.

barge, we expected the same fate every moment; for the sea broke a long way without us. However, we got her head to it, and hove up our grapnel, or I should rather say killick,[6] which we had made to serve in the room of our grapnel, which had been hove overboard some time before to lighten the boat. By this means we used our utmost efforts to pull her without the breakers some way, and then let go our killick again.

Here we lay all the next day in a great sea, not knowing what would be our fate. To add to our mortification, we could see our companions in tolerable plight ashore eating seal while we were starving with hunger and cold. For this month past, we had not known what it was to have a dry thread about us.

The next day being something more moderate, we ventured in with the barge as near as we could in safety to the shore, and our companions threw us some seal's liver; which having eaten greedily we were seized with excessive sickness, which affected us so much that our skin peeled off from head to foot.

Whilst the people were on shore here Mr Hamilton met with a large seal, or sea-lion, and fired a brace of balls into him, upon which the animal turned upon him open-mouthed; but presently fixing his bayonet he thrust it down its throat, with a good part of the barrel of the gun, which the creature bit in two seemingly with as much ease as if it had been a twig. Notwithstanding the wounds it received, it eluded all farther efforts to kill it, and got clear off.

Having lost the yawl, and being too many for the barge to carry off, we were compelled to leave four of our men behind. They were all marines, who seemed to have no great objection to the determination made with regard to them, so exceedingly disheartened and worn out were they with the distresses and dangers they had already gone through. And indeed I believe it would have been a matter of indifference to the greatest part of the rest, whether they should embark or take their chance. The Captain

---

6. Small anchor.

distributed to these poor fellows arms and ammunition and some other necessaries. When we parted they stood upon the beach, giving us three cheers, and called out, God bless the King. We saw them a little after, setting out upon their forlorn hope, and helping one another over a hideous track of rocks; but considering the difficulties attending this only way of travelling left to them (for the woods are impracticable from their thickness and the deep swamps to be met everywhere in them), considering too, that the coast here is rendered so inhospitable, by the heavy seas that are constantly tumbling upon it, as not to afford even a little shellfish, it is probable that all met with a miserable end.[7]

---

7. Nothing more is heard of these gallant fellows, but their names – Corporal Crosslet, Marines Smith, Hales and Hereford – are commemorated on the chart to this day as the names of a group of islands called Islas Marinas.

Chapter 19

NEGOTIATIONS WITH NATIVE INDIANS

Golfo de Peñas, 28th January 1742. Campbell describes the appalling weather that dogged their two-month efforts to get out of the Bay of Sorrows, with food and clothing barely enough to sustain life. In absolute desperation they return to Wager Island as a familiar place to die in. There an Indian agrees to pilot them to Chiloé in exchange for the barge. Tensions and resentment arise against the Captain for not sharing food fairly, even when one man dies of starvation. Six men desert and make away with the barge with all their meagre supplies aboard, leaving five officers stranded and completely destitute.

FROM MIDSHIPMAN CAMPBELL'S ACCOUNT

When we got up to the Cape we found ourselves the third time disappointed there, the wind being always from the north to the west, with such a terrible great sea that it was impossible for any open boat to get round. So we were obliged to return to Marines' Bay, as we called it, on account of the four men left there.

All that night we were obliged to lie on our oars, for it was so dark that we dared not attempt to go ashore, especially in the rough state the sea was in, which would greatly have hazarded the loss of the barge also, and then we must all have infallibly perished.

It is now six weeks since we left Wager Island, during which our chief subsistence has been drawn from under the stones at low water; and we have been every day obliged to remove from place to place to gather shellfish. The loss of the yawl was the more unfortunate to us who belonged in her, as therein we lost all the poor clothes we had except what we happened at that time to have on our backs. All the clothes I had now left were an old shirt, one pair of cloth breeches, one waistcoat, and an old hat, but neither shoe nor stocking.

On 29th January some of the people declared against making a fresh trial to go round the Cape, and insisted on returning to Wager Island. Others were for leaving the barge and attempting to travel overland, which was the maddest thought imaginable, it being impossible to travel in this wretched part of the American continent.[1] For on the coast side it is all wood and swamp, so that if a man should happen to fall he would be in great danger of drowning.

At last all agreed to go back to Wager Island, though we had now lost all hopes of ever revisiting our native country, for we expected to die at Wager Island, looking on that place, which we had been so much used to, as a kind of home.

Before we set out we killed some seal for our voyage. As we came by the place where we had left the four marines, we resolved to go and bring them off. For we considered that if the boat sunk, we then should be free from the miserable life we led, and die altogether. But alas! All we could find of them, or belonging to them, was one musket and their ammunition; and we doubted not but that they had before now perished by some means or other.

Putting to sea from Marines' Bay, we rode away for the headland that we had left on Christmas Day; but it being calm all the day, it was night before we could get into the cove. Then we were obliged to lie all night

---

1. Even today this part of the Chilean coast is extremely inaccessible. Many villages have access only to the sea, and some villages have only paths that are simply wooden walkways along the shoreline. See p286.

upon our oars, keeping the boat's head out to sea, for it both rained and blew very hard.

Next day we set out for Montrose Island,[2] but as soon as we opened the headland that lay to the west of us the vessel almost overset, and filled so fast with water that we were forced to return to the headland and put into the cove, which we called Stone Cove. There we lay weather-bound for two days, after which we again set out for Montrose Island, but could not yet fetch it, and were obliged to put into another harbour. While we lay in this harbour I went on shore, and being very weak my foot slipped so that I fell from one rock to another, then into the water, and was almost drowned, being stunned with the fall from the rocks.

Having lain here one day, we again put to sea, rowing to windward with the wind at north, in order to get to Montrose Island. All this while we had nothing to eat but seal, which was almost rotten, and we could get no slaugh, so that we were in very great distress. It pleased God that the next night brought us to Montrose Island, which was one of the best we could find in this part of the world, though it produced nothing to eat except a berry which tasted like a gooseberry, but it was black and grew on a bush like a thorn.

Here we stayed some time, the weather being exceeding bad, and we had far to go without any harbour in the way. And even when we did put to sea the wind blew so hard that we were forced to put back to the same island we came from. Next day we again put to sea with wind and rain pretty moderate. But we had not been long out before it began to blow hard, and was so thick that we could not see whither we were steering, till we heard the breakers on the shore; and in a little time could see them white all around us. We were then obliged to haul aft the sheet and stand off the shore, which we happily, and I might also say miraculously, cleared. For who could imagine that any boat could carry so much sail in such a storm?

At last it pleased God that we got safe into Redwood Cove. At this time

---

2. Now Isla Javier. See p186.

Mr Byron, Mr Hamilton, and I ate together, and when we came on shore I went with the former to get fish, but Mr Hamilton being sick stayed at home to make a half wigwam. This sort of wigwam consists of three arches about a yard and a half high and two yards wide, covered with bushes or whatever can be got for thatch. We made a fire at the door place, but it proved of no use for the smoke would not suffer us to tarry in the wigwam. And so we called this place Smoke Cove.

Here it was that I was obliged to eat my shoes. They were of seal skin, and they were at that time a very great dainty.

When we set out from Smoke Cove the weather was fair with little wind, which obliged us to row all the way. It pleased God that we got safe into Cheap's Bay the same day about five or six o'clock in the afternoon. We were all in a starved condition, having eaten nothing for three days but tangle and other seaweeds. After landing we moored the barge with her grapnel to the sea and stern fast to the land. Going up to the huts which we left two months before, we found one of them nailed up, and were obliged to break open the door to get in. It appeared that the Indians had been there by the things that were in the hut, particularly a quantity of iron and other materials which we knew they had taken from the wreck of our unfortunate ship.

We found some seal among the bushes which the Indians had thrown away, for it was so rotten that none but men in our condition could have borne the smell of it. We parted it equally among us, ate it all up, and gave thanks to Almighty God for his providential care of us hitherto.

We stayed here 15 days before any of the Indians came to the island. Meantime we endured the greatest hardships imaginable, the weather being so bad that we could neither get shellfish nor seaweeds. In the interim some differences happened between the Captain, Mr Byron, Lieutenant Hamilton, and myself. There had been some misunderstanding among us ever since Christmas Day; this being 12th February by our account. On this day Mr Hamilton walking along shore discovered several pieces of beef washing in the sea, and brought some of them home to Mr Byron and myself, his messmates. Hereupon I went with Mr Byron and we took up several pieces more. The same night we asked the Captain for his frying pan to melt down the fat, in order to preserve it for frying of slaugh or anything else. When we carried it home, with one half of the fat we had found, the Captain would not receive the fat.

Soon after this affair some Indians came with two canoes, and in one of them was a native of the island of Chiloé who could speak a little Spanish. The Surgeon could speak it likewise, and he asked the Indian if he would carry us to Chiloé in the barge, telling him that he should have her for his trouble, with all that was in her, as soon as we came there. The Indian consenting, we immediately fell to providing for the voyage; and were soon ready, for God knows we had neither victuals nor clothing to trouble ourselves with.

6th March 1742. We all except one marine embarked in the barge with the Indian for our pilot. This marine, when we were going on board, came upon the beach and stole a greatcoat belonging to one of the men; which done he hid himself in the woods so that we could not find him, nor had we ever any account of him afterwards.

And now high words arose between the Captain and Mr Hamilton concerning the fat beef he had found some days before; and the difference arose to such a pitch that the Captain threatened to leave the Lieutenant on the island. After this they did not speak to each other for a long time.[3]

The first night of this our new voyage we lay at an island which we called Sheep's Island. Next day the wind came to the south, and we ran to the westward of Montrose Island. This night we lay on our oars for we could not find a harbour for the boat. All this while we were in great want of provisions. On the morrow we went to the bottom of a great bay, where we found our Indian's hut and his wife and two children. Here we stayed

---

3. Both Captain Cheap and Lieutenant Hamilton were determined and difficult men. Cheap had shown it all along, and Hamilton had been removed from the *Centurion* because of a quarrel with another marine officer. He was to show his intransigence again on this nightmare journey when he had a major disagreement with the Indian guide. In the end he and Cheap were reconciled.

two or three days, and then set out with our guide, his wife, children, and another Indian, a young fellow who was either his servant or partner in the canoe. He carried us to the mouth of a river which we were to go up, but this was found impossible, the stream was so rapid. In this river we were pulling and hauling from eight o'clock in the morning till six in the afternoon. When we came out we were almost dead with fatigue and want of sustenance. John Bosman, seaman, one of the strongest men in the boat, died this evening, being the third day since we left the Indian's hut, and in the interim we had had nothing to eat but a little boiled tangle.

This evening we had for supper some wild purslane, boiled with small mussels. As I was lying by the fire I heard the people say that it would be well done to go off and leave the Captain behind for his cruelty. For this day as we lay in the river, and were all faint for want of food, he took out before us all a great piece of boiled seal with tangle, and he and the Surgeon ate it without offering a bit to any one of us, though he knew that poor Bosman perished merely for want of something to eat.

The next day I acquainted Captain Cheap with the murmurs among the people, and that Mr Hamilton also heard what they said – at least he might have heard them if he was not asleep, he being as near to them as I was. Upon this the Captain called Mr Hamilton aside, and taxed him with conspiring to take the command from him.

This day the Indian with his wife and children went out in their canoe to get some seal, for we had nothing to eat; but at the same time he left us the other Indian, his partner, to carry us to a place where we might get some shellfish. As soon as we got thither, everyone went along shore, except Mr Elliot the Surgeon, who was very ill. The men got back to the boat before the officers, and Mr Elliot desired them to go off a little and try if they could shoot him a gull. Hereupon they all, being six in number, got into the barge, taking the young Indian with them for their guide; and we never saw them again, nor could we conceive whither it was that they thought proper to convey themselves.

I leave the reader to imagine what a condition we five poor souls were now in! The country was all rocks and woods, a mere desert, affording us no better house or habitation than the shade of a tree. Nor had we one morsel of victuals; no arms, nor ammunition, nor fire, nor clothing except the few wretched rags on our backs.

Chapter 20

A NIGHTMARE JOURNEY

Golfo San Esteban, 14ᵗʰ March 1742. The Indian guide returns, and conducts them on an exhausting journey to a small Indian settlement. Byron crawls into a wigwam and is befriended by two women, who give him some fish and warm him. They go on a fishing trip together. Their husband returns and is violently angry. The Surgeon is now at his last gasp, and relations with the Indians are deteriorating.

From Midshipman Byron's narrative

At present, no condition could be worse than we thought ours to be. There ran at this time a very high sea, which breaking with great fury upon this coast, made it very improbable that sustenance in any proportion to our wants could be found upon it; yet, unpromising as this prospect was, and though little succour could be expected from this quarter, I could not help, as I strolled along shore from the rest, casting my eyes towards the sea. Continuing thus to look out, I thought I saw something now and then upon the top of a sea that looked black, which, upon observing still more intently, I imagined at last to be a canoe. But reflecting afterwards how unusual it was for Indians to venture out in so mountainous a sea, and at such a distance from the land, I concluded myself to be deceived.

However, its nearer approach convinced me beyond all doubt of its being a canoe, but that it could not put in anywhere hereabouts, but intended for some other part of the coast. I ran back as fast as I could to my companions, and acquainted them with what I had seen.

The despondency they were in would not allow them to give credit to it at first; but afterwards, being convinced that it was as I reported it, we were all in the greatest hurry to strip off some of our rags to make a signal withal, which we fixed upon a long pole. This had the desired effect: the people in the canoe seeing the signal, made towards the land at about two miles distance from us; for no boat could approach the land where we were. There they put into a small cove sheltered by a large ledge of rocks without, which broke the violence of the sea.

Captain Cheap and I walked along shore, and got to the cove about the time they landed. Here we found the persons arrived in this canoe to be our Indian guide and his wife who had left us some days before. He would have asked us many questions, but neither Captain Cheap nor I understanding Spanish at that time we took him along with us to the Surgeon, whom we had left so ill that he could hardly raise himself from the ground.

When the Indian began to confer with the Surgeon the first question was, what was become of the barge and his companion? And as he could give him no satisfactory answer to this question, the Indian took it for granted that Emanuel was murdered by us, and that he and his family ran the same risk; upon which he was preparing to provide for his security by leaving us directly. The Surgeon seeing this did all in his power to pacify him, and convince him of the unreasonableness of his apprehensions, which he at length found means to do, by assuring him that the Indian would come to no harm, but that he would soon see him return safe – which providentially, and beyond our expectation, happened accordingly; for a few days after, Emanuel having contrived to make his escape from the people in the barge, he returned by ways that were impassable to any creature but an Indian. All that we could learn from Emanuel relative to his escape was that he took the first opportunity of leaving them, which was upon their putting into a bay somewhere to the westward.

We had but one gun among us, and that was a small fowling-piece of mine, with no ammunition but a few charges of powder I had about me; and as the Indian was very desirous of returning to the place where he had left his wife and canoe, Captain Cheap desired I would go with him and watch over him all night to prevent his getting away. Accordingly I set out with him, and when he and his family betook themselves to rest in the little wigwam they had made for that purpose, I kept my station as sentinel over them all night.

The next morning, Captain Cheap, Mr Hamilton, and the Surgeon joined us; the latter, by illness being reduced to the most feeble condition, was supported by Mr Hamilton and Mr Campbell. After holding some little consultation together as to the best manner of proceeding in our journey, it was agreed that the Indian should haul his canoe, with our assistance, over land, quite across the island we were then upon, and put her into a bay on the other side, from whence he was to go in quest of some other Indians by whom he expected to be joined. But as his canoe was too small to carry more than three or four persons, he thought it advisable to take only Captain Cheap and myself with him, and to leave his wife and children as pledges with our companions till his return.

As it was matter of uncertainty whether we should ever recover the barge or not, which was stipulated on our side to become the property of the cacique[1] upon his fulfilling his engagements with us, the inducements we now made use of to prevail upon him to proceed with us in our journey were, that he should have my fowling-piece and some little matters in the possession of Captain Cheap, and that we would use our interest to procure him some small pecuniary reward.

We were now to set off in the canoe, in which I was to assist him in rowing. Accordingly, putting from this island, we rowed hard all this day and the next without any thing to eat but a scrap of seal, a very small

1. Chief.

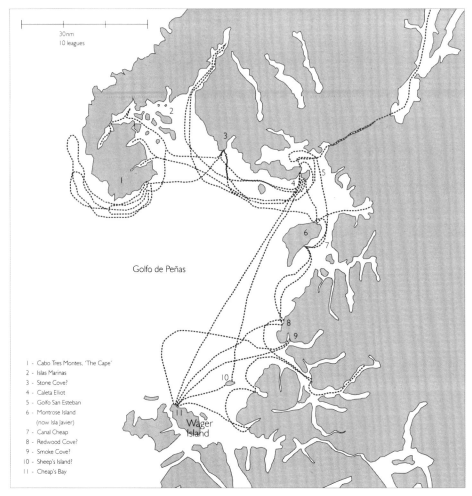

30nm
10 leagues

Golfo de Peñas

1 - Cabo Tres Montes, 'The Cape'
2 - Islas Marinas
3 - Stone Cove?
4 - Caleta Elliot
5 - Golfo San Esteban
6 - Montrose Island
      (now Isla Javier)
7 - Canal Cheap
8 - Redwood Cove?
9 - Smoke Cove?
10 - Sheep's Island?
11 - Cheap's Bay

Wager
Island

This tangle of red lines attempts to reconstruct from survivors' accounts their many valiant endeavours to escape the well-named Golfo de Peñas (Bay of Sorrows). Finally they are guided up a river and cross over land to the north-east.

portion of which fell to my share. About two hours after the close of the day we put ashore, where we discovered six or seven wigwams. For my part my strength was so exhausted with fatigue and hunger, that it would have been impossible for me to have held out another day at this toilsome work. As soon as we landed, the Indian conducted Captain Cheap with him into a wigwam; but I was left to shift for myself.

Thus left, I was for some time at a loss what I had best do, for knowing that in the variety of dispositions observable among the Indians the surly and savage temper is the most prevalent, I had good reason to conclude that if I obtruded myself upon them my reception would be but indifferent. Necessity however put me upon the risk, and I accordingly pushed into the next wigwam on my hands and knees.

In this wigwam, into which I took the liberty to introduce myself, I found two women, who upon first seeing a figure they were not accustomed to, and such a figure too as I then made, were struck with astonishment. They were sitting by a fire, to which I approached without any apology. However inclined I might have been to make one, my ignorance of their language made it impossible to attempt it. One of these women appeared to be young, and very handsome for an Indian; the other old, and as frightful as it is possible to conceive anything in human shape to be. Having stared at me some little time, they both went out; and I, without farther ceremony, sat me down by the fire to warm myself, and dry the rags I wore. Yet I cannot say my situation was very easy, as I expected every instant to see two or three men come in and thrust me out, if they did not deal with me in a rougher manner.

Soon after, the two women came in again, having as I supposed conferred with the Indian our conductor; and appearing to be in great good humour, began to chatter and laugh immoderately. Perceiving the wet and cold condition I was in they seemed to have compassion on me, and the old woman went out and brought some wood, with which she made a good fire. But my hunger being impatient, I could not forbear expressing my desire that they would extend their hospitality a little further and bring me something to eat. They soon comprehended my meaning, and the younger beginning to rummage under some pieces of bark that lay in the corner of the wigwam, produced a fine large fish. This they presently put upon the fire to broil, and when it was just warm through they made a sign for me to eat. They had no need to repeat the invitation; I fell to, and dispatched it in so short a time that I was in hopes they would comprehend without further tokens that I was ready for another. But it was of no consequence, for their stock of eatables was entirely exhausted.

After sitting some time in conference together, in which conversation I could bear no part, the women made some signs to me to lie down and go to sleep, first having strewed some dry boughs upon the ground. I laid myself down, and soon fell fast asleep; and awaking about three or four hours after, I found myself covered with a bit of blanket made of the down of birds, which the women usually wear about their waist. The young woman who had carefully covered me whilst sleeping with her own blanket was lying close by me; the old woman on the other side of her. The fire was low, and almost burnt out; but as soon as they found me awake they renewed it by putting on more fuel. What I had hitherto eaten served only to sharpen my appetite. I could not help, therefore, being earnest with them to get me some more victuals. Having understood my necessities they talked together some little time; after which, getting up, they both went out, taking with them a couple of dogs, which they train to assist them in fishing. After an hour's absence they came in trembling with cold, and their hair streaming with water, and brought two fish; which, having broiled, they gave me the largest share; and then we all laid down as before to rest.

We could not learn what business the men, whose wives and children were left behind, were gone out upon, but about this time their return was looked for. I was therefore determined to enjoy myself as long as they were absent, and make the most of the good fare I was possessed of; to the pleasure of which I thought a little cleanliness might in some measure contribute. I therefore went to a brook, and taking off my shirt, which might be said to be alive with vermin, set myself about to wash it; which having done as well as I could, and hung on a bush to dry, I heard a bustle about the wigwams, and soon perceived that the women were preparing to depart, having stripped their wigwams of their bark covering and carried it into their canoes. Putting on therefore my shirt, just as it was, I hastened to join them, having a great desire of being present at one of their fishing parties.

It was my lot to be put into the canoe with my two patronesses, and some others who assisted in rowing. We were in all four canoes. After rowing some time they gained such an offing as they required, where the water was about eight or ten fathom deep, and there lay upon their oars. And now the youngest of the two women, taking a basket in her mouth, jumped overboard, and diving to the bottom, continued under water an amazing time. When she had filled the basket with sea-eggs, she came up to the boat's side; and delivering it so filled to the other women in the boat, they took out the contents, and returned it to her. The diver then, after having taken a short time to breathe, went down and up again with the same success; and so several times for the space of half an hour. It seems as if Providence has endued this people with a kind of amphibious nature, as the sea is the only source from whence almost all their subsistence is derived.

The divers having returned to their boats, we continued to row till evening, when we landed upon a low point. As soon as the canoes were hauled up they employed themselves in erecting their wigwams, which they dispatch with great address and quickness.

I still enjoyed the protection of my two good Indian women, who made me their guest here as before; they first regaled me with sea-eggs, and then went out upon another kind of fishery by the means of dogs and nets. These dogs are a cur-like looking animal, but very sagacious, and easily trained to this business. Though to appearance an uncomfortable kind of sport, yet they engage in it readily, seem to enjoy it much, and express their eagerness by barking every time they raise their heads above the water to breathe. The net is held by two Indians, who get into the water; then the dogs taking a large compass dive after the fish, and drive them into the net; but it is only in particular places that the fish are taken in this manner. At the close of the evening the women brought in two fish which served us for supper, and then we reposed ourselves as before.

Here we remained all the next day; and the morning after embarked again, and rowed till noon. Then landing, we descried the canoes of the Indian men, who had been some time expected from an expedition they had been upon. This was soon to make a great alteration in the situation of affairs, a presage of which I could read in the melancholy countenance of my young hostess. She endeavoured to express herself in very earnest terms to me; but I had not yet acquired a competent knowledge of the Indian language to understand her.

As soon as the men were landed, she and the old Indian woman went up, not without some marks of dread upon them, to an elderly Indian man, whose remarkable surly and stern countenance was well calculated to raise such sensations in his dependants. He seemed to be a cacique, or chief man among them, by the airs of importance he assumed to himself and the deference paid him by the rest. After some little conference passed between these Indians and our cacique conductor, of which most probably the circumstances of our history, and the occasion of our coming here, might be the chief subject (for they fixed their eyes constantly upon us) they applied themselves to building their wigwams.

I now understood that the two Indian women with whom I had sojourned were wives to this chieftain, though one was young enough to be his daughter; and as far as I could learn, did really stand in the different relations to him both of daughter and wife. It was easy to be perceived that all did not go well between them at this time. Either that he was not satisfied with the answers that they returned him to his questions, or that he suspected some misconduct on their side; for presently after, breaking out into savage fury, he took the young one into his arms, and threw her with violence against the stones. But his brutal resentment did not stop here, and he beat her afterwards in a cruel manner. I could not see this treatment of my benefactress without the highest concern for her, and rage against the author of it; especially as the natural jealousy of these people gave occasion to think that it was on my account she suffered. I could hardly suppress the first emotions of my resentment, which prompted me to return him his barbarity in his own kind. But besides that this might have drawn upon her fresh marks of his severity, it was neither politic, nor indeed in my power, to have done it to any good purpose at this time.

Our cacique now made us understand that we must embark directly in the same canoe which brought us and return to our companions; and that the Indians we were about to leave would join us in a few days, when we should all set out in a body in order to proceed to the northward. In our way back, nothing very material happened, but upon our arrival, which was the next day, we found Mr Elliot, the Surgeon, in a very bad way. His illness had been continually increasing since we left him. Mr Hamilton and Mr Campbell were almost starved, having fared very ill since we left them: a few sea-eggs were all the subsistence they had lived upon, and these procured by the cacique's wife in the manner I mentioned before. This woman was the very reverse of my hostess, and as she found her husband was of so much consequence to us took upon her much haughtiness, and treated us as dependants and slaves. He was not more engaging in his carriage towards us; he would give no part of what he had to spare to any but Captain Cheap, whom his interest led him to prefer to the rest, though our wants were often greater. The Captain on his part contributed to keep us in this abject situation by approving this distinction the cacique showed to him. Had he treated us with not quite so much distance the cacique might have been more regardful of our wants.

The little regard and attention which our necessitous condition drew from Captain Cheap may be imputed, in some measure, to the effects of a mind soured by a series of crosses and disappointments; which indeed had operated on us all to a great neglect of each other, and sometimes of ourselves.

Chapter 21

PRISONERS OF WAR

Golfo San Esteban, 15ᵗʰ March 1742. The Surgeon dies of cold and hunger. The four survivors are taken in canoes by brutal Indians up a river, which requires cruelly hard rowing as it gets more rapid. They make a horrendous trek overland to a lake that connects to the sea. They are starving, wet, barely clothed, chilled to the bone and crawling with vermin. Captain Cheap becomes delirious. Mr Hamilton remains behind. With the canoe in a desperately leaky condition the three officers just manage to get across the Golfo Corcovado to reach Chiloé and civilisation.

FROM MIDSHIPMAN BYRON'S NARRATIVE

We embarked with the Indians, they separating our little company entirely, not putting any two of us together in the same canoe. The oar was my lot, as usual, as also Mr Campbell's; Mr Hamilton could not row, and Captain Cheap was out of the question; our Surgeon was more dead than alive at the time, and lay at the bottom of the canoe he was in. The weather coming on too bad for their canoes to keep the sea, we landed again without making great progress that day.

Here Mr Elliot, our Surgeon, died. At our first setting out, he promised the fairest for holding out, being a very strong, active young man. He had gone through an infinite deal of fatigue, as Mr Hamilton and he were the best shots amongst us, and whilst our ammunition lasted never spared themselves, and in a great measure provided for the rest. But he died the death many others had done before him, being quite starved. We scraped a hole for him in the sand, and buried him in the best manner we could.[1]

Here I must relate a little anecdote of our Christian cacique. He and his wife had gone off at some distance from the shore in their canoe, when she dived for sea-eggs; but not meeting with great success, they returned a good deal out of humour. A little boy of theirs, about three years old, whom they appeared to be dotingly fond of, watching for his father's and mother's return, ran into the surf to meet them. The father handed a basket of sea-eggs to the child, which being too heavy for him to carry, he let fall. Upon which the father jumped out of the canoe, and catching the boy up in his arms, dashed him with the utmost violence against the stones. The poor little creature lay motionless and bleeding, and in that condition was taken up by the mother, but died soon after. She appeared inconsolable for some time; but the brute his father showed little concern about it.

A day or two after we put to sea again, and crossed the great bay[2] I mentioned we had been to the bottom of when we first hauled away to the westward. The land here is very low and sandy, with something like the mouth of a river[3] which discharges itself into the sea. This had been taken no notice of by us before, as it was so shallow that the Indians were obliged to take everything out of their canoes, and carry it over the neck of land, and then haul the boats over into a river, which at this part of it was very broad, more resembling a lake than a river.

We rowed up it four or five leagues, and then took into a branch of it that ran first to the eastward, and then to the northward. Here it became much narrower and the stream excessively rapid, so that we made but

---

1. Now this bay is called "Caleta Elliot". See p186.
2. Golfo San Esteban.
3. Rio San Taddeo, largely fed by melt-water from the adjacent glaciers. See p198.

little way, though we worked very hard. At night we landed upon its banks and had a most uncomfortable lodging, it being a perfect swamp; and we had nothing to cover us, though it rained very hard. The Indians were little better off than we, as there was no wood here to make their wigwams; so that all they could do was to prop up the bark they carry in the bottom of their canoes with their oars, and shelter themselves as well as they could to leeward of it. They, knowing the difficulties that were to be encountered here, had provided themselves with some seal; but we had not the least morsel to eat, after the heavy fatigues of the day, excepting a sort of root we saw some of the Indians make use of which was very disagreeable to the taste.

We laboured all next day against the stream, and fared as we had done the day before. The next day brought us to the carrying place.[4] Here was plenty of wood, but nothing to be got for sustenance. The first thing the Indians did was to take everything out of their canoes and after hauling them ashore they made their wigwams. We passed this night, as generally we had done, under a tree; but what we suffered at this time is not easily to be expressed. I had been three days at the oar without any kind of nourishment but the wretched root I mentioned before. I had no shirt, as mine was rotted off by bits; and we were devoured by vermin. All my clothes consisted of an old short grieko, which is something like a bear-skin, with a piece of a waistcoat under it which once had been of red cloth, both which I had on when I was cast away. I had a ragged pair of trousers, without either shoe or stocking.

The first thing the Indians did in the morning was to take their canoes to pieces. When they have occasion to go over land, as at this time, each man or woman carries a plank; whereas it would be impossible for them to drag a heavy boat entire. Everybody had something to carry excepting Captain Cheap; and he was obliged to be assisted, or never would have

---

4. In 1829 Lieutenant Skyring of HMS *Adelaide*, one of Fitzroy's small squadron which included the famous *Beagle*, followed Byron's route up this river. Skyring's report matches Byron's description closely.

got over this march; for a worse march than this, I believe, never was made. He with the others set out some time before me.

I waited for two Indians, who belonged to the canoe I came in, and who remained to carry over the last of the things from the side we were on. I had a piece of wet heavy canvas which belonged to Captain Cheap with a bit of stinking seal wrapped in it (which had been given him that morning by some of the Indians) to carry upon my head, which was a sufficient weight for a strong man in health, through such roads, and a grievous burden to one in my condition. Our way was through a thick wood, the bottom of which was a mere quagmire, most part of it up to our knees and often to our middle, and every now and then we had a large tree to get over, for they often lay directly in our road. Besides this we were continually treading upon the stumps of trees, which were not to be avoided as they were covered with water; and having neither shoe nor stocking my feet and legs were frequently torn and wounded. Before I had got half a mile the two Indians had left me; and making the best of my way lest they should be all gone before I got to the other side, I fell off a tree that crossed the road into a very deep swamp, where I very narrowly escaped drowning by the weight of the burden I had on my head.

It was a long while before I could extricate myself from this difficulty, and when I did my strength was quite exhausted. I sat down under a tree, and there gave way to melancholy reflections. However, as I was sensible these reflections would answer no end, they did not last long. I got up, and marking a great tree, I then deposited my load, not being able to carry it any farther, and set out to join my company.

It was some hours before I reached my companions. I found them sitting under a tree, and sat myself down by them without speaking a word; nor did they speak to me as I remember for some time, when Captain Cheap breaking silence began to ask after the seal and piece of canvas. I told him the disaster I had met with, which he might have easily guessed by the condition the rags I had on were in, as well as having my feet and ankles cut to pieces. But instead of compassion for my sufferings, I heard nothing but grumbling from every one, for the irreparable loss they had sustained by me. I made no answer; but after resting myself a little I got up and struck into the wood, and walked back at least five miles to the tree I had marked, and returned just time enough to deliver it before my companions embarked with the Indians upon a great lake,[5] the opposite part of which seemed to wash the foot of the Cordilleras. I wanted to embark with them, but was given to understand I was to wait for some other Indians that were to follow them. I knew not where these Indians were to come from. I was left alone upon the beach, and night was at hand. They left me not even a morsel of the stinking seal that I had suffered so much about.

I kept my eyes upon the boats as long as I could distinguish them, and then returned into the wood and sat myself down upon the root of a tree, having eaten nothing the whole day but the stem of a plant which resembles that of an artichoke, which is of a juicy consistency and acid taste. Quite worn out with fatigue, I soon fell asleep.

Awaking before day, I thought I heard some voices at no great distance from me. As the day appeared, looking farther into the wood I perceived a wigwam, and immediately made towards it. But the reception I met with was not at all agreeable; for stooping to get into it I presently received two or three kicks in my face, and at the same time heard the sound of voices, seemingly in anger; which made me retire and wait at the foot of a tree, where I remained till an old woman peeped out, and made signs to me to draw near. I obeyed very readily, and went into the wigwam. In it were three men and two women. One young man seemed to have great respect shown to him by the rest, though he was the most miserable object I ever saw. He was a perfect skeleton, and covered with sores from head to foot.

I was happy to sit a moment by their fire, as I was quite benumbed with cold. The old woman took out a piece of seal, holding one part of it between her feet, and the other end in her teeth, and then cut off some thin slices with a sharp shell, and distributed them about to the other Indians.

---

5. Laguna San Rafael.

She then put a bit on the fire, taking a piece of fat in her mouth, which she kept chewing, every now and then spirting some of it on the piece that was warming upon the fire; for they never do more with it than warm it through. When it was ready she gave me a little bit which I swallowed whole, being almost starved.

As these Indians were all strangers to me, I did not know which way they were going; and indeed it was now become quite indifferent to me which way I went, whether to the northward or southward, so that they would but take me with them and give me something to eat. However, to make them comprehend me I pointed first to the southward, and after to the lake, and I soon understood they were going to the northward. They all went out together, and took up a plank of the canoe and carried it upon the beach, and presently put it together; and getting everything into it they put me to the oar. We rowed across the lake to the mouth of a very rapid river, where we put ashore for that night, not daring to get any way down in the dark, as it required the greatest skill, even in the day, to avoid running foul of the stumps and roots of trees of which this river was full.

I passed a melancholy night, as they would not suffer me to come near the wigwam they had made; nor did they give me the least bit of anything to eat since we embarked.

In the morning we set off again. The weather proved extremely bad the whole day. We went down the river at an amazing rate, and just before night they put ashore upon a stony beach. They hauled the canoe up, and all disappeared in a moment, and I was left quite alone. It rained violently, and was very dark. I thought it was as well to lie down upon the beach, half side in water, as to get into a swamp under a dropping tree. In this dismal situation I fell asleep.

I awaked three or four hours after in such agonies with the cramp that I thought I must die upon the spot. I attempted several times to raise myself upon my legs, but could not. At last I made shift to get upon my knees, and looking towards the wood I saw a great fire at some distance from me. I was a long time in crawling to it; and when I reached it I threw myself

A satellite photograph of the river (left, centre), up which Byron and Campbell had to row, starving and exhausted, before dismantling their canoes and carrying them overland. The glaciers are disgorging icebergs into the lake and the sea, and there was then still 250 miles to row, including a dangerous passage across exposed water, Golfo Corcovado.

almost into it in hopes of finding some relief from the pain I suffered. This intrusion gave great offence to the Indians, who immediately got up, kicking and beating me till they drove me some distance from it. However I contrived a little after to place myself so as to receive some warmth from it, by which I got rid of the cramp.

In the morning we left this place, and were soon after out of the river. Being now at sea again, the Indians intended putting ashore at the first convenient place to look for shellfish, their stock of provisions having been quite exhausted for some time. At low water we landed upon a spot that seemed to promise well, and here we found plenty of limpets. Though at this time starving, I did not attempt to eat one, lest I should lose a moment in gathering them, not knowing how soon the Indians might be going again. I had almost filled my hat when I saw them returning to the canoe. I made what haste I could to her, for I believe they would have made no conscience of leaving me behind.

I sat down to my oar again, placing my hat close to me, every now and then eating a limpet. The Indians were employed the same way, when one of them seeing me throw the shells overboard, spoke to the rest in a violent passion; and, getting up, fell upon me, and seized me by an old ragged handkerchief I had about my neck, almost throttling me, whilst another took me by the legs and was going to throw me overboard if the old woman had not prevented them. I was all this time entirely ignorant by what means I had given offence, till I observed that the Indians, after eating the limpets, carefully put the shells in a heap at the bottom of the canoe. I then concluded there was some superstition about throwing these shells into the sea, my ignorance of which had very nearly cost me my life. I was resolved to eat no more limpets till we landed, which we did some time after upon an island. I then took notice that the Indians brought all their shells ashore and laid them above high water mark.

Here, as I was going to eat a large bunch of berries I had gathered from a tree, for they looked very tempting, one of the Indians snatched them out of my hand and threw them away, making me to understand that they were poisonous. Thus, in all probability, did these people now save my life, who a few hours before were going to take it from me for throwing away a shell.

In two days after I joined my companions again, but I do not remember that there was the least joy shown on either side at meeting.

At this place was a very large canoe belonging to our guide, which would have required at least six men to the oar to have made any kind of expedition. Instead of that there was only Campbell and myself, besides the Indian, his companion or servant, to row, the cacique himself never touching an oar but sitting with his wife all the time much at his ease. Mr Hamilton continued in the same canoe he had been in all along, and which still was to keep us company some way further, though many of the others had left us.

This was dreadful hard work to such poor starved wretches as we were, to be slaving at the oar all day long in such a heavy boat; and this inhuman fellow would never give us a scrap to eat, excepting when he took so much seal that he could not contrive to carry it all away with him, which happened very seldom. After working like galley-slaves all day, towards night when we landed, instead of taking any rest, Mr Campbell and I were sometimes obliged to go miles along shore to get a few shellfish; and just as we have made a little fire in order to dress them, he has commanded us into the boat again, and kept us rowing the whole night without ever landing.

It is impossible for me to describe the miserable state we were reduced to; our bodies were so emaciated that we hardly appeared the figures of men. It often happened to me in the coldest night, both in hail and snow, where we had nothing but an open beach to lie down upon, in order to procure a little rest, that I was obliged to pull off the few rags I had on, as it was impossible to get a moment's sleep with them on for the vermin that swarmed about them. I used, as often as I had time, to take my clothes off, and putting them upon a large stone beat them with another, in hopes of killing hundreds at once, for it was endless work to pick them off. What we suffered from this was ten times worse even than hunger.

But we were clean in comparison to Captain Cheap; for I could compare his body to nothing but an ant-hill, with thousands of those insects crawling over it; for he was now past attempting to rid himself in the least from this torment, as he had quite lost himself, not recollecting our names that were about him, or even his own. His beard was as long as a hermit's, and his face covered with train-oil and dirt, from having long accustomed himself to sleep upon a bag, by the way of pillow, in which he kept the pieces of stinking seal. This prudent method he took to prevent our getting at it whilst he slept. His legs were as big as mill-posts, though his body appeared to be nothing but skin and bone.

One day we fell in with about forty Indians, who came down to the beach we landed on, curiously painted. Our cacique seemed to understand but little of their language, and it sounded to us very different from what

This shows the narrow fjord (Estuario Elefantes) from the place where the survivors came over land to the island of Chiloé. At the northern end there is an exposed and dangerous crossing to Chiloé, civilisation, and imprisonment.

we had heard before. However, they made us comprehend that a ship had been upon the coast not far from where we then were, and that she had a red flag. This we understood some time after to have been the *Anna* pink, whose adventures[6] are particularly related in Lord Anson's *Voyage*; and we passed through the very harbour she had lain in.[7]

---

6. The *Anna* pink had been driven on to the land in continuous gales about 100 miles north of Wager Island in May 1741. She dragged her anchor towards the lee-shore, but managed to find shelter in an unexpected inlet that suddenly opened up in the rocky coast. She remained there two months repairing damage, and then rejoined the Commodore in Juan Fernandez.

7. Byron must here be mistaken. Estuario Elefantes, the long channel in which they were now travelling north, is never closer than 45 nautical miles to where the *Anna* took refuge, called today on the chart Bahia Anna Pink.

The fjord is sheltered, but glaciers debouche into the sea, and it is excessively cold. The survivors' clothing by this time was reduced to lice-infested rags.

As there was but one small canoe that intended to accompany us any longer, and that in which Mr Hamilton had been up to this time intended to proceed no further to the northward, our cacique proposed to him to come into our canoe. He refused, as the insolence of this fellow was to him insupportable. He therefore rather chose to remain where he was till chance should throw in his way some other means of getting forward; so here we left him, and it was some months before we saw him again.

We now got on by very slow degrees to the northward. As the difficulties and hardships we daily went through would only be a repetition of those already mentioned, I shall say no more, but at last we reached an island about thirty leagues to the southward of Chiloé. Here we remained two days for a favourable opportunity to cross the bay, the very thought of which seemed to frighten our cacique out of his senses. Indeed, there was great reason for his apprehensions; for there ran a most dreadful hollow sea, dangerous for any open boat whatever, but a thousand times more for such a crazy vessel as we were in.

He at last mustered up resolution enough to attempt it, first having crossed himself for an hour together, and made a kind of lugsail out of the bits of blankets they wore about them, sewed together with split supple-jacks.[8] We then put off, and a terrible passage we had. The bottom plank of the canoe was split, which opened upon every sea, and the water continually rushed over the gunnel. I may say that we were in a manner full the whole way over though all hands were employed in bailing without ceasing a moment. As we drew near the shore the cacique was eager to land, having been terrified to that degree with this run, that if it had not been for us every soul must have perished; for he had very near got in amongst the breakers, where the sea drove with such violence upon the rocks that not even an Indian could have escaped, especially as it was in the night.

We kept off till we got into smooth water, and landed upon the island of Chiloé, though in a part of it that was not inhabited. Here we stayed all the next day in a very heavy snow, to recover ourselves a little after our fatigue; but the cold was so excessive, having neither shoe nor stocking, we thought we should have lost our feet. Captain Cheap was so ill that if he had had but a few leagues further to have gone without relief he could not have held out.

But it pleased God now that our sufferings, in a great measure, were drawing to an end.

What things our cacique had brought with him from the wreck, he here buried underground in order to conceal them from the Spaniards, who would not have left him a rusty nail if they had known of it. Towards evening we set off again, and about nine the same night, to our great joy, we observed something that had the appearance of a house. It belonged to an acquaintance of our cacique; and as he was possessed of my fowling-piece, and we had preserved about one charge of powder, he made us load for him, and desired we would show him how to discharge it.

---

8. A generic name for climbing shrubs with tough pliable stems, evidently here used as twine.

Upon which, standing up, and holding his head from it as far as possible, he fired – and fell back into the bottom of the canoe. The Indians belonging to the house, not in the least used to fire-arms, ran out and hid themselves in the woods. But after some time one of them, bolder than the rest, got upon a hill, and hollowed to us, asking who and what we were.

The incident of the Indian and Byron's musket.
This fanciful engraving is from a cheap pirated edition of Byron's *Narrative*. The three remaining survivors are being rescued in a canoe by an Indian and his wife. Byron has just given his musket to the Indian, who fires it somewhat uncertainly. Campbell looks on sadly, and Cheap is past caring.

The Indian guide was now among his own people, and Captain Cheap and the two midshipmen were hospitably received in a primitive village. Their generous hosts killed a sheep, brought potatoes and eggs and barley meal, and warmed the strangers with an enormous fire, it being the depth of winter.

The villagers sent a message to Castro, a town some 80 miles north, to inform the Spanish authorities of the arrival of the three men. A few days later a message came back that the prisoners were to be taken directly to a certain place where a party of soldiers would meet them. Their hosts were very concerned to hear this, as they had a great dread of the Spanish. Byron says that they "detest the very name of a Spaniard", and that this is not surprising "for they are kept under such subjection and such a laborious slavery by hard usage and punishments."

The three survivors were taken under guard to Castro and then to Chacao in the far north of Chiloé island, where the Governor resided. Here they were well treated, recovered their strength quickly, and were allowed to go about as they pleased. About three months later Mr Hamilton was brought in by a search party that the Governor had sent south to find him.

Byron learned Spanish as fast as he could, managed to scrounge some better clothing and look less like a scarecrow, and started to observe his surroundings. He was particularly interested in the women of Chiloé. He praises their fine complexions and says that many of them are very handsome. "They have good voices," he writes, "and can strum a little upon the guitar, but they have an ugly custom of smoking tobacco… Women of the first fashion here seldom wear shoes or stockings in the house but only keep them to wear upon particular occasions. I have often seen them coming to the church barelegged, walking through mud and water, and at the church door put on their shoes and stockings, and pull them off again when they come out." He seems to have been a great success with the ladies. He went to stay for three weeks with a lady at a farm who had two handsome daughters, and says that she seemed to be as fond of him as if he had been her own son, and was very unwilling to part with him. And one of the priests offered to convert him to Catholicism and give him his niece in marriage, offering as an inducement his fine wardrobe, which he said would be left to Byron on his death. Byron says the *clothing was, in his present state, quite a temptation.*

They were then put in a ship for Valparaiso, where they were imprisoned in filthy conditions. After a while they were ordered onto a mule train to the capital, Santiago, where they spent the next two years fairly agreeably as prisoners-of-war on parole, staying with a generous Scots doctor, Dr Patrick Gedd.

Byron did not lose his interest in the women of the country. His account can continue the story.

Chapter 22

AN ADVENTUROUS PASSAGE TO FRANCE

Santiago, January 1743. Byron describes Chile, admiring just about everything but particularly the ladies and the wine. Relations with the Spanish in Santiago are friendly, which is ascribed to the humane way Commodore Anson had treated his prisoners. Campbell becomes a Catholic "and of course left us".

In December 1744, under an agreement between Britain and Spain for the exchange of prisoners, the three remaining survivors are told to embark in a French frigate at Valparaiso, and after a six-month delay they reach the Caribbean, where they are chased unsuccessfully by two British ships. The frigate joins a convoy to sail across the Atlantic, and the French Commodore punishes the poor station-keeping of one of his captains by ducking him three times from the yardarm. They arrive in Brest and are delayed several months more awaiting repatriation formalities and a passage home.

From Midshipman Byron's narrative

The women of Santiago are remarkably handsome, and very extravagant in their dress. Their hair, which is as thick as is possible to be conceived, they wear of a vast length, without any other ornament upon the head than a few flowers. They plait it behind in four plaits and twist them round a bodkin, at each end of which is a diamond rose. Their shifts are all over lace, as is a little tight waistcoat they wear over them. Their petticoats are open before, and lap over, and have commonly three rows of very rich lace of gold or silver. They love to have the end of an embroidered garter hang a little below the petticoat. Their breasts and shoulders are very naked, and indeed you may easily discern their whole shape by their manner of dress. They have fine sparkling eyes, ready wit, a great deal of good-nature, and a strong disposition to gallantry.

Their estancias, or country houses, are very pleasant, and have generally a fine grove of olive trees with large vineyards to them. The Chile wine, in my opinion, is full as good as Madeira, and made in such quantities that it is sold extremely cheap. The soil of this country is so fertile, that the husbandmen have very little trouble; for they do but in a manner scratch up the ground, and without any kind of manure it yields an hundredfold. Without doubt the wheat of Chile is the finest in the world, and the fruits are all excellent in their kinds. Beef and mutton are so cheap that you may have a good cow for three dollars, and a fat sheep for two shillings. Their horses are extraordinary good; and though some of them go at a great price, you may have a very good one for four dollars, or about eighteen shillings of our money.

The climate of Chile is, I believe, the finest in the world. What they call their winter does not last three months; and even that is very moderate, as may be imagined by their manner of building, for they have no chimneys in their houses. All the rest of the year is delightful; for though from ten or eleven in the morning till five in the afternoon it is very hot, yet the evenings and mornings are cool and pleasant. In the hottest time of the year it is from six in the evening till two or three in the morning that the people of this country meet to divert themselves with music and other entertainments, at which there is plenty of cooling liquors, as they are well supplied with ice from the neighbouring Cordilleras.

We had a numerous acquaintance in the city, and in general received many civilities from the inhabitants. There are a great many people of fashion and very good families from Old Spain settled here. A lady lived next door to us whose name was Doña Francisca Giron; and as my name sounded something like it, she would have it that we were parientes.[1] She had a daughter, a very fine young woman, who both played and sung remarkably well: she was reckoned the finest voice in Santiago. They saw a great deal of company, and we were welcome to her house whenever we pleased. We were a long time in this country, but we passed it very agreeably.

We found many Spaniards here that had been taken by Commodore Anson, and had been for some time prisoners on board the *Centurion*. They all spoke in the highest terms of the kind treatment they had received; and it is natural to imagine that it was chiefly owing to that laudable example of humanity our reception here was so good. They had never had anything but privateers and buccaneers amongst them before, who handled their prisoners very roughly; so that the Spaniards in general, both of Peru and Chile, had the greatest dread of being taken by the English. But some of them told us that they were so happy on board the *Centurion*, that they should not have been sorry if the Commodore had taken them with him to England.

After we had been here some time Mr Campbell changed his religion, and of course left us.[2]

At the end of two years, the President sent for us, and informed us that a French ship from Lima bound to Spain had put in to Valparaiso, and that we should embark in her.[3] After taking leave of our good friend Mr Gedd

---

1. Relations.

2. This laconic statement would have been full of significance to eighteenth-century readers. For a naval officer, converting to Catholicism in 1744 would have been something like joining the Communist Party in 1960, and a bar to public office, including in normal circumstances being a naval officer. At that date the Pope did not recognise the Hanoverian dynasty as lawful rulers of Great Britain, and the Catholic Church claimed civil jurisdiction in some respects.

In fact Campbell had entirely gone over to the enemy, a fact which can be verified as the story unfolds. His reception on reaching Buenos Aires was quite different from that of other prisoners of war, and this difference was even more marked when they arrived in Spain together and the others were treated brutally (see above p158-9.) His later career is summarised on p267-268.

3. An exchange of prisoners of war had been negotiated between Great Britain and Spain.

and all our acquaintance at Santiago we set out for Valparaiso, mules and a guide being provided for us. I had forgot to say before, that Captain Cheap had been allowed by the President six reals a day, and we had four for our maintenance the whole time we were at Santiago, which money we took up as we wanted.[4]

The first person I met upon our entrance into Valparaiso was the poor soldier who had been kind to us when we were imprisoned in the fort. I now made him a little present, which as it came quite unexpectedly made him very happy.

About the 20th December 1744 we embarked on board the *Lys* frigate, belonging to St Malo. She was a ship of four hundred and twenty tons, sixteen guns and sixty men.

The Lys *joined a small convoy of French ships, but sprang a leak and had to return to Valparaiso for repairs. This was unfortunate for the British passengers, as all the other ships were captured by the Royal Navy or English privateers in the Atlantic, and if the* Lys *had shared the same fate Cheap, Hamilton and Byron might have returned home sooner than they did. As it was* Lys *had a troublesome passage in the Pacific and around the Horn, and there were delays amounting to six months before she headed for the West Indies to replenish her supplies of water.*

One morning about ten o'clock, as I was walking the quarterdeck, Captain Cheap came out of the cabin and told me he had just seen a beef-barrel go by the ship; that he was sure it had but lately been thrown overboard, and that he would venture any wager that we saw an English cruiser before long. In about half an hour after we saw two sail to leeward from off the quarterdeck; for they kept no look-out from the mast-head. We presently observed they were in chase of us. The French and Spaniards

---

4. Money was normally a pressing problem for distressed mariners, but the prisoners in Santiago managed to obtain loans through the kindness of Spanish officers and a British businessman. At this date the Captain's total expenditure was £65, Hamilton's £53, and Byron's £83.

on board now began to grow a good deal alarmed, when it fell stark calm; but not before the ships had neared us so much, that we plainly discerned them to be English men-of-war, the one a two-decker, the other a twenty-gun ship.

The French had now thoughts, when a breeze should spring up, of running the ship on shore upon Puerto Rico; but when they came to consider what a set of banditti inhabited that island, and that in all probability they would have their throats cut for the sake of plundering the wreck, they were resolved to take their chance and stand to the northward between the two islands. In the evening a fresh breeze sprung up, and we shaped a course accordingly. The two ships had it presently afterwards, and neared us amazingly fast.

Now everybody on board gave themselves up. The officers were busy in their cabins, filling their pockets with what was most valuable; the men put on their best clothes, and many of them came to me with little lumps of gold, desiring I would take them, as they said they had much rather I should benefit by them, whom they were acquainted with, than those that chased them. I told them there was time enough, though I thought they were as surely taken as if the English had been already on board.

A fine moonlit night came on, and we expected every moment to see the ships alongside of us; but we saw nothing of them in the night, and to our great astonishment in the morning no ships were to be seen from the mast-head. Thus did these two cruisers lose one of the richest prizes, by not chasing an hour or two longer. There were near two millions of dollars on board, besides a valuable cargo.

On the 8th at six in the morning we were off Cape la Grange; and what is very remarkable, the French at Cape François[5] told us afterwards that was the only day they ever remembered since the war, that the cape had been without one or two English privateers cruising off it. Only the evening before two of them had taken two outward-bound St Domingo-men, and

---

5. Haiti

had gone with them for Jamaica; so that this ship might be justly esteemed a most lucky one.

In the afternoon we came to an anchor in Cape François harbour.[6] In this long run we had not buried a single man, nor do I remember that there was one sick the whole passage. But at this place many were taken ill, and three or four died, for there is no part of the West Indies more unhealthy than this. Yet the country is beautiful, and extremely well cultivated.

After being here some time, the Governor ordered us to wait upon him, which we did; when he took no more notice of us than if we had been his slaves, never asking us even to sit down.

Towards the end of August a French squadron of five men-of-war came in, commanded by Monsieur l'Etendière, who was to convoy the trade to France. Neither he nor his officers ever took any kind of notice of Captain Cheap, though we met them every day ashore.

On the 6th September we put to sea, in company with the five men-of-war and about fifty sail of merchantmen. On the 8th we made the Cayco Grande; and the next day a Jamaica privateer, a large fine sloop, hove in sight, keeping a little to windward of the convoy, resolving to pick up one or two of them in the night if possible. This obliged Monsieur l'Etendière to send a frigate to speak to all the convoy and order them to keep close to him in the night; which they did, and in such a manner that sometimes seven or eight of them were on board one another together; by which they received much damage; and to repair which the whole squadron was obliged to lay-to sometimes for a whole day.

The privateer kept her station, jogging on with the fleet. At last, the Commodore ordered two of the best-going ships to chase her. She appeared to take no notice of them till they were pretty near her, and then would make sail, and be out of sight presently. The chasing ships no sooner returned than the privateer was in company again.

As by this every night some accident happened to some of the convoy

---

6. Now Cap Haitien, Haiti.

by keeping so close together, a fine ship of thirty guns, belonging to Marseilles, hauled out a little to windward of the rest of the fleet; which l'Etendière perceiving in the morning, ordered the frigate to bring the Captain of her on board of him; and then making a signal for all the convoy to close him, he fired a gun and hoisted a red flag at the ensign staff; and immediately after the Captain of the merchantman was run up to the main yard-arm, and from thence ducked three times into the sea. He was then sent on board his ship again with orders to keep his colours flying the whole day in order to distinguish him from the rest.

We were then told that the person who was treated in this cruel manner was a young man of an exceeding good family in the south of France, and likewise a man of great spirit; and that he would not fail to call Monsieur l'Etendière to an account when an opportunity should offer. The affair made much noise in France afterwards.

One day the ship we were in happened to be out of her station, by sailing so heavily, when the Commodore made the signal to speak to our Captain, who seemed frightened out of his wits. When we came near him he began with the grossest abuse, threatening our Captain that if ever he was out of his station again he would serve him as he had done the other. This rigid discipline, however, preserved the convoy; for though the privateer kept company a long time, she was not so fortunate as to meet with the reward of her perseverance.

On the 27th October in the evening we made Cape Ortegal[7] and on the 31st came to an anchor in Brest road. The *Lys* having so valuable a cargo on board was towed into the harbour next morning, and lashed alongside one of their men-of-war. The money was soon landed; and the officers and men who had been so many years absent from their native country were glad to get on shore. Nobody remained on board but a man or two to look after the ship, and we three English prisoners, who had no leave to go ashore.

---

7. Northwest Spain.

The weather was extremely cold, and felt particularly so to us, who had been so long used to hot climates; and what made it still worse, we were very thinly clad. We had neither fire nor candle; for they were allowed on board of no ship in the harbour, for fear of accidents, being close to their magazines in the dockyard. Some of the officers belonging to the ship were so good as to send us off victuals every day, or we might have starved; for Monsieur l'Intendant[8] never sent us even a message; and though there was a very large squadron of men-of-war sitting out at that time, not one officer belonging to them ever came near Captain Cheap.

From five in the evening we were obliged to sit in the dark; and if we chose to have any supper, it was necessary to place it very near us before that time, or we never could have found it. We had passed seven or eight days in this melancholy manner, when one morning a kind of row-gaily came alongside with a number of English prisoners, belonging to two large privateers the French had taken. We were ordered into the same boat with them, and were carried four leagues up the river to Landerneau. At this town we were upon our parole; so we took the best lodgings we could get, and lived very well for three months.

---

8. The official in charge of the port.

Chapter 23

HOME, AND A VOICE FROM THE DEAD

Landerneau, near Brest, November 1745. There is a frustrating delay for the three prisoners, during which Captain Cheap writes home. Orders arrive from Madrid that they are free to go. They take passage in an unreliable Dutch dogger. Arrived at Dover, Byron has insufficient money and is obliged to force his way through the turnpikes on the road to London. He reaches his sister's house in Soho Square, where the porter is reluctant to admit such a disreputable-looking character. Finally he joins his sister, who had thought him dead for five years.

From Captain Cheap's letters
& Midshipman Byron's narrative

Captain Cheap, Midshipman Byron and Lieutenant Hamilton of the Marines spent two months at Landerneau while the French authorities checked with Madrid that the prisoners could be released under the exchange arrangements. It must have been a frustrating delay for three men who for five years had had their endurance tested to the limit. During this period Captain Cheap wrote two letters:

To Thomas Corbett Esquire
Secretary to the Admiralty
12th December 1745, Landerneau

Sir,

You have the trouble of this to desire you'll be pleased to inform Their Lordships that Mr Hamilton, a Lieutenant in Colonel Lowther's regiment of marines, Mr Byron who was a midshipman in the *Wager*, and myself were brought prisoners to Brest in a French ship that sailed from Valparaiso the beginning of March last. We arrived about six weeks ago, and seven or eight days afterwards were sent here by the Intendant in order to be kept (as I am told) until they have directions from the Spanish court how to dispose of us.

It would far exceed the bounds of a letter to give you a detail of the unhappy loss of His Majesty's Ship and the consequence that attended it; therefore I forbear to enter on the subject. But I flatter myself, when I shall have the good fortune to return home, that my conduct will appear unblamable both before and after our shipwreck.

As we have been prisoners so long I hope Their Lordships will be pleased to use their good offices to get us exchanged as soon as possible.

I have the honour to be,
    Sir,
Your most obedient humble servant,
    David Cheap

On the same day he wrote to his former captain, George Anson, who had returned home some eighteen months before. Anson's flagship, the *Centurion*, was the only ship of the squadron to sail round the world and come back intact. David Cheap had started the voyage as the First Lieutenant, and having been promoted by Anson to command could certainly expect his patronage and support. He therefore wrote to him in terms which in the flowery language of the day would not have seemed as obsequious as they do today:

12th December 1745, Landerneau

Sir,

I should be unpardonable if I let slip this opportunity, which is the first that I have had, of congratulating you on your safe arrival in your native country after so tedious and fatiguing a voyage, and your having obtained the preferment you so justly deserve in the opinion of all mankind. Even your enemies speak well of you – I mean the enemies of Great Britain for I believe you have no personal ones – and at the same time I take the liberty to assure you that no man on earth wishes your prosperity with a warmer heart than I do.

You are no doubt already informed of some of our misfortunes, because I have been told that some of the officers and men are got home, but they know only a few of them and probably have not told the truth. For what can be expected of such poltroons who rather than do their duty by endeavouring to join you (which might easily have been done) and look the enemy in the face, chose to expose themselves to the fatigue of so long a navigation and perishing of hunger, after most inhumanly abandoning us and destroying at their departure everything they thought could be of any use to us that they could not carry with them.

However, sir, I will say no more upon that head until I have the happiness of seeing you. Only give me leave to add that if the rest of the marine officers had done their duty as well as Mr Hamilton, who is here with me, I have very good grounds to believe I should have brought the mutineers to reason. And although we are unluckily miscarried in that and some subsequent projects, yet I hope you will be persuaded it was not for want of inclination.

You will see by the letter that I wrote to Mr Secretary Corbett the time of our sailing from Chile and arrival at Brest, and the Intendant sending us here to await the result of the Court of Spain which we daily expect; and hope it will bring us leave to return home. But if we should be disappointed and kept longer here, I must beg your favour and protection which I flatter myself I shall have whilst I behave myself as I ought, and when I behave otherwise I shall expect neither.

Some time before we left Chile the Jesuits offered us what money we wanted and said it was by order of their General at Rome. I do not know from what quarter the credit came; however, we took no more than we wanted to pay off a debt we had contracted with one of the supercargoes of the ship, which was 900 pieces-of-eight.

Messrs Byron and Hamilton (my two faithful companions and fellow sufferers) beg leave to kiss your hand, and I am,

    Sir,

Your most humble and obedient servant,
    David Cheap

Byron's narrative now brings them home:

Landerneau, 5th February 1746. Then an order came from the Court of Spain to allow us to return home by the first ship that offered. Upon this, hearing there was a Dutch ship at Morlaix ready to sail, we took horses and travelled to that town, where we were obliged to remain six weeks, before we had an opportunity of getting away. At last we agreed with the master of a Dutch dogger[1] to land us at Dover, and paid him beforehand. When we had got down the river into the road, a French privateer that was almost ready to sail upon a cruise hailed the Dutchman, and told him to come to an anchor; and that if he offered to sail before him, he would sink him.[2] This he was forced to comply with, and we lay three days in the road, cursing the Frenchman, who at the end of that time put to sea, and then we were at liberty to do the same. We had a long uncomfortable passage.

---

1. Fishing boat, as used in the North Sea off the Dogger Bank.
2. This threat was presumably made to avoid intelligence of the privateer's departure being passed to a patrolling British warship.

About the ninth day before sunset we saw Dover, and reminded the Dutchman of his agreement to land us there. He said he would; but instead of that, in the morning we were off the coast of France.

We complained loudly of this piece of villainy and insisted upon his returning to land us, when an English man-of-war appeared to windward, and presently bore down to us. She sent her boat on board with an officer, who informed us the ship he came from was the *Squirrel*, commanded by Captain Masterson. We went on board of her, and Captain Masterson immediately sent one of the cutters he had with him to land us at Dover, where we arrived that afternoon, and directly set out for Canterbury upon post-horses; but Captain Cheap was so tired by the time he got there that he could proceed no further that night.

The next morning he still found himself so much fatigued that he could ride no longer. Therefore it was agreed that he and Mr Hamilton should take a post-chaise and that I should ride; but here an unlucky difficulty was started, for upon sharing the little money we had it was found to be not sufficient to pay the charges to London; and my proportion fell so short that it was, by calculation, barely enough to pay for horses, without a farthing for eating a bit upon the road, or even for the very turnpikes. Those I was obliged to defraud by riding as hard as I could through them all, not paying the least regard to the men who called out to stop me. The want of refreshment I bore as well as I could.

When I got to the Borough I took a coach and drove to Marlborough Street, where my friends had lived when I left England, but when I came there I found the house shut up. Having been absent so many years, and in all that time never having heard a word from home, I knew not who was dead or who was living, or where to go next; or even how to pay the coachman.

I recollected a linen-draper's shop not far from thence, which our family had used. I therefore drove there next, and making myself known, they paid the coachman. I then inquired after our family, and was told my sister had married Lord Carlisle and was at that time in Soho Square.

I immediately walked to the house and knocked at the door; but the porter not liking my figure, which was half French, half Spanish, with the addition of a large pair of boots covered with dirt, he was going to shut the door in my face, but I prevailed with him to let me come in.

I need not acquaint my readers with what surprise and joy my sister received me. She immediately furnished me with money sufficient to appear like the rest of my countrymen; till that time I could not be properly said to have finished all the extraordinary scenes which a series of unfortunate adventures had kept me in for the space of five years and upwards.

Soho Square, where Midshipman Byron had a dramatic reunion with his sister, Lady Carlisle, on 14th or 15th March 1746.
This view, dated 1731, looks north, and the fine open country in the background indicates why Soho received its hunting-cry name. Carlisle House, now demolished, can be seen on the right and south of the break in the houses caused by Sutton Street (now Sutton Row).

PART 5

Consequences at Home

Chapter 24

THE SHADOW OF MUTINY

The *Wager* survivors straggled back to England over a period of three and a half years. Baynes and his party were first. He had managed to send a letter home from Barbados, and parts of it were published in *The Gentleman's Magazine* in September 1742:

> Having rounded Cape Horn we were separated by a violent storm from the Commodore, and in the night our ship bilged on the east side of an island in latitude 47:08 S, which we judged to be the island of Chiloé. All that were sick between decks were drowned, but the Captain and 311[1] more of us got safe to the island, where the natives brought us refreshments several times. The Captain was for staying to see if Commodore Anson might not call there and take us in, but the majority being for going away in the long-boat, dissensions arose, and the Captain shot one of the most mutinous dead on the spot. Having afterwards lengthened the long-boat by pieces of the wreck, and stowed some provisions in her, the greatest part went aboard, leaving the Captain and some others behind. After having passed the Straits of Magellan, meeting with almost insurmountable difficulties, we

---

1. A surprising error or misprint. The true total was 140.

arrived safe at Rio de Janeiro; from whence we were brought in His Majesty's ship the *Advice* to Barbados.

This was the first news anybody at home had had of the *Wager* for two years.

Baynes returned in November 1742, having passed through Lisbon where, as we have seen, he gave out a version of events which blamed Bulkeley. On arrival in England he reported to the Admiralty, and his astonishing story of shipwreck, starvation, shooting, and abandonment must have been very badly received. He was ordered to write down what had happened, and was then examined by a Board of Officers consisting of "three commanders of ships, persons of distinguished merit and honour." Accounts refer to it both as a Court of Enquiry and a Board of Enquiry.

Bulkeley states that at this enquiry Baynes accused him of making away with the long-boat and leaving the Captain behind. It is regrettable that no documentation has come to light. It would be interesting to see how Baynes could have attempted to exonerate himself and blame Bulkeley when he had been the senior officer present, and had actually taken a part (albeit a shadowy and indecisive one) in the arrest of the Captain.

The Boatswain was also examined, and a somewhat wild account of this appeared in *Aris's Birmingham Gazette* on 3rd January 1743:

> On Thursday Mr King, Boatswain of the *Wager* storeship, and 13 others belonging to the said ship, which was one of Commodore Anson's squadron, and was lost in the South Sea, were before the Lords of the Admiralty, and gave their Lordships an account of their sufferings, they being several days at sea on a frame made out of the wreck of the said ship.

Already public interest was being aroused by the *Wager* story, and the still-continuing Anson expedition of which it was a part.

At exactly this moment HMS *Stirling Castle* returned home, and communications between the Admiralty and Spithead must have worked fast because the three warrant officers, Bulkeley, Cummins, and Young, were confined on board while the Board of Enquiry examined Baynes and King. The warrant officers were detained two weeks on board, which after a two-year absence and within sight of their own homes must have been hard to bear. They were then allowed ashore, and subsequently reported to the Board with their own account of events, refuting such allegations against them as had been made by Baynes.

The Admiralty was then faced with a confused and incomplete disaster story that included the likelihood of mutiny and an allegation of murder. The few survivors were at odds with each other and giving contradictory and mutually incriminating reports. Not unreasonably, judgment was

This extract from the muster book shows the Admiralty's attempt to account for all personnel lost in the *Wager* disaster, including "Heny. Cusens Midsn. Shot by the Captain about the end of June 1741."

reserved until Commodore Anson or Captain Cheap should come home. No arrears of pay would be allowed to any of the survivors until the whole matter had been clarified.

This last decision seems a severe one and must have caused hardship to all, but it is roughly in line with the way the wages of eighteenth-century seamen were handled, with arrears usually being paid at the end of a commission.

Bulkeley was in financial straits, but interest in the *Wager* story was still growing, and he had his journal. Reports of Anson's successes in capturing Spanish ships in the Pacific and taking much bounty were now beginning to reach the press, and this created great public excitement in compensation for a long and tedious war. Bulkeley showed his journal to a publisher who immediately recognised a best-seller. But Bulkeley was extremely aware that his position with respect to the Admiralty was dubious and his future uncertain. Ever punctilious in matters of procedure and form, he wrote to Their Lordships as follows:

> My Lords,
> We are offered a considerable sum by the booksellers of London for the copy of our journal, to publish it to the world. Notwithstanding money is a great temptation to people in our circumstances, still we are determined to abide by Your Lordships' resolutions.

He received a verbal reply from one of the Admiralty messengers: "The journal is your own and Their Lordships have nothing to do with it, so you may do as you will with it."

It was then published by Jacob Robinson at the Golden Lion in Ludgate Street, price three shillings and sixpence. It was a publishing sensation, and serialised month by month in the *London Magazine*. There was much discussion, and opinion on the conduct of the survivors was divided. The public saw Bulkeley as a heroic seadog whose epic voyage had succeeded against all odds, odds which included the Captain's unreasonable plan and

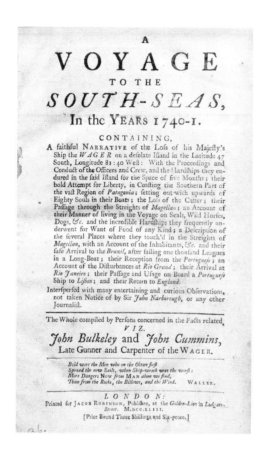

Title-page of Bulkeley's Voyage to the South Seas, *1743.*

Although he puts his shipmate Carpenter John Cummins on the title-page as co-author, the book was almost certainly written entirely by Bulkeley. Its day-by-day account of what is probably the greatest castaway survival voyage of all time is unmatched.

vicious behaviour. But the body of naval opinion must surely have been suspicious of this view. However much justification Bulkeley might bring forward, the fact was that the Captain's authority had been collectively defied and his orders disobeyed. He had been surprised, tied up, deprived of his command, and then abandoned to his fate while his men made off with the principal boat. It is extremely hard to see how any court-martial board of eighteenth-century captains and admirals could have judged this as anything other than mutiny,[2] and a mutiny of this seriousness could be

---

2. The word mutiny was not then used exclusively in its modern sense of "a collective refusal of duty", but sometimes to describe lesser crimes that would today come under the heading of insubordination, striking a superior officer, etc. However the *Wager's* mutiny would have been judged an extremely serious one in any age.

expected to result in the ringleaders (in this instance Lieutenant Baynes and the warrant officers Bulkeley, Cummins and King) being hanged from the main-yard. Any defence based on the fact that when a ship was lost the men's pay ceased, and that therefore they were no longer under naval discipline, would surely not have detained a court-martial board for long; and in any case such an argument could not apply to officers, who went on half pay.

Bulkeley had another line of defence up his sleeve against the charge of mutinously making away with the long-boat, which is so curious and absurd that it is only worth quoting to show how far legalistic minds can go:

> There was one great good man that gave his judgement in our favour so far as to say she was not the King's long-boat, giving these reasons: at the first wrecking of the *Wager*, they cut the masts away, which rendered them incapable of hoisting her out; but some time after the Captain gave orders to his officers and people to go off to the wreck and bring the long-boat on shore. They obey his orders, go off to the wreck, saw the gunnel down, launch the boat, and bring her on shore; when there, the Captain orders her to be hauled up at a proper place for lengthening; his orders are obeyed; after which he orders the Carpenter to saw her asunder; the Carpenter goes to work, and obeys the Captain's orders. Now, it is to be observed, that the long-boat is in two parts, and by Captain Cheap's orders; by which orders he has not only made her useless to the whole body of the people on the island, but as useless to himself as the wreck in the sea, and by his own orders. But the Carpenter, with the assistance of the people, have gone into the woods, cut their own timber, sawed their own plank, and brought her into a position of 23 tons.

So for a time, amid all these uncertainties, the matter rested uneasily. Anson's long-awaited return came in June 1744. During a remarkable voyage he had captured a Spanish treasure ship, and after many adventures he reached Spithead amid nation-wide excitement. The treaure was loaded on to 32 wagons, the first one displaying the British colours superior to the Spanish flag, and taken by the *Centurion's* ship's company, with a regiment of soldiers as escort, from Portsmouth to London. Three hundred chests packed with pieces-of-eight, eighteen chests of gold bars, barrels of gold dust, fine swords and candelabra, amounting to the most valuable prize ever taken by the Navy up to that date, accompanied by "kettle drums, trumpets and French horns" – it must have been a stirring sight, paraded like a Roman triumph through cheering crowds along Piccadilly and St James's Street and into Pall Mall. There the procession was greeted by the Prince of Wales with Anson in attendance, and it then moved slowly along the Strand into the safety of the Tower of London.

Anson's voyage was rightly seen at every level as an important achievement, and seemed to have opened up far-reaching prospects for the Royal Navy. Moreover the nation needed a victory after four years of a war that appeared interminable and unrewarding, and Anson provided a dramatic one. There were a few dissident voices to point out that he had lost seven of his eight ships and 1666 of the 1854 men[3] he had set out with, but in general the mood was one of ecstatic public acclaim and hope for the future.

Anson was received by the King, awarded a knighthood, and promoted to Rear Admiral of the Blue. Within a week or two he would no doubt have been consulted about proceeding against the *Wager* mutineers, but he would have had little further information to contribute, and still there was no news of Captain Cheap. It was therefore decided by the Admiralty that the evidence had become no clearer, and that matters were best left where they were pending Cheap's return. This had the welcome advantage of not spoiling the current wave of euphoria and the sense that a great victory had been won against the Spaniards in far seas that they had hitherto regarded as their own.

---

3. Professor Glyn Williams assesses four were lost from enemy action, a few from accidents, and the rest from disease and starvation.

Baynes and Bulkeley and the other warrant officers must have been extremely relieved by this decision. No word had been received from Captain Cheap for three and a half years, and his survival and return must have seemed improbable.

But then Cheap, Hamilton, and Byron, as we have seen, reached London in early 1746, and the Admiralty Board, of which Anson was now a member, could defer action no longer. On the 24th March 1746 an Admiralty Order was issued for a court-martial. Baynes and Bulkeley would have been dismayed to read in the *Penny London Post*[4] of 26th March 1746:

> Admiralty Office, 25th March 1746
>
> Vice-Admiral Stewart being directed to hold a court-martial at Portsmouth for enquiring into the cause of the loss of His Majesty's late ship the *Wager*, the Lords Commissioners of the Admiralty do hereby direct the officers, petty-officers, and foremast-men who belonged to the said ship, to repair immediately down to Portsmouth, and apply to Mr George Atkins, Deputy Judge Advocate of His Majesty's Fleet, for his directions.
>
> Thomas Corbett, Secretary to the Admiralty

Bulkeley's account of these critical days is as follows:

> One of the Proctors of Doctors'-Commons asked me what news now our Captain was come home? I told him I was going to Portsmouth to the court-martial. He then asked me if I knew nothing more than the advertisement for the court-martial. I hold him no; at which he told me, that the Monday before the advertisement was published there were four messengers dispatched from the Marshal of the Admiralty, in order to take up the Lieutenant, the Boatswain, myself and the Carpenter. On this I replied, if that is fact I will go and deliver myself up to the Marshal here in town.

---

4. It appeared in other papers on later dates too.

Finding me fixed in my resolution, he desired me to go and dine at the Paul's-Head Tavern in St Paul's Church-Yard, where the Deputy Marshal was to dine that day. Accordingly I went, and after dinner applied to him, desiring to know his opinion in regard to the officers of the *Wager*, as their Captain was come home; for I had a near relation which was an officer that came in that long-boat to Brazil, and it would give me concern if he should suffer. His answer was that he believed we should be hanged. To which I replied, for God's sake for what, for not being drowned? And is a murderer[5] at last come home to be their accuser? I have carefully perused the journal, and can't conceive that they have been guilty of piracy, mutiny, nor anything else to deserve it. It looks to me, if so, that their adversaries have taken up arms against the power of the Almighty for delivering them. At which he said, Sir, they have been guilty of such things to Captain Cheap whilst a prisoner, that I believe the Gunner and Carpenter will be hanged, if nobody else.

As I was not known to him, on these words I told him, then I was one of the men that must suffer, for I was the unfortunate Gunner of the *Wager*. After he was convinced he told me I was then become his prisoner; he had me to his house, where I was confined until the rest of the officers were brought up to town, which, as soon as they came up, he wrote to Their Lordships to inform them that he had us all in custody; but that I had delivered myself up to him here in town; desiring their Lordships' farther directions concerning us. The answer received was, to send us to Portsmouth and there to deliver us up on board Admiral Steward (HMS *Prince George*), to take a receipt, and to take particular care that the Gunner and Carpenter did not make their escape.

After we went on board of Admiral Steward, we were told we were to be hanged, nay, not a letter came from any of our friends, but there were these words mentioned, you are to be hanged. When the Captain came down to Portsmouth, some of my friends waited on him, desiring

5. This part of Bulkeley's journal was not published until after Cheap had died.

to know what he had to allege against us? His answer was, Gentlemen, I have nothing to say for nor against the villains, until the day of trial, and then it is not in my power to be off from hanging them. This expression occasioned the whole place to believe it would be so.

One by one the survivors, some under escort, travelled to Portsmouth and assembled aboard the flagship, HMS *Prince George*, at anchor off Spithead. Cheap and Byron were there; Bulkeley and Cummins also; Lieutenant Baynes, Lieutenant Hamilton of the Marines, Boatswain John King and the Mate, John Jones, had answered the summons too. Of our main characters only Midshipmen Morris and Campbell were yet to return, and Captain Pemberton, no doubt a prudent man, was nowhere to be found.

On 14th April signed statements or depositions, which would be read out at the court-martial, were made by all *Wager* survivors who had been traced, and these depositions were attested by the Deputy Judge Advocate, George Atkins. Captain Cheap had signed his narrative on 11th April, and it is not known whether it would have addressed the breakdown of discipline and his reasons for shooting Cozens. It was certainly read out in court in its entirety, but, significantly and most regrettably, it is the only document which has not been retained in the Court-Martial Record.

When Bulkeley came to make his deposition on 14th April he complained that he was being kept prisoner without knowing the details of the charges against him. To his astonishment, in view of what he had heard of the opinions of Cheap and everyone else, the Deputy Judge Advocate told him that the court-martial was only for the loss of the ship. No charges of mutiny were to be brought.

Once again, he and the others must have been mightily relieved.

It seems likely that this surprising decision not to proceed with charges of mutiny was taken by the Admiralty Board on the advice of its highly respected new member, Rear Admiral Sir George Anson. On his famous voyage Anson had experienced storm, shipwreck, fearful scurvy, and finally triumph. He had lost ninety percent of his men. His *Voyage Round the World* was being written, and would soon become one of the best known travel books of the time, raising public awareness in Britain of the benefits of a properly maintained Navy with a worldwide reach. Maps of South America were being published, some of them even showing the supposed position of the wreck of the *Wager*.

This map of South America, with some interesting boundaries depicted, was published in the *The Gentleman's Magazine* of 1749, in response to the increasing public interest that Anson's *Voyage* had engendered. It includes the words "Here about the *Wager* was lost". The position is, not surprisingly, only approximate.

Charges of mutiny would inevitably have brought up unwelcome questions about Captain Cheap's conduct, questions that Anson may have thought were perhaps better left unasked.

Such speculation appears to be on firmer ground in view of the absence of the Cheap narrative from the Court-Martial Record, and the fact that it was dated three days before the others. Perhaps a possible sequence of events might have been:

16th March 1746. Cheap reaches London, exhausted.

17th - 20th March. Cheap recovers somewhat; buys clothes; calls on his old captain, Rear Admiral Sir George Anson, at the Admiralty. He is ordered to write a report, perhaps with a narrative dealing with the loss of the ship separate from the rest of the story.

22nd March. The Admiralty Board, or some of them, meet to make a decision on the long-running *Wager* business. They decide to call all witnesses for a court-martial into the loss of the ship, which was the normal procedure and which would also have the effect of tracing and assembling the main suspects. Awkward difficulties in proceeding against the mutineers are discussed.

23rd March. Sunday.

24th March. The Admiralty Order for the court-martial is issued.

25th March. The summons for witnesses to report to Spithead is issued.

26th March and on several subsequent dates. The summons is published in newspapers.

11th April. Cheap completes his narrative, probably in London, and proceeds to Portsmouth for the court-martial. If Bulkeley is to be believed, at this moment Cheap and everyone else fully expect that a trial for mutiny will follow the court-martial for the loss of the ship.

12th April. The Admiralty Board scrutinise Cheap's narrative, and debate the merits and demerits of proceeding with charges of mutiny. In this debate Anson's personality, in which there was a generous element of humanity and fairness, would surely have played a major part. Of course he would have strongly disapproved of mutiny, and no doubt would have supported the Navy's extreme punishment for the most serious cases of it, but he may have thought, very privately, that the mutineers could bring forward on their side an uncomfortable whiff of justification. A charge of mutiny, once brought, would almost certainly have been proved, and four men might swing. He may also have reflected that David Cheap, his own appointee and previous First Lieutenant, had suffered enough and should be protected from public criticism, especially as his faults were the result of an inflexible determination to come to grips with the Spanish enemy. Altogether, in this exceptional and unprecedented case, there would have seemed to be good reasons for passing over the mutiny question, and he may have recommended this to his fellow Board members. They therefore decide on balance not to proceed with mutiny charges, and send a message to this effect to the Deputy Judge Advocate in Portsmouth.

13th April. Sunday.

14th April. The Deputy Judge Advocate tells Bulkeley that no charges of mutiny are to be brought.

All this, in the absence of documentation, is speculation. But the loss of a ship required a definite formal enquiry, and this necessitated the court-martial which now went inexorably ahead.

Chapter 25

THE COURT-MARTIAL

The court-martial took place on 15ᵗʰ April 1746. Sworn statements had been taken previously by the Deputy Judge Advocate, and were read out in court and confirmed by all witnesses. These statements were subsequently attached to the minutes in the Court-Martial Record, and have been inserted here at the point where they were read out in order to show the evidence exactly as the court heard it.

It is occasionally not immediately obvious from the Record as to who is asking and answering the questions, and the minutes, which were taken down in shorthand at the time and copied out later, have other confusions and obscurities which have been rectified as far as possible.

Minutes of a court-martial held on board His Majesty's ship *Prince George* at Spithead the 15ᵗʰ April 1746, for enquiring into the cause of the loss of His Majesty's ship *Wager*, cast away on a sunken rock on the coast of Patagonia in the South Seas on the 14ᵗʰ May 1741, pursuant to an order from the Right Hon. the Lords Commissioners of the Admiralty dated 24ᵗʰ March 1745.

Admiralty Warrant[1] dated 11ᵗʰ October 1744, empowering Vice Admiral

---

1. This Warrant and the Admiralty Order are not in the Court-Martial Record, but they are presumably the documents that defer investigation into the loss of the *Wager* until Captain Cheap should return home.

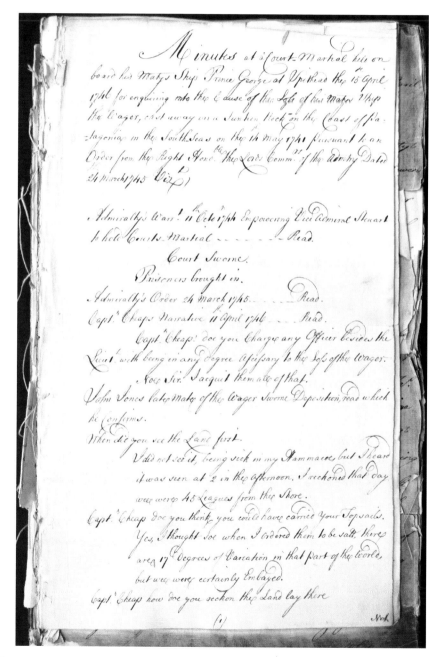

The minutes of the court-martial show that Captain Cheap's narrative was read out to the court; but it is not there now, whereas all the others are. The binding of the book has been broken at this point. Has the narrative been intentionally removed?

Steuart[2] to hold a court-martial, read. Court sworn. Prisoners brought in. Admiralty Order dated 24th March 1745 read.

Captain Cheap's narrative dated 11th April 1746 read.[3]

Captain Cheap, do you charge any officer besides the Lieutenant with being in any degree accessory to the loss of the *Wager*?
No, Sir. I acquit them all of that.

John Jones, late Mate of the *Wager*, sworn, his deposition read as follows: On the 14th May 1741 between the hours of 4 and 5 in the morning, the ship struck on a rock or shoal, I then being in my hammock, and had not been out of it to do any duty for several days before. When I came on the deck I found the fore and main courses set, it then blowing very hard, and had our men been all well, whereas we had not above six men in a watch to the best of my remembrance, in my humble opinion we were not able to carry any more sail, our mizzen-mast being gone. We always with our foresail set carried our helm a-lee. I looked at the compass and found after she got off the shoal that she lay up to the west, and I told them she lay with her head off shore. The Carpenter's Mate came and said that there was six foot of water in the hold. We had our starboard tacks aboard, and the wind variable from the N to the NW. The Lieutenant proposed letting go the anchor, but I told him there was not room to bring the ship up and if we should swing clear of the rocks she must sink as the water increased so much on us. I went to Captain Cheap, who was then in the Surgeon's cabin, and had the evening before by a fall very much hurt his shoulder, I think I have heard the Doctor say it was dislocated which rendered him incapable to give his necessary orders. He told me that if the people's lives were saved, he had no regard to his own. The second or third time

---

2. Stewart often became Steuart or Stuart, the French being reluctant to use a w. Admiral Stewart used all three spellings indiscriminately.
3. Captain Cheap's narrative has been removed from the Court-Martial Record.

she struck she broke the rudder, after which accident we were forced to back and fill her to keep clear of the shoals and I believe the current set true through them or else it were impossible for the ship to come where she sunk.

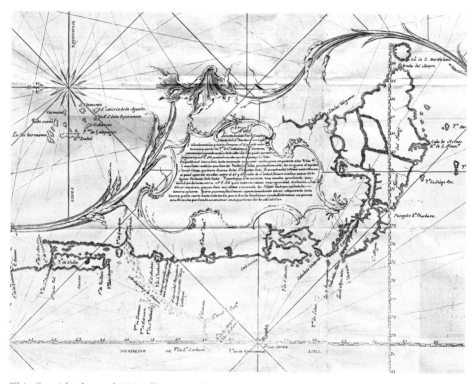

This Spanish chart of 1744 illustrates the navigational problems, discussed here at the court martial, that all seamen encountered in the South Seas at that date. The wreck of the *Wager* is marked, but some 70 nautical miles from its proper position. A translation of the Note includes this dire warning:

"We cannot be certain about the line of the coast, but as far as the islands are concerned we can be, at least from information given by the Indians of Chiloé, who have seen them, and which is confirmed by Captain David Cheap from one of the frigates of Admiral Anson's Squadron, who was wrecked amongst them between 46 and 47° latitude, believing himself more than 80 leagues distance from the coast. And since that position is known for certain, it is very likely that the coast also runs NE/SW; and until it is possible to have more certainty, or observations are made which can provide confirmation, pilots should take care to remain well outside. And in order to make it easier to know how to proceed, we have shown both one and the other version of the map up to Cabo Corzo, which is where opinions differ as to its direction, rather than giving a unanimous view on the direction from there to the south." (See inside cover for the full chart.)

When did you see the land first?
I did not see it, being sick in my hammock, but I heard it was seen at 2 in the afternoon. I reckoned that day we were 45 leagues from the shore. There are 17 degrees of variation in that part of the world, but we were certainly embayed.[4]

Captain Cheap, do you think you could have carried your topsails?
Yes, I thought so when I ordered them to be set.

Captain Cheap, how do you reckon the land lay there?
North and South.

Jones states SW by S, NE by N, from the Straits of Magellan to the place where we were lost.

On the 13th May, what latitude did you judge your selves in?
46:40 to the best of my remembrance.[5]

Was there any dispute among the officers about the course you steered?
Yes, I heard some of the officers, the Lieutenant and Gunner and others, uneasy at steering for Socorro, for fear we should fall in with a lee-shore, therefore we wished to have gone to Juan Fernandez.

Captain Cheap says by his reckoning they were 55 leagues from the shore and all the officers except the Mate made it farther, some even 90.

What was the last land you made before you were lost?
Sometime about the beginning of April we made land, which Frazier calls the Passage of Santa Barbara. We had an observation two days

---

4. This observation may have been made by the Captain.
5. Jones speaking.

before we were lost.

Were you desirous to make the land?
Yes, the land of Socorro, but this was to the southward of it.

What time did the ship strike?
Between 4 and 5 a.m.

Was everything done for the preservation of the ship and the people's lives?
Yes, everything was done.

Captain Cheap asks, did you remember that the Carpenter told the Lieutenant he saw the land on the 13th?
Yes, I heard the Carpenter say so, after the ship was lost.

Did you ever hear any reason given why the Captain was not acquainted with your seeing the land?
I cannot tell. I never heard any reason, only that it could not be the land because it bore NNW.

Did you ever hear anybody say that they hove the lead after you wore the ship?
No, I never heard of it.

Lieutenant Baynes asks Jones if he does not remember that on the 1st May, the wind being fair for Juan Fernandez, which we could have fetched if we had not lain by 3 or 4 days with the wind westerly, SSW. I asked the Captain why he would not go thither, and Captain Cheap said his rendezvous was at Socorro, and there he would go if possible.[6]

---

6. Apparently this question is not answered by Jones.

Did you know the rendezvous before that time?

No, it never was public.

Captain Cheap, after you told the Lieutenant the rendezvous was at Socorro, how did the Lieutenant behave then?

I can lay nothing to his charge after that. He obeyed my orders.

The Hon. John Byron sworn, his deposition read as follows:

13th May at 8 a.m. when I came upon deck, I saw several bunches of rock-weed pass by the ship, upon which I called to the Carpenter who was by me and showed him them. He told me he believed he had seen the land and had showed it the Lieutenant. 14th May at half past 2 p.m. saw the land bearing NNW distant 4 leagues. We were then lying-to under a reef mainsail with the larboard tack aboard and the foreyard down; upon which the Captain wore ship, and laid her head to the westward, the wind at NNW. The Captain going forward to give directions for the fixing of new straps to the jeer blocks,[7] they being broken, and four of our starboard fore chain-plates,[8] he fell down the after hold, all the gratings being unlaid, and dislocated his arm. He was brought up and laid in the Surgeon's cabin, as being thought by the Surgeon more proper than his own for the reducing his arm. As soon as he came a little to himself, he sent for the Lieutenant, and hearing the wind was at NW by N he ordered him to set the topsails and keep all hands upon deck all night, as the Captain has often told me. At half past 4 a.m. the ship struck, but having received no damage the officers upon deck were immediately for loosing the topsails. But it then being too late, the Captain ordered them to let go the anchor, but it not being clear, we drove upon a second reef, which broke the head of our rudder, and we had seven foot of water in the hold. So afterwards steering with our head

---

7. The jeer blocks were tackles (small pulleys) which, being made fast to the masthead by straps, enabled the hands on deck to lift the heavy yards into position. Without them it would have been extremely difficult to have swayed up (lifted into position) the yard.

8. The chain plates take the athwartship stress of the sail and mast.

sails, till we stuck fast on a bank near the island we got ashore upon. I do think that with the strength we had, we could have set our topsails and hauled the sheets home.

Did you tell the Captain that the Carpenter had seen the land?
No, I did not think it my place.

Did you ever tell the Lieutenant?
I cannot say whether I did or not.

Did you endeavour to make more sail after the foreyard was swayed up?
We set our foresail, but never attempted to set the topsails. Our yard was swayed up about 7 or 8 p.m. before we struck.

When you put the ship about did you see any bay within you?
Yes, a very deep bay, but we had but just entered it.

After you wore did you ever know or hear whether the lead was hove?
Yes, I do think there were soundings, but I cannot remember them.

Captain Cheap says Campbell the Midshipman told him there was no water in 20 fathom of line.

Did the ship go off from the shore after you wore?
I believe not. I think she went wholly to leeward.

Do you think the ship would have bore her topsails?
Yes, with all the reefs in I do think she would. At least it should have been tried, I think.

Thomas Hamilton, Lieutenant of Marines, sworn, his deposition read as follows:

Some days before our shipwreck I was told we were in or near the latitude of our rendezvous, the island of Socorro. We lay-to at night and made sail in the day. On the 13th May I heard the officers talking of seaweed which they saw, and at 3p.m. of the 14th was told they saw land, and had wore the ship, and stood to the westward. I went upon deck and saw the land upon our weather bow, bearing about NW, 4 or 5 leagues as I imagine. The Captain was upon deck and uneasy about the rigging of the foremast, being disabled; he gave orders about it and at last went forward himself. He fell down the after hatchway, pitched upon head and shoulders. Both were much bruised, and his left shoulder put out, so that the head of the bone came down below his armpit. After the shoulder was reduced with infinite difficulty and torture to the Captain, as soon as he recovered himself and was a little easier, he sent for the Lieutenant, but I know not what passed. The Surgeon gave the Captain a composing cordial, and he fell asleep. About 9 or 10 all was quiet and no officer came to the Captain, nor I heard of no apprehension of danger, but about 4 a.m. the stroke of the ship upon the rocks awaked me. I ran to the Captain; he bid me send the Lieutenant. Not finding him, I returned, and the Captain bid me order to let go the anchor, but it was not clear. We struck again, and set fast till the tide rising hove us off. I think it was here we broke our rudder, and our headsails and a strong tide carried us clear when we were just upon the rocks, almost touching. At last we set fast on a small island. I understood from the Captain that our misfortune was owing to the Lieutenant not setting the topsails as ordered, and which I believe was the truth, for I never heard it contradicted.

After you wore ship, did you see or know whether they hove the lead?
No, I know not, nor did I hear the Captain's orders to the Lieutenant to set the topsails. I have heard some of the people say that the Lieutenant disobeyed the Captain's orders by not setting the topsails and saved their lives.

John George, Mariner, sworn, his deposition read as follows:

On the 14th May 1741 it was my watch upon deck, when about 4 o'clock a.m. the ship struck upon a rock on the coast of Patagonia. It blew very hard right on the shore, and we had but eight men in the watch and those very weak. We had our courses set, and the ship crippled very much with that sail, but it was as much in my opinion as she could bear, but we were forced to carry what sail we could, to endeavour to claw it off the shore. I do think we were too weakly handed to have set the topsails and hauled the sheets home, but if we could have done it, I don't think the ship could have carried them.

Did you ever know, or see, or hear that the lead was hove when you wore the ship?

No.

Why do you think you could not carry your topsails?

Because there was a great sea, violent squalls of wind, and the ship lay gunnel-to with reefed courses.

Could the ship at any time have carried her topsails when you first wore, till she was lost?

No, it blew a hurricane of wind, but it was my first voyage, and I can't say much, but her gunnel was even with the water, and I don't think she could bear more sail.

John King, Boatswain, sworn, his deposition read as follows:

On the 14th May 1741 between 4 and 5 a.m., it blowing very fresh and we under our courses, the ship ran upon a sunken rock from whence she beat to a small island and there lay fast. I know of no order for setting our topsails, but had we had orders to set the main-topsail I am of opinion the ship would not have carried him, there was such a gale of wind. I think the ship could not bear him set, nor had we strength enough I think to do it. At this time the Captain had put out his shoulder and was not upon deck.

Did you ever hear the lead was hove from your wearing the ship to your striking?
I can't remember the lead ever was hove till we had struck, then we hove the lead and had 14 fathom water.

Could the lead have been hove and you not heard of it or known it?
No, certainly it could not, for I was then upon deck.

Did you ever hear the deep-sea line ordered to be stretched forward after you wore?
No, I never did.

Did you ever hear that the Captain ordered the Lieutenant to set the topsails?
The Lieutenant came upon deck and said the Captain had ordered if it was possible to set the topsails. I said it was impossible to loose them in the brails, they would have split to pieces, nor could the ship carry them, nor had we any strength. We had not above three seamen in one and four in the other watch besides marines.

How many marines had you in a watch?
I don't know.

How many persons had you in each watch, marines and seamen?
Sixteen in both watches, as well as I remember.

Have you anything to say against your Captain, of remissness or neglect, or being any ways deserving censure for the loss of the ship?

No, the Captain behaved very well. I have nothing to say against him or any other officer.

Were you upon deck when you wore ship, or were you on the Sick List?
Yes, I was upon deck. I assisted in fitting the jeer blocks, and swaying the foreyard up. I saw the Captain in the steerage, when he had received his hurt, and was upon deck when the ship struck, and had done my duty two or three days.

John Bulkeley, Gunner, sworn, his deposition read as follows:
14th May at 2 p.m., being on the foreyard assisting in handing the foresail, saw the land bearing NW half N, at the sight of which I acquainted Captain Cheap, on which he instantly gave orders to sway the foreyard up, set the sail and wear the ship to the southward which we were three hours about. The Captain seeing the weakness of the people and want of strength, he coming forward to assist himself, fell off the ladder and unhappily dislocated his shoulder. At 8 o'clock of the same evening the Captain sent for the Lieutenant and myself, and said, Gentlemen, you are sensible of the danger the ship is in and the necessity of making sail being on a lee-shore; therefore I desire you will use your utmost endeavour to crowd her off, and if possible set the main-topsail. But the violence of the gale would not permit of making more sail without endangering the ship. At 4 a.m. the Master and myself relieved the Lieutenant, he having had the middle watch. About an hour after the ship struck, at which time we could not discern half her length for the storm of wind and rain. The ship striking, the Captain sent several times up with orders to let go the anchor, which was impossible to be done. The ship a short time after bilged and grounded where it was impossible ever to get her off. We could not if the weather had permitted have set our topsails for want of strength, for in the two watches we could muster no more than 13 hands, petty officers and all.

Did you ever hear any directions for stretching the deep-sea line or was the lead hove when you made the land NW half N?
No.

Why did you not heave the lead?
The Master was in the watch with me, and it was his business.

After the ship struck upon the first rock and went off again, how did you keep her?
Upon a wind close-hauled till we struck again, which broke our tiller, then we steered with our sails, and she ran ashore the third time before the wind.

How came you not to let go your anchor?
The cable was foul.

Captain Cheap says the cable was across the cathead.[9]

How long after you struck the first time was it before you struck the second time?
Half an hour.

Do you know if the Lieutenant acquainted the Captain from time to time of the bearings and of all the transactions?
It was so dark no bearings could be seen. I don't know what he did with the other transactions.

Was the Boatswain upon deck, and did he keep all hands upon deck?
Yes.

---

9. The cathead is a strong projection on either bow, used to ensure the anchor is raised clear of the bow. An anchor cable that, through weather damage or poor securing, had come across the cathead would make the anchor incapable of being used until it was cleared.

Have you anything to object to the conduct of the Captain or officers, or to his proceedings in all respects for the good and preservation of the ship and crew?
I believe not. I can lay nothing to the charge of any officer.

Did you ever hear any reason given for not heaving the lead?
No, never. I believe it was forgot.

Do you believe the ship could at any time, from the time of wearing to her striking, have carried even her main-topsail?
I think she could not till 12 at night, then my watch was out.

John Cummins, Carpenter, sworn, his deposition read as follows:
On the 13th May 1741 about nine in the morning I went to inspect the chain-plates on the starboard side. After going on the forecastle, I saw the land, and showed it to the men of the forecastle, and immediately acquainted the Lieutenant with it, he not allowing it to be land because the bearing was NNW. I answered, Sir, may we not be embayed. The Hon. John Byron answered, True, Carpenter. About 4 in the afternoon the Captain going down the ladder of the quarterdeck fell down and dislocated his shoulder, and was laid in the Surgeon's cabin. About 8 at night the Captain sent to me to acquaint me I must take the middle watch with the Lieutenant. I was called out at 12 o'clock, went on deck, but dismal dark. Pumped ship at seven glasses.[10] At 4 the Gunner relieved the Lieutenant. About half past, being between sleep and waking, I felt a shock as though the sea took the ship under the main chains. Immediately the Gunner acquainted me the ship had struck, I got out of bed, called to my Mate to step in the well and see what water. He answered, No water. I was for letting go the anchor; Mr. Jones, Mate, answered, If you let go the anchor we shall perish. The ship ran till about half past 5 then set fast. I heard nothing of setting the

---

10. 3.30 a.m.

topsails but am of opinion we had not strength enough to have set them and hauled home the sheets, nor would the mast have borne the sail for it blew a hurricane.

There was no examination of the Carpenter following the reading of his deposition. The court then questioned the Lieutenant.

Mr. Baynes, how came you not to acquaint the Captain that the Carpenter saw land?
I did not think it was land, it looked like dark, between two heavy clouds, which very soon disappeared.

The Carpenter says the sight of it was soon gone, though it must be the land.

Did you hear the lead ordered to be hove?
No; not till after we had struck.

Lieutenant Baynes is asked how he came not to cast the lead.
He says he could not believe it was land, it so soon disappeared, and by his reckoning they were 70 leagues off.

Have you anything to lay to the charge of the Captain or any of the officers, for neglecting the preservation of the ship?
No.

Mr. Baynes, how came you not to have your cable clear?
They were bent[11] about a fortnight before we came in sight of land, and I know not how the cable came over the cathead.

After the ship had beat over the first reef of rocks why did you not let go

11. That is, the end of the cable was tied to the anchor ready for letting go.

an anchor?

I was for it, but Mr. Jones the Mate said we should all perish if we did, nor do I think there was trust to be put in the cables. Captain Cheap says the best bower had been bent not above nine or ten days before.

After you first struck, how long might it be before you came upon the second reef of rocks?

An hour I believe, but upon the first rock we struck twice very soon one after the other, and the rudder after that could not be traversed, so that we were obliged to steer with our sails.

Mr. Baynes, when you were obliged to steer with your sails, how came you not to haul the mainsail up?

We did at last, but we were a long while about it.

Lieutenant Fielding of Frazier's Marines, sworn.

Do you know anything of the *Wager* at the time of her going ashore, or before it?

I know nothing of it, more than that the ship was in a terrible condition, there could not be above three soldiers in each watch I think, they were all down with the scurvy. I heard some of the people say they saw the land, and I looked where they did, but could not see it, nor can I say anything to the matter.

The President tells Lieutenant Baynes he has heard what his Captain's charge was, and what was said by the several evidences.

What have you to say in your defence?

I never could set the topsails, it blew so very hard. I did not believe it was land that the Carpenter saw, otherwise I would have certainly told the Captain. As to heaving the lead, the Captain and Master were then upon deck and they did not order it, and neither from the signs of the land, nor from my own reckoning could I suppose it to be land, therefore it did not come into my thoughts to heave the lead.

Withdraw everybody and the Court debated the sentence.

THE FINDING[12]

At a Court-Martial held on board His Majesty's ship *Prince George* at Spithead the 15th April 1746, pursuant to an Order from the Rt. Hon. the Lords Commissioners of the Admiralty dated 24th March 1745;
Present:

> Jas. Steuart Esq., Vice-Admiral of the Red Squadron of His Majesty's Fleet and Commander-in-Chief of all His Majesty's Ships and Vessels at Spithead and in Portsmouth Harbour, President
> Commodore Chas. Windham Esq.
> Captains Solo. Gideon
> Thos. Harrison
> Edwd. Rich
> Clark Gayton
> Jno. Hume
> Chas. Watson
> Thos. Philpott
> Wm. Parry
> Timthy. Nucella
> Thos. Stanhope
> Robt. Harland

All duly sworn according to Act of Parliament.

---

12. The finding of the Court is recorded in the handwriting of the Deputy Judge Advocate, George Atkins.

The Court proceeded to enquire into the cause of the loss of His Majesty's late ship the *Wager* on the 14th May 1741 upon a sunken rock on the coast of Patagonia, & having heard Captain Cheap's narrative read, as well as what Lieutenant Robert Baynes had to say in his own defence, the depositions of such of the officers & crew of the said ship as could be met with, & what they had all to say on the occasion, & maturely considered the same, were unanimously of opinion, that Captain David Cheap had done his duty, & used all means in his power to have preserved His Majesty's ship *Wager* under his command, & as he says he has no charge to lay against any of the officers of the said ship, save only against Lieutenant Baynes, therefore the Court do acquit him the said Captain Cheap & all the officers & ship's company, except the said Lieutenant Baynes, & they are hereby acquitted accordingly for the loss of the said ship *Wager*. And the Court, having maturely considered the case of Lieutenant Baynes, are unanimously of opinion that he was to blame in not acquainting the Captain when the Carpenter told him he thought he saw the land, in never heaving the lead, nor letting go the anchor, but in regard to the weakly condition of the ship, the cable being foul, and but thirteen sickly hands to clear it, as well as the little reason he appeared to have to believe it could have been the land which the Carpenter fancied he saw, either from its appearance, or from the distance his own & the general reckonings of the ship made them from the land, therefore the Court do adjudge him the said Robert Baynes to be acquitted for the loss of the said ship *Wager*, but to be reprimanded by the President for such omission, & he is hereby acquitted accordingly, & ordered to be reprimanded.

Chapter 26

AFTERMATH

After the court-martial Cheap's promotion to captain was speedily confirmed, and a month later he was appointed to command the 5th Rate HMS *Lark*, 44 guns, and ordered to cruise off Madeira to intercept Spanish shipping. HMS *Gloucester*, a new 5th Rate commanded by his old shipmate from the *Centurion*, Captain Charles Saunders,[1] was in company. We find him having difficulty with provisions and masts, problems he was extremely familiar with:

> To the Secretary to the Admiralty
> *Lark* in Madeira Road
> 24th July 1746
>
> Sir,
>   I have the honour to acquaint you for Their Lordships' information that I arrived here on the 22nd current with His Majesty's ship the *Lark* and *Gloucester*, and pursuant to my instructions I applied to the Consul for a supply of provisions to complete me for four months, of all species, which he could not do as you will see by a copy of his letter

---

1. Later First Lord of the Admiralty.

which I send you enclosed.

I shall put the ships' companies to short allowance and proceed to sea as soon as we can get our wine and water aboard and repair the *Lark's* mainmast which I found to be sprung in two places, and then to continue cruising for two months...

The next letter in the Admiralty files is of an altogether different nature. David Cheap, like Anson, was not a great letter-writer, but he would have enjoyed penning this one:

To the Secretary to the Admiralty
Lark, Plymouth Sound
13th January 1747

Sir,

My last letter to you was from the island of Madeira which I believe is not yet come to your hands. I have now the honour to acquaint you (for Their Lordships' information) that I sailed from thence the 21st December last, in company with His Majesty's ship the *Gloucester*. We met with nothing until the 25th, when at break of day we saw a sail standing to the eastward and gave chase. About two o'clock in the afternoon the *Gloucester* came up with her and began to engage. She resisted about half-an-hour and then struck. She is called *Le Port de Nantez*, John le Depencier Master, bound to Cadiz from Vera Cruz and the Havana, from the last of which places she sailed on the 18th November. We found on board of her 105 chests of silver, several of which are marked Rey[2] and (as they say) each chest contains three thousand pieces-of-eight, which I thought advisable to take out of her and put on board the *Lark* and *Gloucester*, her cargo besides is very valuable consisting of cochineal, indigo, vanillas, Havana snuff, and sugar.

---

2. Therefore money belonging to the Spanish King or government.

She is a new ship built at Nantes about four years ago, 650 tons burden, mounted with 32 guns, and has on board 200 men, two of which were killed. Amongst the prisoners is a Spanish Second Lieutenant and two Lieutenants of Infantry belonging to the garrison of the Havana.

Finding her so valuable a prize I determined to proceed to Spithead with her without loss of time, which I hope Their Lordships will be pleased to approve, and likewise of my giving Captain Rogers orders whom I spoke with last Sunday to the westward of Scilly, to keep in company as he was bound to the same port. We were this morning at daybreak off the Start but the winds coming SE by E obliged me to bear up for Plymouth because of the badness of the prize's sails and rigging.

I intend the first fair wind to proceed to Spithead with the prize, there to wait Their Lordships' further orders.

I have the honour to be,

    Sir,

Your most obedient humble servant,

    David Cheap

P.S. All the information I can get from the prisoners is that they sailed on 15th October in company with eight sail of Spanish ships of war who had on board eight million pieces-of-eight and were bound for Europe, but happening five days after they set out to meet with an advise boat from Cadiz who informed them of the King of Spain's death, they determined to return to Havana and wait there for fresh orders from Spain.

This is what some of the common seaman say for the officers pretend to know nothing of the matter.

The Secretary to the Admiralty has written in the margin of this letter "16th January answered, glad of his success."

In a follow-up letter Cheap, a Scot but not of course a Jacobite, writes:

I forgot to tell you in my last that I had the satisfaction to find that our prize and some part of her cargo belonged to Mr Walsh of Nantes, a man well-known in France for his services done to the Young Pretender in the late expedition to Scotland.[3]

David Cheap then represented to the Admiralty that his health was so much weakened as to make him "quite incapable of doing my duty." It seems likely that his health had never been properly restored after the exceptional rigours of the previous five years. He asked to be relieved of his command on grounds of asthma and gout. This request was soon granted, and with his share of the prize money amounting to more than £56,000[1] he retired a rich man. He was never employed at sea again, and perhaps neither his health nor his inclinations would have allowed it.

The following year he bought the estate of Sauchie, near Stirling, and married Anne Clark or Clerk,[5] daughter of Sir John Clerk of Penicuik.[6] Cheap was one of the founder members of the illustrious golf course at St Andrew's, and subscribed to the silver club which is generally taken as the beginning of the Royal and Ancient Golf Club. There were no children of the marriage, and he died in 1752 aged 59.

David Cheap's strongest characteristic was steadfastness of purpose, resulting in an inflexible – but surely in some respects admirable – refusal to be diverted from his orders even after his ship was a broken wreck. His plan to go northward with a hundred well-armed men to capture a Spanish ship by stealth[7] might just have worked, if he could have weathered Cabo Tres Montes – a big proviso, but certainly possible in the lengthened long-boat. If he had been successful this would have put his initiative and determination

---

3. That is, in the famous rising, or infamous rebellion, in 1745-1746 by Prince Charles Edward Stuart, who came quite close to restoring the House of Stuart to the thrones of England and Scotland.

4. This equates to £11,000,000 or more in modern money. See Appendix C.

5. Both spellings were used.

6. One of her brothers wrote a somewhat controversial book on naval tactics in 1782, which interested Nelson.

7. Further north there were plenty of ships of all sizes, as Anson found.

and daring on a level with Cochrane or the young Nelson.

But Cheap was no Cochrane or Nelson, because he lacked the most important of all the subtle ingredients of naval command: the ability to inspire and motivate his men, and thus rally them to a common cause in the face of adversity. This failure of leadership allowed a worsening situation

Captain David Cheap.
This fine portrait by Allan Ramsay was probably painted in 1748 when Ramsay was at the height of his powers and rapidly establishing himself as one of the country's foremost portrait painters. In the background HMS *Lark* is visible in the act of capturing the Spanish ship *Le Port de Nantez* off Madeira in 1746, thereby making David Cheap's fortune and enabling him to retire, buy an estate, acquire an heiress wife, and have his portrait painted.

on Wager Island to degenerate into resentment and then open mutiny. His aloof and uncompromising personality told against him too, and he made no attempt at consultation or explanation, let alone attempting to persuade anyone of the feasibility of his plan; and even his officers were kept in the dark. His action in shooting a drunk man can at best be described as supremely rash. Dealing sensibly with belligerent drunkenness is something that comes within the experience of naval officers in all ages, and Cheap was not an inexperienced youngster. Far from re-establishing his command over a deteriorating situation, this impetuous action gave disaffected and desperate men an excuse for a mutiny which subsequently no one on the Board of Admiralty wanted to investigate too closely.

John Byron, now aged 22, found he had been promoted to Lieutenant during his five years' absence, and with Anson on the Board of Admiralty could expect, under the eighteenth-century system of patronage and preferment, some advancement to his career. He was in fact promoted Captain on 30th December 1746, and given command of the *Syren* frigate. From Midshipman-prisoner to Post Captain[8] within a year – he may have mused on the dramatic swings of fortune that go with a naval life, but his personality seems to have been one that takes everything as it comes in a phlegmatic and level-headed way. In 1748 he married Sophia Trevanion of Carhays in Cornwall, a famous beauty for whom "men would have willingly run through fire." Their second son was christened George Anson after Byron's old Commodore, and indeed the names George Anson continued in the Byron family until 1941. Sophia wrote of her husband:

> *Tho train'd in boisterous elements, his mind*
> *Was yet by soft humanity refin'd.*[9]

8. A Post Captain is an officer of captain's rank appointed in command of a ship.
9. Written by her in the flyleaf of Byron's own copy of his *Narrative*.

During the next twenty years he commanded many ships of different sizes, and as he moved up the seniority list he was often in command of small squadrons as the wars with France and Spain continued. We find him in 1757 destroying shipping and privateers off the coast of France; and in 1760 in the Baie de Chaleurs, New Brunswick, he sank an entire French convoy of 20 ships which had been sent for the relief of the garrison in Montreal.

In 1764 he was appointed Commodore and Commander-in-Chief of all His Majesty's Ships and vessels in the East Indies, a title whose sole purpose, no doubt with the experiences of 1740 in mind, was to put foreign intelligence systems off the scent. He was given a small squadron consisting of the frigate *Dolphin*,[10] the sloop *Tamar*, and a stores-ship *Florida*, and they set off apparently for the Cape of Good Hope in July. Only after leaving Rio de Janeiro did he reveal his secret orders, which were a direct result of Anson's expedition 24 years previously. Anson had been acutely aware that operations in the Pacific would have been very much facilitated with a base from which to repair and replenish, and it must have been obvious to all that any further expeditions without such a base would be perilous. Anson's book, *A Voyage Round the World*, makes the point strongly:

> It is scarcely to be conceived of what prodigious import a convenient station might prove, situated so far to the southward, and so near Cape Horn... I doubt not but a voyage might be made from Falklands Isles to Juan Fernandez and back again, in little more than two months. This even in time of peace might be of great consequence to this nation, and in time of war would make us masters of those seas.

Byron's secret orders, therefore, were to establish the existence of Pepys's Island, claim the Falkland Islands for Britain, and then proceed through the Straits of Magellan. Once in the Pacific he was to head north and search for

---

10. Probably the first Royal Naval ship to be sheathed in copper.

Foulweather Jack.
The *Wager* story has few heroes, but Midshipman John Byron, grandfather of the poet, is certainly one of them. He subsequently had a distinguished (but perhaps unlucky) career, founded the first settlement in the Falkland Islands in 1765, and was promoted to Vice Admiral. Bad weather seemed to follow him around and his nickname, Foulweather Jack, has gone down in history.

   This portrait by Sir Joshua Reynolds of Byron as a Commodore is reproduced by courtesy of the 13th Lord Byron.

the elusive North-west Passage through the Arctic ice north of Canada. If this could not be found he was to make his way home going west across the Pacific. His orders also invited him to inquire after any survivors from the *Wager*,[11] but only if he could do so without antagonising the Spanish, with whom we were now at peace. His ship's company were to "receive double pay for their better encouragement" – a generous provision which caused the Admiralty some difficulty when it was cited as a precedent for subsequent expeditions.

Byron and his small squadron headed south, and encountered atrocious weather, with a particularly vicious squall which caused some damage. Ferocious weather seemed to follow Byron around, and his nickname on the lower deck, Foulweather Jack, seems to have been current from this date. He certainly experienced a very large number of tempests and mishaps during a long career at sea, and his nickname was to stay with him for the rest of his life. It is still the name by which history remembers him.

Pepys's Island, marked on the charts about 300 miles north of the Falklands,[12] turned out not to exist at all. It had been all along a strange navigational aberration, having been confidently reported by Captain Cowley in his voyage round the world in 1686, and confirmed by no less than the famous astronomer Dr Halley in 1701. For these reasons its existence was regarded as certain until various eighteenth-century navigators had zig-zagged across its supposed position and found nothing. It is hard to credit, but both Cowley and Halley must have been reporting the Falkland Islands and must have made their latitude some four-and-a-half degrees in error.

Byron arrived off the Falkland Islands on 12th January 1765 and anchored in the fine harbour between Saunders and Keppel Islands, which he named Port Egmont in honour of the First Lord of the Admiralty. With a suitable little ceremony, the flag was raised and possession of the Falklands

---

11. Captain Fitzroy, in the *Beagle* in 1832 with Darwin aboard, was also invited by the Admiralty to make enquiries about the fate of any *Wager* survivors. No one found any traces, but see p288 below.
12. See chart p47.

claimed for King George III. During his stay Byron established a settlement on Saunders Island by planting gardens and making a start at building, and examined the north and north-west coasts of the Falklands. In the next few years Port Egmont was visited and improved by many British ships, and it developed into a small dockyard where a ship was built and commissioned as HMS *Penguin*. The site was excavated in 1992. The ruins that can now be seen include a Governor's house, a barracks, store houses, harbour walls, a mole, gun emplacements, a wedge-shaped dock, a furnace, and vestiges of vegetable plots started by the Surgeon of the *Tamar*.

One of many lasting effects of Anson's vision and Byron's survival was that the Falkland Islands became a crucial British base during the long Pax Britannia and in both twentieth-century World Wars. It continues be a delightful outpost of British civilisation to this day.

Part of the considerable remains of the 1768 British settlement and dockyard at Saunders Island, Falkland Islands.

Byron then took two months to pass through the Straits of Magellan into the Pacific, battling against his customary bad weather. But once through the Straits he ignored the next part of his orders – the search for a North-West Passage – and headed off across the Pacific to make what discoveries he could. This action seems bizarre and almost unaccountable, but he was never officially censured for it, and it seems probable that he had had verbal instructions to modify his orders if he saw fit. He was renowned for humanity and solicitude for his men, no doubt with many memories of the suffering of the *Wager*'s ship's company, and this may have been the reason for his change of plan. In fact he discovered very little of importance during his voyage across the Pacific, but he reached home after a passage of 22 months – the fastest yet – having suffered very few deaths from scurvy.

In 1768, with the *Wager* story still of great interest to the public, he published his excellent *Narrative*. As we have seen, he criticises his old Captain at many points, which he would not have wished to do while Cheap was alive.

In 1775 he was promoted Rear Admiral and offered the appointment as Second-in-Command on the North American station, but he asked the First Lord for leave to call on him to explain why he wished to decline on grounds on health. This was communicated to King George III who wrote to the First Lord:

> He is too gallant an officer to pretend illness without sufficient reason; therefore I expect, when you see him, that he will not change his opinion; in which case I am clear that Sir Peter Parker[13] is the properest person you can pitch upon.

In 1778, with his health improved, he was promoted Vice Admiral. That same year it became known that the French Admiral Comte d'Estaing was

---

13. Sir Peter Parker came from a well-known naval family, and his son Christopher (later Vice Admiral Christopher Parker) married Byron's daughter Augusta.

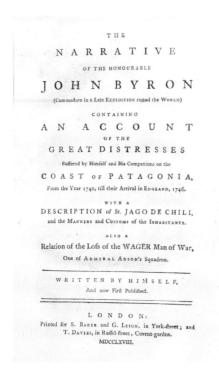

The title-page of Byron's *Narrative*, a best-seller in its day.

John Byron's wife, Sophia, has written in her own copy of his *Narrative* a moving tribute to her husband and the hardships he suffered:

Had some good angel op'd to me the book
Of Providence, and let me read my life,
My heart had broke, when I beheld the sum
Of ills which one by one I have endur'd

taking a squadron from Toulon to support the American rebels in the War of Independence, and Byron in his flagship *Princess Royal* was given thirteen ships and ordered to intercept. Foulweather Jack lived up to his name, and his squadron was severely damaged by gales. Nevertheless, he repaired and augmented his ships and chased the French south along the eastern American seaboard. He caught up with them in the West Indies, where d'Estaing was forced to abandon St Lucia. Byron was too late to prevent the French capturing the island of Grenada, and an inconclusive battle against a superior French fleet resulted in Byron withdrawing and the island lost. He then left his fleet to Admiral Parker and took passage home, suffering from "disorder and disease," to face some criticism for the loss of Grenada. He was not employed again, although it is said that he was offered command in the Mediterranean after the peace in 1783, and declined it for health reasons. He died in 1786 aged 62.

The general assessment by naval historians is that Byron was a fine officer who had more than his fair share of bad luck. The naval biographer John Charnock, writing in 1797, seems to sum him up fairly: "(he had) the universal and justly acquired reputation of a brave and excellent officer, but of a man extremely unfortunate."

The poet Byron, who never knew his grandfather, wrote to his sister:

> *Reversed for me our grandsire's fate of yore, –*
> *He had no rest at sea, nor I on shore.*[14]

Don Juan, shipwrecked and starving, had his dog suffer a fate similar to John Byron's:

> *So Juan's spaniel, spite of his entreating,*
> *Was kill'd, and portion'd out for present eating.*[15]

And when Juan is on the point of expiring with hunger and thirst, the poet writes with typical detachment and bathos:

> *... his hardships were comparative*
> *To those related in my grand-dad's 'Narrative.'*[16]

There are echoes of Foulweather Jack's experiences elsewhere in Byron's works. The splendour and havoc and uncaring viciousness of the sea are clearly close to the poet's heart, as in the famous apostrophe to

---

14. *Epistle to Augusta,*1830.
15. *Don Juan,* 1819, Canto II, lxx. See p77.
16. *Don Juan,* Canto II, cxxxvii.

the ocean at the end of *Childe Harold*:

> *Roll on, thou deep and dark blue Ocean – roll!*
> *Ten thousand fleets sweep over thee in vain;*
> *Man marks the earth with ruin – his control*
> *Stops with the shore; – upon the watery plain*
> *The wrecks are all thy deed, nor doth remain*
> *A shadow of man's ravage, save his own,*
> *When, for a moment, like a drop of rain,*
> *He sinks into thy depths with bubbling groan,*
> *Without a grave, unknell'd, uncoffin'd, and unknown.*[17]

Gunner John Bulkeley became a successful merchant navy captain, and emigrated to America where he probably had relations, still no doubt in a seafaring capacity of some sort. We find him producing the first American edition of his book in Pennsylvania in 1757, with a dedication to the Honourable William Denny esquire, Lieutenant Governor of the province of Pennsylvania. Compared to the 1743 edition it contains a good deal of additional material, including what he calls Captain Cheap's account of his proceedings, although this turns out to be only a close paraphrasing of the version in Anson's *Voyage*, which itself was mostly based on Campbell's account. He also includes long extracts from Isaac Morris's book, and a comparison of these extracts with the original is revealing. Bulkeley has excised the crucial passage where Morris describes the falseness of Bulkeley's claim that the long-boat was prevented by weather from recovering the castaways. Morris had stated – almost unchallengeably – that the weather was fair, and went on to declare that the real reason for being abandoned was to ensure that the remaining survivors would thereby have more room aboard and a greater share of extremely limited provisions.

---

17. *Childe Harold's Pilgrimage*, 1818, Canto IV, clxxix.

Bulkeley was an exceptional seaman, and his voyage of 2500 miles from Wager Island to Rio de Janeiro in the *Wager's* long-boat deserves more credit than it has received in the long annals of the sea.[18] As a feat of seamanship it surely exceeds Captain Bligh's celebrated warm-water voyage from Tofua to Timor 48 years later. Bulkeley possessed leadership qualities of a high order, and this enabled 29 men[19] to survive in circumstances so extreme that one almost rubs one's eyes with disbelief. But his strong and obstinate personality was a major contributor to the breakdown of the Captain's authority, which formed so large a part in the whole disaster that was the *Wager's* fate. Bulkeley's graphic journal, mostly written on the voyage, reveals his character probably more than he intended: a difficult, self-opinionated man, mentally and physically tough, dispassionate to the point of callousness about the fate of his shipmates,[20] and with the classic sea-lawyer's determination to prove himself right and justify his actions in accordance with the rules and regulations of the Navy.

Bulkeley settled permanently in America. Descendants of his carried on a tradition of naval service: one fought with John Paul Jones and one with Nelson. A distinguished descendant was Vice-Admiral John D. Bulkeley USN, one of the most decorated officers of World War II. An Arleigh Burke class destroyer was named after him in 2001.

Midshipman Campbell's behaviour in Santiago and his favoured treatment by the Spaniards on the way home had already aroused suspicion, as we have seen. He protested in his book published in 1747 that he was not in the Spanish service, which may have been legally true at that exact moment, but Spanish sources make it clear that at some time while he was in Santiago during the period 1744 to 1746 he had actually applied to the Governor of Chile to join the Spanish navy, and was then "employed as a volunteer in the service of squadron-chief Pizarro." In any case, on his

---

18. See Appendix D.
19. Thirty reached Rio Grande, and one died in hospital soon afterwards.
20. There are many examples of this, e.g. his description of the death of Mr Harvey the Purser on p106.

return to England he failed to convince Their Lordships, as he had failed to convince his Captain, that his conduct had not been much too friendly towards the enemy. His book was quickly withdrawn from publication, presumably under threat of criminal or libel proceedings, and today only a few copies are known to exist. That same year he left for Portugal, where he started to recruit English and Irish soldiers to fight for the King of Spain; in this disgraceful act of treason he claimed to have suborned 47 men. He was then given a commission in the Spanish army with the rank of Infantry Lieutenant. In 1751 he married Cathalina Rico in Lima, and in 1757 we find him as Director of Works for the rebuilding of Lima Cathedral after an earthquake. He was naturalised a Spanish citizen in 1759 and became Corregidor (an important official, similar to magistrate or mayor) of Chillán, Chile, in 1766. He is last heard of in 1770, by which time he had become a Lieutenant Colonel and was engaged in action against the Araucanos, a native tribe in the north of Chile.

Lieutenant Baynes went on to half-pay and is not heard of again. After being reprimanded at the court-martial, and after the weakness of character and failure of leadership so often revealed in this story, it is to be hoped that he found some more suitable form of employment before he died in 1755. Carpenter Cummins and Cooper Young drop out of sight. Midshipman Morris joined the merchant service, and one wishes him well.

This is where the *Wager* story might be expected to end, but its influence continued, and in fact still continues. Anson remained on the Board of Admiralty almost continuously until he died in 1762, and his naval reforms were so prolific and far-reaching that he has justly been called the Father of the Navy. His improvements included two that were directly the result of the *Wager* disaster. One was a Bill to include in the Articles of War measures "for extending the discipline of the Navy to the crews of His Majesty's ships wrecked, lost or taken, and continuing to them their wages under certain conditions." This ensured that never again would there be any grey area of doubt about the legality of naval discipline continuing when ships were lost.

The other *Wager*-inspired reform addressed the difficulty whereby embarked marines came under their own authority and discipline independent of the naval line of command. Legislation was introduced to bring the Marine Regiments under Admiralty command, and to ensure that the captain had authority over them while they were embarked. This led directly to the formation in 1755 of the Marine Corps, which in 1802 became the Royal Marines, an elite part of the Naval Service to this day.

The appallingly high incidence of scurvy in the *Wager* and the rest of Anson's squadron led to a successful investigation into its causes and cure. When the Seven Years' War broke out in 1756 a regular supply of fresh victuals had been accepted as an essential part of keeping a fleet at sea, and scurvy had been almost eliminated as an operational factor.

Even there the *Wager* story does not end, and in December 2006 that old wreck suddenly came to life again. But it would first be interesting to see what the colonial Spanish made of it.

PART 6
The Wreck Returns

Chapter 27

THE SPANISH ATTEMPT SALVAGE

Revisiting the Place of Disaster: Salvage Operations, Missionary
Voyages and Exploration Expeditions to Wager Island.

*By Chilean maritime archaeologist Diego Carabias Amor, Director of the
Wager Research Project.*

The loss of the *Wager* had important consequences in the life of Colonial
Southern Chile, and contributed significantly to knowledge of the
geography of Western Patagonia and its indigenous inhabitants.

Survivors from the wreck reached the island of Chiloé during the
winter of 1742. Their arrival increased a long-standing concern among
the Spanish authorities: could the British be establishing settlements in
Western Patagonia, somewhere between the Gulf of Peñas and the Straits of
Magellan? During the second half of the previous century two expeditions
had already been sent to search for foreign settlements in the southernmost
part of the Spanish Empire, led respectively by Bartolomé Gallardo (1674-
5) and Antonio de Vea (1675-6). Anson's narrative, published in 1748,
described the discovery of a secure harbour in the Chonos Islands, named
Inchin, where the *Anna* pink had sheltered for two months, and suggested
the advantages of seizing this port for Britain to assist expanding British
interests in the Pacific Ocean.

This alarming situation was the motivation behind three new
expeditions sent from Chiloé by the Spanish Crown to the Gulf of Peñas:

the first, commanded by Mateo Abraham Evrard, was despatched in 1743 to recover the remains of the wreck, and will be addressed in detail later; a second one was led by Manuel Brizuela in early 1750; and finally, another was led by Evrard at the end of that same year, which would establish a short-lived Spanish fort at Inchin, named San Fernando de Tenquehuen.

The Gulf of Peñas represents, to a seaman, the main geographical obstacle of Western Patagonia, and was a convergence zone for several linguistically-different indigenous groups. The Guayaneco Islands were of major importance due to their location at the edge of the archipelago and near the crucial Messier and Fallos channels. In time, the *Wager* wreck-site came to be known as the "Pérdida de Guayaneco" (the Loss at Guayaneco Island), and it became the centre of operations for the exploration and evangelisation of the unknown territories of extreme Southern Chile. These expeditions enhanced social interaction, and the landscape of Western Patagonia began to be seen in a multi-ethnic context, both by the Spanish population and by the indigenous groups of the area.

The first European to visit the wreck of the *Wager* seems to have been the Jesuit priest Father Pedro Flores, probably in 1742. On his return he was arrested and accused of bringing off nearly 100 kilos of iron from the wreck which was to be used in the construction of a new church for the Society of Jesus on the island of Achao, Chiloé. After a controversial trial in Castro, Father Flores was eventually released.

Clearer documentary evidence, probably dating from 1743, reveals the Governor of Chiloé, Juan Victorino Martínez de Tineo, organising an important salvage operation to recover the guns, anchors and nautical gear of the *Wager*, all of which were very scarce in the region and highly sought after. Chiloé was a relatively poor settlement, and the supplies for the expedition had to be collected from the population of the city of Castro. The expedition amounted to no less than 160 men, and this total included Spanish regular troops, allied Indians from Chiloé, and Chono people serving as pilots. They were transported in eleven *dalcas*, the traditional sewn-plank canoes that are described by Byron. Command of the expedition was given to Evrard, who was a Second Lieutenant of the Calbuco Fort, and Royal Purser José Uribe was appointed Commissary Judge. The force set off from Huenao, in Quinchao Island, Chiloé, with supplies for six months.

This salvage operation was a complex task, and it may still be seen as an outstanding achievement considering the difficulties faced. These included sailing more than 300 nautical miles in open canoes, crossing the Ofqui isthmus through more than five kilometres of marsh and bog, recovering extremely heavy and bulky objects from the bottom of the sea, and then returning with them to Chiloé. For the underwater salvage the Spaniards probably employed Chono and Caucahue Indians owing to their remarkable free-diving skills. The objects recovered included ten iron six-pounder and four bronze three-pounder guns, an anchor, over a hundred cannon balls, over a thousand musket shot, three copper cauldrons, and various pieces of lead, iron and steel. Hauling over the swampy ground of the *desecho* the one ton six-pounders and the rest of the artillery, with frequent rains, must have been an extremely trying and arduous task.

Evrard probably established two forts on the west coast of the eastern Guayaneco Island, now called Wager Island. The expedition returned successfully to Chiloé four months after setting off, apparently without any casualties. According to the Governor's report the inappropriate size of the *dalcas* and lack of provisions prevented the recovery of other materials, leaving in place fourteen guns, iron ballast, nautical gear and anchors.

The operation was considered a complete success by the Spanish authorities. The guns went straight to the Royal Treasury, and the other objects recovered paid for the expenses of the expedition. The Governor stressed the quality of the bronze three-pounder guns, probably light artillery field-pieces destined for the assault of Valdivia and other Spanish cities of Chile and Peru, remarking "Without exaggeration, I can say that I have never seen such perfect and refined artillery." Then the Governor made an order forbidding all movements in the area before the rest of the materials could be recovered under orders of the King of Spain.

In 1744 the guns salvaged from the *Wager* had carriages specially made from local timber, and were set up to reinforce the defences of the main military post in the island, the fortress of Chacao.

Although no direct documentary evidence has been identified so far, some administrative documents indirectly suggest several other salvage operations to Guayaneco were performed between 1743 and 1748 during Governor Martínez de Tineo's administration. Besides these Spanish expeditions, and in spite of the Governor's restriction order, the remains of the *Wager* were also from time to time exploited by the local nomadic Indian groups which Byron and Campbell describe. During this period, Officer Pedro Mansilla was sent to Boca del Guafo, south of Chiloé, in search of Chono Indians "who had started recovering iron, anchors and wax that (the *Wager*) had on board". After a long hunt through the islands, the Indian runaways were captured, their canoes claimed and the illegally salvaged materials were brought to the Spanish authorities in Chacao. Indian salvage efforts must have been considerable, for over half a ton of iron was recovered.

An important consequence of Evrard's 1743 expedition to Guayaneco was the accidental rediscovery of the Caucahues, an ethnic group which might be identified with the modern Alakaluf Indians. The Caucahues, along with other local indigenous groups living between the Gulf of Peñas and the Magellan Straits – Tayjatafes, Calenches, Leycheles, Requinagueres – would be from 1743 systematically Christianised and relocated by the Jesuit missionaries in the Island of Kaylin in southern Chiloé, which became the Kaylin Mission in 1764.

From his voyages to the Guayaneco and Chonos Islands in 1743-4 and 1750, Evrard, now First Sergeant of Chiloé, prepared a chart which is indirectly known from three sources: the narratives of Pilot Francisco Machado, Jesuit Father José García Martí, and the *Historia Geographica e Hidrographica*, a report prepared for the King by the Spanish Governors of Chile. Evrard's chart was in turn the basis for a map prepared by

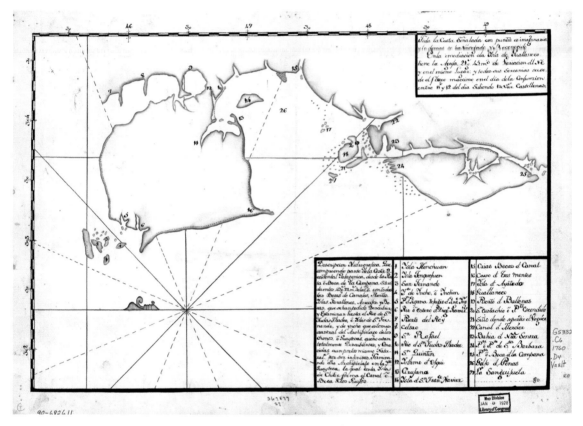

The date of this map is unknown, but it must be about 1770 (north is to the left: the Golfo de Peñas is in the centre.) The key to no. 21 reads "Sitio donde se perdio el Vaguér" (The place where the *Wager* was lost; Spanish does not use the letter W, which in the case of foreign names is usually replaced by V.)

The map also shows the overland route, no. 12, by which the four survivors eventually escaped from the well-named Golfo de Peñas (Bay of Sorrows).

The map was probably made for the Governor of Chiloé to accompany his report to the King of Spain about the *Wager* incident and its subsequent salvage operation. The wreck site is placed very accurately for latitude, but about 100 nautical miles in error for longitude, which was then based on the meridian of Lima.

276

Father García from his own observations. The journal of García's second expedition (1766-7), with Caucahue Indians from the Kaylin Mission, to Guayaneco in search of pagan Indians of the Calen and Tayjataf tribes, represents an invaluable ethnographical document. It was first published in Germany in 1809 in a German-Spanish edition by C.G. von Murr, and it includes a map in which the position of the wreck of the *Wager* is located between the two main Guayaneco Islands, which are named "Guayaneco" and "Ancanzcan".

Father García visited the wreck site in January 1766, nearly 25 years after the loss of the ship, identifying the spot as "Port Teumaterigua", which he described as "pampa without high mounts and looking fine for crops and potatoes" and finding "plenty of evidence of the lost ship and the numerous Englishmen who died there". From some of the Caucahue Indians who claimed to have been in the area when the *Wager* was lost he obtained interesting accounts of the activities of the marooned English survivors.

This missionary remarks that Ancanzcan Island (modern Byron Island) is called "Guayaneco" among the Indians, but this term is used by the Spanish to name the wreck-site, which in turn is called by the Caucahues "Camarigua".

A year after García's visit (1767-8), the wreck was visited by another expedition led again by Second Lieutenant Pedro Mansilla with Pilot Cosme Ugarte, sent by the Governor of Chiloé, Manuel Fernández de Castelblanco, to explore the Guaitecas Islands and the isthmus of Ofqui. On 2nd February 1768, in the Gulf of Peñas, Mansilla's party met Jesuit Father Juan Vicuña who was returning to his mission in Chiloé bringing converted Tayjatafe Indians. The missionary accompanied Mansilla and Ugarte in their exploration southwards to latitude 53° S, a six-day journey which would be very much criticized by geographers of the time. On his way back to Chiloé on the 27th February 1768 Mansilla recovered part of a large anchor which had already been cut in two by a previous Government expedition. On the return trip Father Vicuña's canoe was wrecked and

Cannon at Juan Fernandez (see chart p161).
When Anson watered and refitted the remnants of his squadron at Juan Fernandez it was undefended, and indeed uninhabited. His voyage made the Spanish aware of the vulnerability of their Pacific possessions, and they urgently set about strengthening them, here and elsewhere.

The cannon shown in this photograph almost certainly include some taken from the wreck of the *Wager* in the salvage expeditions that took place during the period 1743-1769. The Governor of Chiloé admired the British workmanship, saying, "Without exaggeration, I can say that I have never seen such perfect and refined artillery."

he was drowned, in what was to be the last Jesuit missionary voyage to Patagonia of the eighteenth century.

One year later (1768-9) a new hydrographic and military expedition to the Magellan Straits sailed from Chiloé, led this time by Pilot Francisco Machado and Officer José de Sotomayor, sent by Governor Carlos de Beranger.

Sotomayor disobeyed his orders to take his ship round the Taitao Peninsula, and carried on southwards across the traditional Ofqui isthmus track exclusively with *dalcas*. Machado was a fine seaman and skilful cartographer, and he surveyed and named several places in the area around the Gulf of Peñas, which can be seen on an unpublished Spanish chart of about 1770 (see p276).

Back in Chiloé, the Governor, displeased with the results, ordered an investigation, and the expedition officers were sent for trial. Machado's innocence was proved and he was released. Machado had visited the place of the wreck which he calls "Desposorio de Guayaneco" on 21ˢᵗ February 1769, which he describes as "not a port, nor anything but a haven for native canoes". He observes that the *Wager* was wrecked at the west end of Guayaneco Island, characterised by an extended and dangerous reef system, near a shallow haven.

After the Society of Jesus was expelled from the Americas in 1767 by King Charles III, Jesuit missionaries were replaced by Franciscans. The Franciscan Order of San Idelfonso of Chillán arrived in Chiloé in 1769, and they were in turn subsequently replaced by the Franciscans of the Colegio Santa Rosa of Ocopa, Lima.

In consequence, nearly ten years later, the Guayaneco Islands were visited again by a missionary expedition searching for "indios gentiles" (heathen Indians), this time led by Fray Benito Marín and Fray Julián Real. On 5ᵗʰ January 1779 they rounded Guayaneco Island from the west with the intention of identifying the place where the ship belonging to Anson's fleet was lost. They found evidence of an Indian settlement formed by four dwellings which had been recently constructed in front of the wreck. The next summer season (1779-80) Fray Francisco Menéndez and Fray Ignacio Vargas repeated this voyage to the Gulf of Peñas, and verified from local information that the *Wager* wreck-site was still being visited by nomadic waterborne Indians. This is the last occasion when the place is mentioned in Spanish Colonial documents.

Nearly half a century later, during the surveying voyages of the Patagonian channels and the coasts of Tierra del Fuego, ordered by the British Admiralty in the years 1826 to 1830 and carried out by HMS *Adventure* (Captain Philip Parker King) and the famous HMS *Beagle* (Captain Pringle Stokes, later Captain Robert Fitzroy), the first modern hydrographic charts of the Gulf of Peñas were completed.

By using the information of the Franciscan expeditions to Guayaneco contained in González Agüero's *Descripción Historial de la Provincia y Archipiélago de Chiloé* and Byron's narrative, the two islands where the *Wager* was lost were identified and named Wager and Byron Islands by Captain Parker King. Several other geographical features commemorate the *Wager* story: Canal Cheap, Speedwell Bay, Caleta Elliot, and the islands Hereford, Crosslet, Hales, and Smith, named after the Marines left to their fate in the north of the Gulf in 1742. All these names remain on the charts to this day as a tribute to our shared heritage.

In 1829 Captain Parker King appointed Lieutenant W. G. Skyring to command the sloop HMS *Adelaide* and to survey the Guayaneco Islands, but despite his efforts to locate the exact place of the wreck along the northwest coast of Wager Island, no remains were found. Parker King described meeting a very old man in Chiloé, Pedro Osorio, who had participated in the last missionary expeditions to Guayaneco and who even claimed he remembered the *Wager* survivors: "Don David" (Captain David Cheap); "Don Juan" (John Byron); "Hamerton" (Hamilton); and "Plasta" (Alexander Campbell?).

During the late twentieth century, there were several informal reports of finds in the area by fishermen and yachtsmen. Finally, in November 2006 two different and independent expeditions coincided in the islands, one formed by a party of British exploration divers and another by a group of Chilean marine archaeologists. Although with very different aims and approaches, both were extremely interested in the *Wager* events. With some on-the-spot collaboration, they were able to start unravelling a new chapter of this fascinating story.

Chapter 28

THE FINDING OF THE *WAGER*, 2006

By Major Chris Holt, MBE

It is not every day that one is asked by the legendary British explorer John Blashford-Snell of the Scientific Exploration Society to lead an expedition to find a lost warship, in a completely remote and uninhabited island off Patagonian Chile. During my service in the Army I had been employed as a commando and a military diver, which meant that I was relatively well equipped to plan and mount such a challenging expedition. However, it has to be said that the planning for *Wager Quest* was paper thin, owing to the sparseness of contemporary information about the wreck site.

The Scientific Exploration Society (SES) had been hoping to mount an expedition to find the wreck of the *Wager* since the mid-1980s. The arrival of Commander Charles le May as the Chilean Naval Attaché to London was the catalyst needed to make things happen. Commander le May took a personal interest in the search to find this piece of shared heritage, and with his help and that of other Chilean authorities, the SES was finally able to gain the practical support required to undertake such an ambitious project.

As for leads to follow, we had little more information than is available in the preceding chapters of this book. While tremendously helpful with the planning of safety and logistics, neither the Chilean authorities nor the locals had any information relating to conditions on the extremely remote island which is now called Isla Wager. More importantly, no one in the world of maritime history or archaeology was prepared to risk a reputation to give me even a vague indication of where the *Wager* might lie along some ten miles of rugged and rocky coastline on the northern shores of Wager Island.

The only slight lead was through a Chilean historian named Fernando Hartwig, who indicated in an email that the wreck had been salvaged by the Spanish with the assistance of some local Indians in about 1745. They had recovered some cannons, the ship's forge, and some other items of value to them such as iron nails, but the detail was sketchy.

Having trawled through the historical accounts, scanned satellite imagery, spoken to round-the-world yachtsmen, made contact with Chilean historians and studied general academic information about the area, we concluded that there were three possible locations where the *Wager* might have come to rest. These three locations were chosen primarily because of information gleaned from the accounts of Bulkeley and Byron and are shown in Figure 1.

The plan before departure was fairly simple – and had to be. With such flimsy information, it was necessary to remain as flexible as possible, and the only certainty seemed to be that any plan would have to adapt to changing circumstances. In outline the key details were as follows:

○ The team would consist of twelve divers from the SES and two divers from the Armada de Chile. The divers would include a maritime archaeologist, Andrew Torbet, a doctor, Richard Booker, and our camera lady Lynwen Griffiths.

○ Once in Chile, we would travel by land to the logging village of Tortel on the Rio Baker, and then, using two small fishing boats, we would make the 120km journey to Isla Wager, where we would stay for around three weeks.

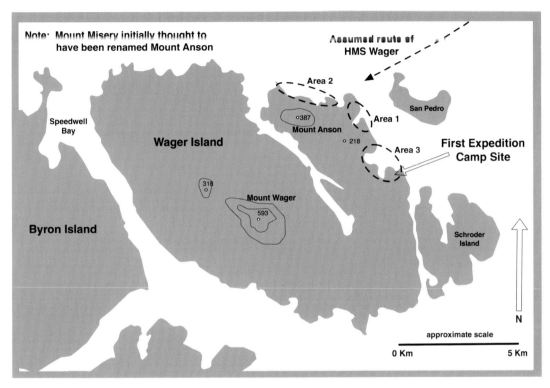

Figure 1.
Our initial assessment of where we would find the *Wager* led us to identify three search areas.

Wager Quest Team.
Standing left to right: Chief Diver Jaime Soto (Armada de Chile), Dr Richard Booker, Lynwen Griffiths, Eric Neime, Andy Torbet, Jamie Hannah, Newton Hau, Mathew Buckland-Hoby, Davy Carson, Mike Smeaton, Lt Martin Guajardo (Armada de Chile), Paul Blunt. Seated left to right: Chris Hunter, Chris Holt.

◦ We would camp on the beaches of the island as close as possible to what we felt was the survivors' beach (Cheap's Bay), and mount our searches from there using small inflatable craft.

◦ Once established on the island, we would dive in the areas that were consistent with the descriptions in the accounts of the time, and, if something was located, conduct a simple survey to act as a start point for a professional archaeological expedition.

◦ In the case of a medical emergency, we would rely first on assistance from the Armada de Chile and second on the civilian emergency rescue organisation Mariscope, operating in Patagonia. Either way, we could expect to be at least twenty-four hours away from medical evacuation should things go wrong. If the weather was bad, this could be as long as five days.

As is always the way with SES expeditions, there would also be a local aid element to our trip. In addition to the diving team, a land party would take part in the expedition and would operate in the area of Tortel. This land team would take scientific observations of two glaciers, and would also assist with a water supply and sanitation project for the village.

Having said our goodbyes in the UK and negotiated hard about excess baggage, we headed off for a month, not really sure what might happen or whether we had any chance of success. I kept a journal during the expedition and it forms a useful summary of our activities.

> *5th November 2006*
> *… I spent the time before take-off wondering whether I had done enough in the way of preparation. This has been a recurring concern particularly in the week running up to departure. The conclusion I keep drawing is that there is very little I can do in terms of planning and that the basis of the plan is pretty much to make one up when we get there! I am of course entirely comfortable with this; it is after all the way I seem to run my life.*

Arriving in Chile, we moved straight to our 'base camp' in Coyhaique, which is the gateway to Chilean Patagonia. This small town runs on logging, salmon farms and tourism. It was here that we made our first contact with CONAF, the Chilean National Forest Corporation. They would provide us with facilities and manpower to assist with the drawing-together of our equipment and were hugely useful throughout the entire trip, particularly to the land-based team. We also became aware of a group called CIEP who were the focal point for all scientific research activity in Patagonia. After two days in Coyhaique making friends with the locals, we headed off early on the morning of 7th November for the tiny logging village of Tortel.

> *The scenery was breathtaking and the sense of remoteness increased when the tarmac ran out. We travelled all morning through mountains with snow covered peaks towering above us. The countryside changed almost every 30 minutes from lush mountain pasture to deep deciduous wood, all broken with crystal clear lakes filled with an abundance of fish . . .*

Tortel is unlike anything I had ever seen before. Perched on the steep sides of a fjord, it has no roads and no cars. Wooden walkways above the water link the houses and buildings, and, apart from walking, the main form of transport is a flotilla of small boats, which seem to be used for just about every purpose. The locals are well built and seemed to puff just as much as we did constantly going up and down hundreds of steps to get from accommodation to restaurant or town hall to local shop. We had two days here to get our kit sorted and head out on two of the larger local boats. There was also the possibility of a Chilean naval vessel assisting with our expedition, but, as is often the way, it was not quite clear what had been promised or merely hinted at, or when precisely the naval vessel might turn up. Keen to be ready, we spent a day preparing kit and packing it in watertight containers in expectation of a gruelling three weeks on the island. The townspeople could not have been more friendly or welcoming

The extraordinary village of Tortel, showing the wooden walkways that take the place of roads. There are over two kilometres of walkway, including flights of 250 steps and more.

The Mayor took time to explain to us exactly why they were so pleased to have us and the significance to them of the *Wager* story. The town has had a road approaching it for about two years, has a new school and receives some routine assistance from the likes of Raleigh International (it is the village where Prince William was filmed cleaning the toilets), but as yet it has had very little in terms of tourism or external visitors. This means that the economy still relies heavily on logging, and the locals are keen to diversify as soon as possible. In addition to their interest in the *Wager* story, there was something else, something I had not considered. Such a remote and insular community can trace its heritage in the area for generations. As in many South American communities, it is possible to see the bloodlines of Spanish and indigenous Indians in the faces of the locals. The Mayor was in no doubt that descendants of people involved in some way in the *Wager* story would be living now either in Tortel or nearby. Basically, *Wager* was an important part of their history and they were just as keen as we were to locate her resting place.

On 8th November I met the skipper of the boat that was supposed to be taking us to Wager Island. *Buzetta* was described to me as a seafaring vessel that would easily take our team and all our kit, although the toilet was not quite ready.

Louis appeared more like a horseman than a sailor. His wide brimmed gaucho hat combined with his height (short), forearms (Popeye-like) and moustache (Adolfian) meant that he looked interesting. Sadly the initial descriptions of just the toilet not being quite ready were stretching the truth a little:

'Louis, this cabin is not ready – is it the toilet?'

'No –galley.'

'What about the bridge, Louis?'

'No ready.'

'The hold?'

'No ready.'

'What about the engines, Louis?'

'Eeeees a no ready.'

It became immediately clear that we would not be leaving Tortel in a local boat for at least four days, if not a week, and that we would now need to rely on the Chilean Navy if we were to get any useful time on Wager Island.

I delivered the news to the team and there followed a fairly quiet lunch, but then our deliverance arrived in the form of the Chilean Navy and the patrol vessel *Puerto Natales*. Forty metres long and equipped with small boats, excellent navigation and communication equipment, and orders to assist us in any way they could, she was a wonderfully welcome sight. The ship arrived with not only a willing and able crew, but also our two Chilean Navy divers. Lieutenant Martin Goajardo and Chief Diver Jaime Soto were both impressive characters but for entirely different reasons. It was clear from the outset that Martin, a young officer, was a highly intelligent and articulate man; his communication skills would come in very useful during the entire expedition. Jaime was impressive for more obvious reasons. The size of a well-fed bison, and with an infectious smile, he immediately became a central figure in the team and someone who could be relied upon if something heavy needed shifting or an unpleasant job finished off.

We carried endless loads of equipment aboard *Puerto Natales* and, after finding the best we could offer the crew in terms of hospitality, snatched a few hours' sleep before an early morning departure. Knowing as little as we did about the island, I was keen to have as much time as possible in daylight to select a site and set up camp. At 0800 on the morning of 9th November, as we were about to leave Tortel, I had a chance meeting with a local diver by the name of Carlos Wager. His surname immediately grabbed my attention, as did his knowledge of the diving conditions in the area. Standing beside an old oil drum with a chart laid on top, he jabbed at the area of Wager Island with a grubby finger, and my interpreter started to translate:

> *There are a number of wrecks along this northern coast of Wager Island. I found a wreck here, British I am sure and man-of-war, very well preserved. She lies in about 12 metres of water only a hundred metres or so away from the shore. Most interestingly she lies in between two giant white rocks…*

Needless to say my heart raced; the description was exactly what I was expecting. Could it be that this man had already found the *Wager* and that all we had to do was survey the remains? I asked him to point out exactly where this particular wreck was? As he looked in more detail at the chart, he picked out Penguin Island, lying about ten miles south of Wager Island: '*She's here – Penguin Island.*' Here was a new factor of uncertainty: there was now reported to be a British wreck far from Wager Island in a location sounding very much like that described by Bulkeley and Byron. Was it possible that, over time or with some bizarre fatigued stroke of a pen in the hydrographic department of the Admiralty, Wager Island had been wrongly named? It would be a cruel twist of fate.

I boarded our support vessel and waved goodbye to Tortel with as much uncertainty as it is healthy to have, desperately hoping that a solution would present itself once I arrived at the island.

The fjord formed by Rio Baker is stunning, and our passage was a memorable one. It was even more satisfying because of the climate, which was being very kind to us. Patagonia in November can be compared to a windy and wet spring in northern Scotland. We were fully expecting limited visibility and almost permanent rain showers, but as we left our moorings the sun was beating down on a mountain and glacier landscape that was truly unforgettable.

The combination of excitement and the raw untouched beauty of the scenery was a heady mixture. Most of us spent the entire trip grinning stupidly at each other. This was only made more so by the presence of dolphins playing in our bow-wave for the latter part of the journey. The crew are amazing. Captain Crawford's team are slick; being on the bridge was like watching a well-oiled machine. Unexpectedly they served us with a fantastic lunch and at just after 12 o'clock we saw Mount Anson and Wager Island for the first time – it was a good moment.

From a short comment in one of the stories written loosely about the *Wager* story, we had accepted the assumption that Mount Misery had been renamed Mount Anson. No one had disagreed with this assumption during our research, so over time it developed credibility. Using this as a start point, we planned to ask the Captain to position *Puerto Natales* between San Pedro and Wager Island, and make an initial long-range recce of where the survivors' beach might lie. This should have been relatively simple; according to one account, the northern side of Cheap's Bay is formed by Mount Misery, and the waves lap the foot of the mountain. All we needed to do was find the bay directly south of Mount Anson. Sadly, the ground did not lend itself exactly to the description, but there was one large bay that was rapidly presenting itself as the best option:

The bay that we think is Cheap's Bay has what looks like two sandy beaches on the north shore. These are the only beaches of any sort we have seen while travelling north in the channel between Wager and San Pedro. Initially the relationship between this large bay and Mount Anson did not seem correct, so we have pushed further north. From the ship one can see an area that on the chart does not appear to be a bay, but which presents itself as a possible option. After loading kit, Andy and I will set off to recce for a camp site, first in the northern bay and then in the large bay with the beaches.

Knowing that you are probably the first British citizens to step on an Island for 260 years is an unusual feeling. On one hand, my mind was racing, assessing possible options for a safe and sustainable camp site, but on the other I was more than aware of the gravity and significance of our return to the spot where so many men had met their end. As we moved into the northern bay in a small Navy inflatable, Andy and I both knew that it was finally time to set foot on Wager Island:

The temptation to go ashore was too great and at about 1400 I was the first of our group, followed quickly by Andy, to set foot on Wager Island. We walked around for a couple of minutes and saw an enormous bird of prey happy to remain in its spot even though we walked within 10 or 15 feet of the creature. Perhaps the size of a large buzzard, it had a peculiar beak and in the complete absence of any ornithological knowledge we decided to nickname it a Parrot Eagle – I'm sure its real name is far more impressive! Out of sight of our small launch we shook hands and toasted our arrival with a swig of Linie[1] from my wife's hip flask.

---

1. Linie is a Norwegian aquavit that has been shipped to Australia and back, thereby crossing the equator or "linie" twice.

Returning to the ship, now at anchor in the area we would call Driftwood Cove, we both agreed that one of the beaches in the larger bay would make an ideal camp site. In the absence of anything screaming out 'Cheap's Bay', we needed to get people established safely on the island before darkness fell. That first afternoon was a blur of activity as we established a fairly comfortable camp, and I soon realised that I had been blessed with a team of highly competent and team-spirited individuals. But for an accident of time, I have no doubt that each one of them would have been familiar with the smell of gunpowder and the lure of voyages to the New World.

We woke on the morning of 10th November to life on Wager Island and the harsh realities of the next three weeks. Our camp was in position S 47 degrees 43 minutes 11.3 seconds, W 074 degrees 54 minutes 13.3 seconds. A bracing wash in the small stream near our camp was followed by the experience of sharing a 'toilet', more accurately described as a log seat over a deep ditch. There is little place for modesty or privacy on such a trip, and people very quickly developed a healthy sense of humour.

To maintain us, the bulk of our diet while on the island would consist of rice, pulses and bean feast, a meat substitute product. While this combination led to most of us losing weight, it did little for haute cuisine. There are only a finite number of combinations for such basic ingredients, and unsurprisingly, after the more attractive items had been consumed, the menu in the latter weeks became a bit monotonous. Accommodation was also very basic. Apart from the two-man tents that we all slept in, we had an old Army 12 x 12 foot tent to which we added a lean-to constructed of timber and two large tarpaulins. Over the coming weeks we would be exposed to just about everything: burning sunshine, heavy rain, and extreme hail storms that rendered us pinned down by their ferocity. This small area, perhaps 20 feet long and 12 feet wide, became home for 14 people during daylight hours and almost permanently during inclement weather. Not only did we store allour equipment and food in the shelter, we also cooked, ate, serviced our equipment, conducted meetings, dried wet clothing and relaxed in this tiny space.

There are a number of qualities required of people who embark on these trips, but for me the most important are a sense of humour and the ability to get on with others. After three weeks without a shower, eating rice, fruitless searching, and days of constant rain while wearing wet clothing, the ability to smile is the most valuable qualification one can have. At one point or another I think everyone has a down moment on a truly arduous expedition such as this; but the thing that separates those who shine in such an environment from those who merely cope is almost always the ability to laugh.

With all our basics provided for and a full rehearsal made of our emergency procedures, we started the job of actually looking for HMS *Wager*. Our first dive was a shake-out dive to confirm that everyone's kit was in full working order and that our safety procedures worked satisfactorily. As one would expect, there were a couple of minor issues (we ended the day with one fin less than we had started with) but overall it was a success. We had made our first searches in the bay we believed to be Cheap's Bay and now had another priority. Our expedition coincided with 11th November – Armistice Day – and it seemed appropriate that we should conduct a service to remember those who had lost their lives a long way from home.

> *Captain Crawford of the* Puerto Natales *and his men joined us and we travelled together in a small flotilla across the bay. At 1100 we held our service on the northern beach of the bay in brilliant sunshine. Rather than sing a hymn I read the poem "The Soldier" by Sub-Lieutenant Rupert Brooke, RNVR:*
>
> > *If I should die, think only this of me:*
> > *That there's some corner of a foreign field*
> > *That is forever England…*

I'm glad we did it properly. We left a wreath from the British Legion and had a chance to remember lost friends, my thoughts returning to some personal memories.

Afterwards we returned to our camp and offered the Chilean Navy the best we could in terms of hospitality: coffee, biscuits and a seat around our fire. We had spent so long learning about the fate of the *Wager* that formally marking our respects for the crew was a deeply touching moment for me. I was not the only one who was genuinely moved by the experience.

Over the next week we mounted extensive searches both in the water and over land to search for the remains of the wreck and any signs of human habitation. Diving conditions were pretty average, normally between eight and ten metres of depth with visibility of around two or three metres. The bottom was particularly silty in the large bay, which meant that, if contact was made with the bottom, a cloud of brown gloom would quickly reduce the visibility and render any hope of effecting a decent search almost impossible. Overland conditions were just as severe, the following being a fairly average excursion:

Near the shore the vegetation is dense and unforgiving. It saps the energy and snags on buckles and bootlaces – it takes one frustratingly long to get through. Once through it (around 50 metres or so can take about 20 minutes) the ground is reminiscent of Scotland. The rocks protrude through tight moss and tuft grass, and lichens grow on them in abundance. After just over an hour of walking, the weather became particularly aggressive. The rain was drenching and driven by a powerful and gusting wind that nearly swept me from my feet. Andy, the doctor and I gathered in a hollow and discussed the options. Clearly there was little point in the whole team being exposed to such conditions and potential risk.

After a week of early starts, energy-sapping daily searches and no progress, we needed to take stock of our situation. We had all reached similar conclusions about the island. First, the area we were occupying did not lend itself naturally to the descriptions made by Bulkeley and Byron Secondly, the northern shore of the island was far more treacherous than areas on the east and seemed more appropriate to the wrecking of ships. This, combined with some background information we had relating to seismic activity in the area, led me to a decision point. It was time to review our progress and to establish an acceptable position on the way forward. Before our arrival on the island we had all agreed that the north-east corner of the island presented the most likely location, the main research and opinions coming from Andrew Torbet, our archaeologist, Paul Blunt, who had tirelessly researched the historical accounts, and Davy Carson, who had looked in depth at the probable effects of wind and tide in the Golfo de Peñas on *Wager* in her final hours. As best as I could, I locked these men together in our living space and told them not to come out until they knew where the *Wager* lay.

We re-read the accounts (rather than the books about the accounts) and came up with the following pieces of information that we felt were important:

1. The ship was only 'feet from making clear water' and missing the island before she struck.

2. When the men first launched the lengthened long-boat Speedwell, *they immediately turned away from the wind and across the 'inlet' to Speedwell Bay (something in the accounts we had somehow previously all missed).*

3. From Mount Misery looking towards land (i.e. east), it was not possible to see if they were on an island because of greater hills in the way.

All of these points lead us to believe we need to be not on the north-eastern but on the north-western shore.

Figure 2 shows how these three facts relate to each other and why we decided we were probably in the wrong place. In hindsight it seems remarkable now that we had all missed the passage about the long-boat bearing away into Speedwell Bay, and that no-one had checked that Mount Misery had really been renamed Mount Anson. However, to a certain extent, the joy of such an adventure is that one is conducting genuinely on-the-hoof detective work from the first day you start to draw the information together. As individuals we had all made similar assumptions and had read only portions of the information available. It was only when we were finally able to sit together (this had not been possible prior to departure) that collective logic and mental horsepower could be bought to bear.

In addition to revisiting the information in the survivors' accounts, we also went back to the information that Davy had discovered about the earthquakes in the area. Between 1741 and 2006 there had been a total

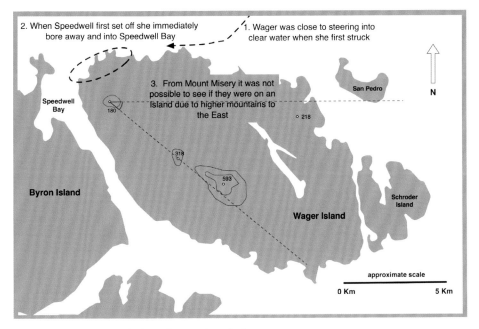

Figure 2. Reassessment of where the wreck might be.

of ninety-four earthquakes recorded in the Golfo de Peñas. On 22nd May 1960 the largest-ever recorded earthquake, 9.5 on the Richter scale, hit the Chilean coast within a few miles of Wager Island. The Chilean authorities have little practical interest in Wager Island or the archipelago it sits in, so no accurate data exist as to how this earthquake affected the island. It would be up to us to make an educated guess – and without the help of a qualified geologist. The tectonic plate on which Wager Island sits is advancing at around 20–70mm per year, and information we could lay our hands on suggested that it had moved at more than 20mm per year before the 1960s event. This, we think, led to an advance of around 5.5 metres during the quake. Converted into a vertical height as the plate rode up over the South Americas, this gave us a rise of somewhere between three and seven metres! We made some observations ourselves and also compared the historical charts with modern satellite imagery. While there is always some discrepancy in old charts, it was clear that Wager Island was a very different shape now from what it had been in 1741 – it was larger, and to our eyes it looked very much as though it had been pushed up and out of the ocean, and by an amount that was nearer to seven metres than to three (see Figure 3). The very real possibility dawned on us that not only could we be in the wrong spot, we might also not be on a diving expedition anymore! The bay that presented itself most readily in the north-western corner of the island on the old chart as Cheap's Bay no longer existed; all that was visible on the satellite photos was a large sandy beach and acres of forest.

At breakfast each morning I would brief the team on the plan for the day, and after dinner we would summarise the day's activities and discuss options for the following day. After dinner and over a long discussion, the team all came to the same conclusion: we needed to get to the other side of the island. The following morning I called John Blashford-Snell on the satellite phone and requested a move. Having discarded thoughts of an initial recce using the inflatables on safety grounds, we would now be at the mercy of a fishing boat, the *Santa Fe*, and the weather, to advance our search.

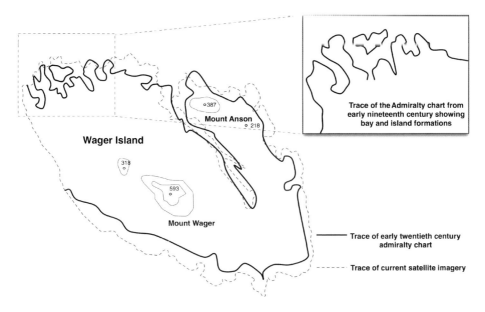

Figure 3. The outline of the island has changed considerably owing to the 94 earthquakes that have occurred since the ship was wrecked.

Cheap's Bay from Mount Misery, looking north.
The dotted lines show approximately where the shoreline would have been before the great earthquake of 1960 (the largest earthquake ever recorded) which raised the land seven metres. The wreck was found just below present-day sea level, midway between where the dotted lines touch the sea.

At this point, when we really needed a break in the weather, we were hit by a storm that lasted for three days and prevented all but the most basic of activities. It was our first taste of the kind of treatment that the Golfo de Peñas can mete out, and all of us were glad we had constructed such a robust camp. Once the storm had cleared and *Santa Fe* was able to move, we had one more day to fill before she arrived. It is always important to keep people occupied on these trips and we decided we should placate the sea gods and name our two boats:

> *Many of the Chilean locals still believe in an evil sea serpent called Kai Kai, and a more passive land serpent. After the severe earthquake in the 1960s, a six year-old boy was beaten to death and offered as a sacrifice to the sea. One of our boats had to be named* Speedwell *and we decided that the other should have a girl's name and probably a Chilean one. Having consulted with Martin and Jaime, we came up with* Rosita. *This was after one of Jaime's female instructors – apparently a loveable and reliable woman, but one who did nothing in a hurry. We held a brief ceremony, and Lynwen blessed each boat with a dribble of whisky from a hip flask.*

Finally our salvation arrived in the form of *Santa Fe*, and we loaded all our equipment and people onto what was a very small vessel. Those with a sense of mortality kept their dry suits on, and halfway through our journey it seemed that their pessimism might have been well placed. I watched as the boat's engineer disappeared into a smoke-filled space below my feet. I looked in with interest until what I saw led me to think I was better off not watching. The smoke cleared to show our engineer working in a tiny space, but with a clearly rising water level. Two large truck batteries were floating in sea water and, as they arced gently against the side of the large metal fuel tank, the engineer relit his constantly present cigarette. I looked for my dry suit and, not finding it, grabbed a life jacket and joined the rest of the team sitting on deck enjoying the view and in a position where, if necessary, we could swim for the shore. The engineer emerged

Wager Quest, Camp 2.

after twenty minutes with a handful of worked timber, some electrical circuitry and two grubby bits of engine that looked to me like fuel pumps. He showed them to the captain, exchanged a few brief words and then threw them all overboard! Obviously non-essential components. Our offerings to the sea gods must have worked, because two hours later we were on a mile of white sand beach with all our equipment and some less tense divers.

From almost the moment of arrival, our second camp site had a certain feeling of rightness. We pitched camp high on the flood plain of a fresh-water stream, and the team constructed windbreaks to protect our new home from more expected bad weather. We utilised the few days of good weather and set about making searches, both diving along the northern shore and also travelling inland to high vantage points in an effort to identify Mount Misery and to search for signs of past habitation. This was a magical couple of days, particularly because all our dives and boat excursions were accompanied by a pod of porpoises:

> *On the way back in the boats and with time to spare we played again for about 15 minutes with the porpoises. It was a fantastic experience, which had everyone, including me, animated. The animals were also clearly enjoying themselves, and, as we circled around to create a wake for them to play in, they were not only jumping out of the water close to the boats to get a good look at us, but even brushing up against the boats and puffing so close that I could smell their breath. If for no other reason, today made the entire trip worthwhile.*

As tick follows tock, our three splendid days of good weather were followed by a three-day storm that prevented us from achieving anything. We were again pinned down in the tents and could do nothing useful in terms of searching at all. It was deeply frustrating, particularly as we were all convinced that we were at last in the right spot. A consequence of this storm was that the small stream next to which we had camped expanded from a two metre wide trickle into an eight or ten metre wide torrent. We were camped on a sandy flood plain a few hundred metres behind the sand bar that separated the fresh river water from the ocean. It was the only relatively flat spot available and we had camped there safe in the knowledge that in the fullness of time, we might have to move – the alternative being to hack a clearing in the dense undergrowth or to live on the beach exposed to the relentless wind. Twice a day the high tide would breach the sand bar and the now swelling stream would come into our camp. It was a fairly unpleasant and damp time.

At last our luck changed: on 20th November the weather broke and we sent teams inland and into the water to recommence the search. After a successful but fruitless day, we sat around the camp fire and all agreed that the next logical step was to get a team to the top of the nearby mountain that was 400 metres inland, and fast becoming the top candidate for Mount Misery.

The following morning a large team headed upstream; the river was vastly expanded because of the heavy rain, and we could use it as a highway. The mountain was only 400m inland, but by the stream the journey was closer to a kilometre. The members of the team planning to climb the mountain were dressed in walking gear and sat in the boat during the deeper sections. The remainder of us wore dry suits, to enable us to haul the inflatables up and over two sets of rapids. It was hot and hard work. Once the climbing team led by Andy had set off, we tied up the boats, swam the kilometre or so back to the camp and waited a call on the radio to replay the whole performance in reverse.

Andy is not someone who is drawn into false optimism; he is a 'professional Scotsman' and proud of it. When I met him back at the boats, he was excited about the correlation between what he had seen from the top of the mountain and the descriptions in the accounts. He finished off his debrief to me by saying: 'I think I've just been to the summit of Mount Misery, which means that the *Wager* is somewhere here.' The whole team was excited, and the journey downstream and back to the camp seemed to take half the time and effort – none the less it was again hot and heavy work. As the buoyant land team stepped out of the boats at our camp site, there was one task left before everyone could get out of their suits and relax for the evening: having nearly lost one of the inflatables to the wind, we religiously removed the boats from the water at the end of every day and tied them down firmly. As I was leaning on the bow of one of them, I heard a flurry of ripe language from the stern. Chris Hunter, one of the serving members of the Armed Forces on the team, had painfully stubbed his toe on something, and the heat and effort were not helping. 'Just a minute fellas, I'm going to move this damned thing, otherwise I'll only do it again.' On his hands and knees, he cleared away the sand around the offending item and tried to move it away from his now throbbing toes. It was an unusual moment, one of those where everyone goes quiet at the same time and you cannot really remember who spoke first, but, as he continued to fan with his hand, slowly but surely the outline of a large worked piece of timber became visible. More hands joined his, and within three or four minutes we had uncovered about one and a half metres of hull planking. An unusual feeling came over me, much like when you have known the answer to a question all along, but for some reason have forgotten to tell anyone. We were literally ten metres away from my tent, in the very spot where for a week we had been washing our pots, pans, clothes and bodies, and it was entirely likely that we had just stumbled over the wreck of HMS *Wager*. The storm that had come close to washing away our morale had also scoured away large amounts of sand on the bottom of the stream, exposing the smallest edge of timbers that must have remained buried for decades.

HMS Wager, *found after 265 years.*

Regrettably the logistical constraints of getting food and equipment to the island meant that we were only able to toast our success with a bottle of wine between 12 people – but we were all on top of the world. By the time we finished an initial investigation of the area to establish the likely size of the find, we had uncovered a piece of wreckage roughly 5 x 5 metres. With the light fading, we decided on an early start to begin a detailed survey that we could then hand over to a professional archaeological team.

The following morning Andy reminded the team of the basics of a simple survey and we set to work. Concurrently, we also began to build a small coffer dam of boulders and rocks upstream from the find to prevent the excavation being back filled with sand flowing downstream.

The wreckage was in a remarkably well preserved condition under about 50cm of water and 10cm of sand. We had found four frames of a hull section with at least eight pieces of hull planking attached. Constructed completely of timber, the joints were made with trenails, wooden fixing pins, that could be clearly seen. This would be consistent with *Wager's* construction, but more importantly the size and shape of the timbers were consistent with what we had been told we should expect to find. There were a number of interesting areas: three rectangular cut blocks that could either be repairs of a split timber or evidence of her conversion from an East Indiaman to a warship, some ceramics applied to one of the timber ends, perhaps as a waterproofing putty used when she was repaired in Brazil, and finally evidence of rough cutting and burning at the edges of some of the timber planks. Sadly there was only one artefact, a musket ball that Matt Buckland-Hoby discovered wedged between two of the frames.

Over the next two days we made a complete survey of the timbers using the old fashioned method of tape measure, pencil and paper, and took a series of photos using an underwater camera to create a photo mosaic of the entire find. So it was that with three days remaining on the island, we had effectively completed what we set out to do: to find evidence of the *Wager's* final resting place and make a survey that could be used to start a follow-up expedition by an archaeological team.

Divers carefully sifting sand to uncover timbers of the *Wager*.

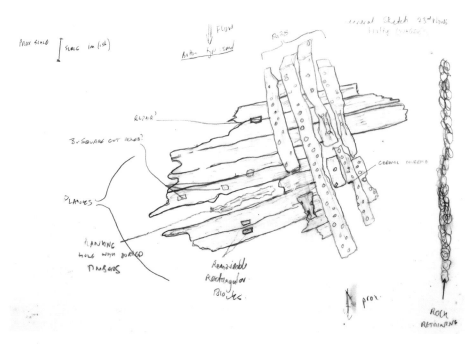

Diver's sketch of a fragment of the *Wager*, about 5 x 5m in size.

Section of planking with neat trenails (wooden dowels hammered into hand-drilled holes). This is likely to have been part of the original construction.

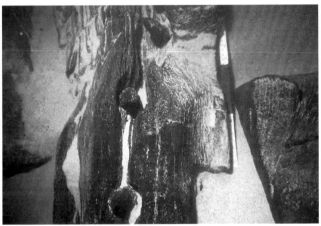

More trenails, where the wood around them has been eroded.

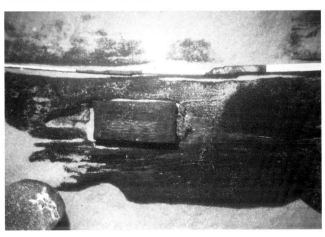

This could be a piece of damage repair (by Carpenter Cummins?) On the right hand side of the block a piece of fibrous material can be seen, no doubt packed around the edges as caulking to make a better seal.

Chris Holt holds a musket ball found embedded in the timbers, possibly one fired by the drunken ship's company, led by the Boatswain, who at first refused to leave the wreck.

I awoke in the morning to one of the team telling me that a small boat was in the bay. Assuming that this was some kind of elaborate practical joke I walked out onto the beach to see, sure enough, a small inflatable with six people in it pulling into what we were now convinced was Cheap's Bay. It is worth remembering at this point that we were on an island at best 24 hours from the nearest village and that the Golfo de Peñas is one of the most treacherous parts of the ocean, particularly in a small boat. I knew that the Chileans were considering sending an archaeological research team to the island at some point, but details were fairly thin. Once we had helped our guests to haul up their boat onto the beach, some introductions were called for. The two group leaders gravitated towards the front of both groups, and as we shook hands he said, 'So you are Chris Holt?'

Diego Carabias and his team from ARKA Consultants had been funded to conduct a two-year study into Wager and Byron Islands, and specifically into the relevant indigenous Indian history. Finding *Wager* was something that was pivotal to their research. They had heard of our expedition, but somehow we had failed to communicate with each other prior to our departure from the UK. Once he had heard of our imminent arrival, Diego had planned a period of field work on the island and hoped that at some point our paths might cross. It seems remarkable to me now, but until the moment we met, we were two completely separate expeditions in a wildly remote part of the world with only the slightest chance of bumping into each other. We had a lot to talk about!

I showed Diego and his team our find and clearly they were as excited about it as we were. After a brief period of deliberation it was concluded that the Chileans should join us at our camp, and as we waved them off to collect their equipment from the opposite side of the island, we prepared a camp site for them. This spirit of mutual assistance would continue for the remaining time on the island.

For our team this was the perfect ending. Not only had we found what we felt sure was part of the *Wager*, but we were now in a position to see a professional archaeological team start their research, and tell us more about the site and what happened after the shipwreck.

Once Diego and his team had returned we had time to chat about his research and compare notes on what we each did and didn't know about the *Wager* story. Here in the UK we are well equipped with the accounts of the survivors, and the records held in places like the National Archive in London, the UK Hydrographic Office in Taunton, and the Naval Historical Branch in Portsmouth had been invaluable in our research. The Chileans had access to the records of the Spanish outposts from the time and local Indian accounts. After a brief period talking to Diego it became clear to me and the team that *Wager* was not only an epic story for the Royal Navy, it is also a pivotal part of the history of the relationship between the Spanish and the local Indian tribes, and therefore an important part of Chilean history.

The site where the *Wager* was wrecked is a spot that had been used by the local Indians for some time, and the wrecked ship became for them an additional reason to visit. Even after all the British had left, the site continued to be used, and where possible items were salvaged. The local tribe, which operated in the archipelago of islands to the south of Wager Island, was known as the Alakaluf; they had not yet made formal contact with the Spanish, and were still operating as a hunter-gatherer maritime culture. In around 1745 the Spanish at Chiloé, having been alerted to the presence of the wreck by the arrival of Cheap and Byron, went off with a local Indian workforce to salvage the site for its metallic content. During this salvage expedition a Spanish camp was established near the wreck site, and first contact was made between the Spanish and the Alakaluf. For a period of over 50 years, the Spanish sent a Jesuit priest to the camp on Wager Island to convert the Alakaluf, and eventually they were subsumed into the Christian way of life.

Interestingly, the Indians were used by the Spanish to conduct the salvage and they used a traditional and relatively low-energy method to extract the maximum metallic content from the vessel. *Wager* was in relatively shallow water and as far as we can tell, firmly stuck not far from shore. The accounts that exist apparently suggest that large sections of the ship would be hacked free and then dragged up onto the beach. Here they would be burned if necessary to free them from rigging or other snags and the metallic content liberated without too much care for the timber, which was essentially worthless. The fact that our find was a 5 x 5m section of hull planking with rough cuts and evidence of charring at the edges supported this theory of working, and encouraged our firm belief that we had found part of the *Wager*. The only question really remaining is where the other sections are and, more interestingly, where the keel section and unrecovered cannon may lie.

We felt strongly that we wanted to assist the Chileans in any way we could with their research. Having arranged for them to join us aboard the Chilean Navy vessel coming to collect us, we set off on daily missions to search for signs of the Spanish camp, or the actual site of the wreck, whilst Diego and his team made detailed studies of the wreckage. This should have been a period of two or three days, but again the weather turned and we were pinned down by a ferocious storm that prevented even the Navy from reaching the island. After four unplanned extra days in the wet, food was scarce and we were all delighted and relieved to see the patrol vessel in the inlet between the Islands of Wager and Byron.

During these final days Diego and his team were able to make detailed studies of the area where the wreckage was found, and we were able to locate what we believe to be the site of a large encampment.

After nearly a month on the island we had not only found what we believed to be part of the famous *Wager*, but had also learnt about her amazing after-story. We embarked in the Chilean patrol vessel and, as Cheap's Bay and Mount Misery disappeared into the distance, we all felt a sense of achievement and, I think, not a small amount of sadness to be leaving a very special place.

Everyone's hope, on both sides of the Atlantic, is that this unique piece of our shared heritage should be investigated as completely as possible,[2] and that the amazing story of HMS *Wager* should be available for future generations to appreciate. All of the team from the SES expedition feel proud of what we managed to achieve, but most of all we have been touched by a remarkable story and an amazing island called Wager.

2. Since the discovery of these remains, the wood has been identified as of European origin, with a radiocarbon date consistent with the construction of the *Wager* in 1734. Other discoveries have included ceramics, glass, barrel staves, iron bolts and musket balls of calibre 0.68 as used in English muskets of the time.

Appendix A

WAGER'S BOATS

Wager's boats and their various capacities are an important part of the story. In the following table I have estimated sizes and carrying capacities from W. E. May's *The Boats of Men of War* (1974), from the National Maritime Museum's collection of ship models, and by various indications in the accounts of survivors. David Joel's excellent *Charles Brooking* (2000) is also very informative about boats of that era, as Brooking never got this sort of detail wrong.

Although the Admiralty made many attempts over the years to standardise boats carried in ships, in 1740 there was still such a wide variation that there has necessarily been a certain amount of guesswork and extrapolation in this table.

Name of boat	Length in feet	Max. number of men	Her fate
Long-boat	36	?35	Sawn in half by Carpenter Cummins and lengthened.
Long-boat after lengthening	48	59	Epic voyage of 2500 miles to Rio Grande. 29 survivors. Probably then sold for a pittance to provide passage money for survivors.
Cutter	25	12	Lost with 11 men on Patagonian coast in vicinity of Isla Duque de York.
Barge	24	10 (12 in extremis)	Taken by 6 deserters who absconded in Golfo San Esteban. Presumed lost.
Yawl	18	7	Sunk in Golfo de Peñas. One survivor.

Appendix B

THE AUTHORSHIP OF THE INDIAN INSURRECTION ACCOUNT

Morris's account of the Indian insurrection aboard the *Asia* is a close copy of a description of the same event in Anson's *Voyage*, and indeed he acknowledges the source and puts the extract in quotation marks. At first sight it seems surprising that Morris, who was present, should quote the author of Anson's *Voyage* (Walter or Robins) who was not.

Morris and Campbell came home during the period April to June 1746. Campbell's self-serving book, with his version of the insurrection, came out in 1747, but was quickly withdrawn from the bookshops and suppressed, presumably under threat of libel from Captain Cheap, or possibly because Campbell was already being recognized as a traitor.

Anson's long-awaited *Voyage* was published in 1748. While ignoring Campbell's version of events, it was careful to say that the account of the Indian insurrection was "taken from the mouth of an English gentleman" who was present. It seems highly likely that the gentleman referred to is Morris, and since he had published nothing at that date it must be that he had described the incident to Walter or Robins, probably Robins, who then wrote the graphic account quoted here.

When Morris came to publish his own book three years later, it would then have been natural in those copyright-free days for him to consider that he had every right to use the *Voyage* account, as it had been based entirely on his own description.

Whenever Morris and Campbell disagree, Morris, a modest and thoughtful man with no axe to grind, seems the more reliable.

Appendix C

PRIZE MONEY

HMS *Lark* (Captain David Cheap) and HMS *Gloucester* (Captain Charles Saunders) captured the Spanish ship *Port de Nantez* off Madeira on Christmas Day 1746. The 105 chests of silver and a mixed cargo were officially valued at £300,000. This was called "Bounty Money", and would have been allocated by law as follows:

1. Bounty money to be divided in 8 parts.

2. Captain to have three parts (but if under command of a Flag Officer, to give Flag Officer one part of this).

3. Lieutenants, Captain of Marines if borne, Master – one part divided equally.

4. Boatswain, Gunner, Purser, Carpenter, Master's Mate, Surgeon and Chaplain – one part divided equally.

5. Midshipmen, Carpenter's Mates, Surgeon's Mates, Coxswain, Quartermaster, Master at Arms, Corporals – one part divided equally.

6. Able Seamen, Ordinary Seamen, Stewards, Cooks, Armourer, Gunsmith, Cooper, Swabber, Barber, Soldiers – two parts divided equally.

   Cheap and Saunders therefore, on an independent cruise with no Flag Officer present, shared 3/8ths of £300,000, or £56,000 each.
   It is difficult to relate this to modern money, but I have tried two methods of doing so. First, taking the inflation tables of the Composite Price Index, the multiplier from 1750 (when the tables start) to 2012 is 193. Cheap's £56,000

in 1746 therefore would equate to nearly £11 million today.

Secondly, £56,000 can be related to the naval pay of a junior captain in 1746, which was £142 per annum. This amount of prize money therefore made Cheap richer by 394 years of naval pay. Applying this principle to the 2012 pay of a Commander on promotion gives an equivalent in today's money of £27 million.

These two calculations are far apart, but however one looks at it the Captain of the *Lark* had a handsome Christmas present and was now a rich man.

Appendix D

CASTAWAY SMALL-BOAT VOYAGES

The table overleaf of castaway small-boat voyages has been compiled in an attempt to compare Bulkeley's achievement in the *Speedwell* with others' since. The list omits purely drift-survival situations, of which there have been many amazing ones in all ages: for example, Steven Callahan's solo 1800-mile journey in a life-raft in 1982, the Baileys in 1973, Poon Lim in 1942, and the appalling *Medusa* saga of 1816. It also omits non-castaway voyages: for example, Captain Slocum's unique feats of navigation, seamanship, and boat-building with the *Spray* and the *Liberdade*, which were premeditated, adequately stored, and supported by friendly assistance at many ports. Dr Alain Bombard is in a class of his own, but hardly merits inclusion for some of the same reasons.

There are so many factors of differing importance in castaway voyages that there has to be a good deal of subjective judgement in any attempt to evaluate them.

There is a second-hand account in William Travis's *Beyond the Reefs* (1959) of a voyage by an American named Rowe who was wrecked on an uninhabited island in the Chagos archipelago in 1951. He is said to have built an eight-foot sailing boat out of boxwood with no nails or cordage and sailed and paddled 1200 miles to Alphonse Island in the Seychelles. I have been unable to find any confirmation of this extraordinary story, but if authentic it would certainly merit inclusion here.

Captain, ship, route, date	Days at sea	Distance run in nms	Type and size of boat
Gunner Bulkeley, HMS *Wager*, Wager Island to Rio Grande 1741-2	107	2500	Long-boat *Speedwell*, lengthened at Wager Island from 36 ft to 48 ft
Captain De Long, *Jeannette*, Arctic, 1881	?76	500	Cutter 26 ft 2nd cutter 16 ft Whaleboat 25 ft
Captain Pollard, *Essex*, Pacific, 1820	60	4000	3 whaleboats, 25 ft
Captain Bligh, HMS *Bounty*, Tofua to Timor, 1789	41	3600	Launch 23 ft
Captain Brookes, *Isabella*, Falklands to Buenos Aires, 1813	40	1200	"Long-boat," 18 ft
Dougal Robertson, Yacht *Lucette*, Pacific, 1972	38	750	Life-raft, then 9ft 6in fibreglass dinghy with jury-rigged sail
Shackleton/Worsley, *Endurance*, Elephant Is. to South Georgia, 1916	15	800	Whaler *James Caird*, 22 ft
Captain Theaker, *Lord Eldon*, Indian Ocean to Rodriguez, 1834	14	1000	Long-boat ?30 ft, 2 quarter boats

Number of survivors	Number lost from all causes	Remarks
29	52	Ferocious sub-Antarctic weather and treacherous waters. No chart or chronometer. Supreme feat of seamanship and endurance.
13	20	Boats sledged for about one third distance. De Long + 11 died of starvation and exposure. 2nd cutter lost with 8 men.
5	15	Cannibalism. Warm water. 3 marooned and rescued later.
12	2	Warm seas. No chart or chronometer, but "a book of latitudes and longitudes". Hostile natives. Outstanding feat of navigation.
6	0	Successful rescue mission. Quadrant and chart and probably chronometer of some kind carried.
6	0	Yacht sunk by killer whales. Relatively fair weather. No compass, chart, or sextant. 21 days in dinghy after life-raft was holed and abandoned.
6	0	Vicious seas and gales, mostly from astern. Dramatic rescue mission.
46	0	Warm water, ample provision. Severe overloading after one quarter boat sank.

BIBLIOGRAPHY AND SOURCES

ANON. *A Voyage to the South Seas*, 1745. Mostly recycled Bulkeley.

ANON. *Loss of the* Wager *Man of War, One of Commodore Anson's Squadron…* Printed for Thomas Tegg, London 1809. Mostly recycled Byron.

ANSON, George. *A Voyage Round the World in the Years MDCCXL, I, II, III, IV by George Anson Esq; Commander in Chief of a Squadron of his Majesty's Ships, sent upon an Expedition to the South-Seas…Compiled… and published under his direction, by Richard Walter, M.A., Chaplain of his Majesty's Ship the* Centurion… London, 1748. There has been much discussion about the true authorship of this book, and Professor Williams has shown that Benjamin Robins is likely to have written more than Walter.

BARROW, Sir John. *The Life of George Lord Anson*, 1839.

BULKELEY, John. *A Voyage to the South-Seas in the Years 1740-1. Containing a faithful Narrative of the Loss of his Majesty's Ship the* Wager… *By John Bulkeley and John Cummins, Late Gunner and Carpenter of the* Wager… *The whole compiled by Persons concerned in the Facts related.* London, 1743.
– First American Edition with Additions, Philadelphia, 1757.

BYRON, John. *The Narrative of the honourable John Byron …containing an Account of the Great Distresses suffered by himself and His Companions on the Coast of Patagonia…* London, 1768.

CAMPBELL, Alexander. *The Sequel to Bulkeley and Cummins's Voyage to the South-Seas, or the Adventures of Captain Cheap etc…by Alexander Campbell, late Midshipman of the* Wager, London, 1747. Suppressed soon after publication under threat of libel; only a handful of copies are known to exist.

CARABIAS AMOR, Diego. *Encuentro de Dos Mundos,* 2009

CHARNOCK, John. *Biographia Navalis,* 1797.

CHEAP, David. *Letter to Richard Lindsey* in the Joseph Spence papers, James Marshall and Marie-Louise Osborn Collection, Beinecke Rare Book and Manuscript Library, Yale University. Not published.
– *Letters* to the Secretary to the Admiralty, Public Records Office, Kew, ref. ADM 1/1602, ADM 1/1603. Not published in full.
– *Letter* to Rear Admiral Sir George Anson. Ibid. Not published in full.

EDWARDS, Philip. *The Story of the Voyage – Sea Narratives of Eighteenth-Century England,* 1994.

FITZROY, Captain Robert. *Narrative of the Surveying Voyages of His Majesty's Ships* Adventure *and* Beagle *1826-1836...* 1839. The part that concerns this story was edited by Fitzroy but written by others.

HARLAND, John. *Seamanship in the Age of Sail,* 1984

JOEL, David. *Charles Brooking,* 2000. This book is informative about boats of this period.

MAY, W.E. *The Boats of Men of War,* 1974.

MILLER, David. *The Wreck of the Isabella,* 1995

MORRIS, Isaac. *A Faithful Narrative of the Dangers and Distresses that befell Isaac Morris, late Midshipman of the* Wager, *and Seven more of the Crew...* Not dated, but almost certainly 1751.

NAISH, G.P.B. National Maritime Museum's *Book of Ship Models,* 1953.

OXFORD DICTIONARY OF NATIONAL BIOGRAPHY, 2004 Edition.

PACK, S.W.C. *The* Wager *Mutiny*, 1964.

RODGER, N.A.M. *The Wooden World*, 1986.

SHANKLAND, Peter. *Byron of the* Wager, 1975.

SLOCUM, Victor. *Castaway Boats*, 1938.

SOMERVILLE, Vice Admiral Boyle. *Commodore Anson's Voyage into the South Seas and around the World,* 1934.

WALKER, Violet W. *The House of Byron*, 1988.

WILLIAMS, Glyn. *The Prize of All the Oceans,* 1999.

YOUNG, John. *An affecting Narrative of the Unfortunate Voyage and Catastrophe of his Majesty's Ship* Wager, *one of Commodore Anson's Squadron in the South Sea Expedition...* London, 1751. Published anonymously; the author can only be John Young the Cooper, although this has been disputed. Possibly some parts were ghosted.

IMAGE CREDITS

The author and publisher gratefully acknowledge the permission granted to reproduce the copyright material in this book. Every effort has been made to establish all copyright holders, but should there be any errors or omissions, the publisher would be pleased to insert the appropriate acknowledgement in any subsequent printing of this publication.

Front cover: reproduced with kind permission of Commander David Joel
Back cover: reproduced with kind permission of Sir William Molesworth-
    St. Aubyn
Front inside cover: reproduced with kind permission of Geoff Hunt
Back inside cover: reproduced with kind permission of Anthony Terry
Cannon (p18) reproduced with kind permission of Anthony Terry
Press Gang (p30) image courtesy of Bridgeman Art Library
Dockyards (p33) artist unknown
Sir Charles Wager (p35) artist unknown
Deserters document (p37) National Archives, London; photo: Felicity Price-
    Smith
Memorial (p38) C.H. Layman
Books (p40) collection: Colin Paul; photo: Michael Blyth
20th December engraving (p44) collection: Colin Paul; photo: Michael Blyth
7th March engraving (p45 top) collection: Colin Paul; photo: Michael Blyth
Wager sketch (p45 bottom) collection: Colin Paul; photo: C.H. Layman
Anson's Route map (p46) collection: Colin Paul; photo: Michael Blyth
Rounding Cape Horn chart (p47) collection: Colin Paul; photo: Michael Blyth
Wager Embayed chart (p49) Felicity Price-Smith
HMS *Wager* in Extremis (p51) reproduced with kind permission of Commander
    David Joel; photo: Dave Thompson
The Wreck of HMS *Wager* (p54) reproduced with kind permission of
    Commander David Joel; photo: Dave Thompson
Frontispiece (p56) collection: Colin Paul; photo: Michael Blyth

Loss of the *Wager* engraving (p59) collection: Colin Paul; photo: Michael Blyth

A critical moment (p68) collection: Colin Paul; photo: Michael Blyth

Bulkeley's journey map (p112) Felicity Price-Smith

Discharged Dead document (p124) National Archives, London;
    photo: Felicity Price-Smith

Routes across South America map (p161) Felicity Price-Smith

Bay of Sorrows chart (p186) Felicity Price-Smith

Rio San Taddeo (p198) Google: Map data ©2014 Google, Inav/Geosistemas
    SRL, Mapcity

Route through the Fjord (p201) Google: Map data ©2014 Google, Inav/
    Geosistemas SRL, Mapcity

Glaciers (p202) Shirley Critchley

Byron's musket engraving (p204) collection: Colin Paul; photo: Michael Blyth

Soho Square (p220) collection: Amanda Barker-Mill; photo: Felicity Price-Smith

Muster book extract (p224) National Archives, London;
    photo: Felicity Price-Smith

Bulkeley title page (p226) collection: Colin Paul; photo: Michael Blyth

South America map (p232) reproduced with kind permission of Anthony Terry

Court-Martial document (p236) National Archives, London;
    photo: Felicity Price-Smith

Spanish chart (p238) reproduced with kind permission of Anthony Terry

Captain David Cheap (p257) reproduced with kind permission of the
    Strathtyrum Trust; photo: C.H. Layman

Foulweather Jack (p260) reproduced with kind permission of the 13th Lord
    Byron; photo: C.H. Layman

Saunders Island settlement (p262) C.H. Layman

Bryon title page (p264 left), collection: C.H. Layman; photo: Michael Blyth

Sophia's tribute (p264 right), collection: C.H. Layman; photo: Felicity Price-Smith

Bay of Sorrows map (p276) reproduced from an original in the collections of the
    Geography & Map Division, Library of Congress

Cannon (p278) reproduced with kind permission of Anthony Terry

Figure 1 (p283) Chris Holt

Wager Quest Team (p283) Chris Holt
Tortel walkways (p286) Shirley Critchley
Figure 2 (p295) Chris Holt
Figure 3 (p297 top) Chris Holt
Cheap's Bay (p297 bottom) David Carson
Wager Quest camp 2 (p299) Mike Smeaton
HMS Wager wreck (p302) Chris Holt
Divers (p304 top) Chris Holt
Sketch (p304 bottom) Chris Holt
Wooden wreckage (p305 top) David Carson
Wooden wreckage p305 centre) Chris Hunter
Wooden wreckage p305 bottom) Chris Hunter
Musket ball (p306) Chris Holt

GLOSSARY

Terms which are used once only and explained in a footnote are not repeated here.

Athwart, athwartships – at right angles to the fore-and-aft line.

Back and fill – to brace the yards so that the wind blows on the forward part of the sail.

Bale goods – cargo in bales.

Barge – see Appendix A.

Beam-ends – a ship on her beam ends is heeled over till her deck beams are nearly vertical.

Bend – to join two ropes together, or tie a cable to an anchor.

Bilged – a ship is said to be bilged when she is holed in her lowest part.

Boats – see appendix A.

Bower anchor – the largest anchor carried in a ship. The *best bower* is the one on the starboard side.

Bowsprit – the spar that extends over the bows to take forestays and jibs.

Brace – a rope attached to the outer end of a yard whereby the sails are angled to the wind.

Brails – ropes which gather in the sails, usually for a short time.

Breaker – a small barrel or cask. Sometimes spelt *barricoe*.

Bulkhead – a vertical partition in a ship.

Cable – 1. any heavy rope, particularly the ship's anchor rope.

      2. as a measure of distance, 200 yards.

Cant – to turn or swivel something.

Careen – to beach a ship and heave her down on one side to clean the bottom.

Cathead – a short strong beam projecting horizontally over the ship's bows and approximately athwartships. It serves to hoist and let go an anchor without fouling the ship's side with the anchor flukes.

Chain-plates – metal plates secured to the ship's side to take the strain of the shrouds that hold the masts in place.

Claw off – to attempt to beat to windward to avoid a lee-shore.

Close-hauled – sailing as close to the wind as possible.

Commodore – until recently a temporary rank, senior to captain and below admiral, created for a special mission or service.

Courses – the lowest sails in a square-rigged ship.

Crowd – to carry as much sail as possible, or perhaps too much.

Cutter – see Appendix A.

Deep-sea line – see *lead*.

East Indiaman – a ship built for one of the East India Companies.

Embayed – driven into a bay and unable to escape the lee-shore by weathering either headland.

Fathom – the seaman's old unit of measurement for depths and lengths of rope, equal to six feet or 1.8 metres. Now replaced by metres.

Forecastle, foc'sle – the foremost part of the upper deck of a ship.

Groyne – the old seafaring name for La Coruña in northwest Spain.

Gunnel or *gunwale* – the upper edge of a ship's side.

Hand (verb) – to furl a sail.

Headsails – sails forward of the foremast, e.g. jibs and staysails.

Jeers, jeerblocks – the assemblage of tackles by which the yards of a ship are hoisted into position.

Larboard – the old term for the left-hand side of a ship when facing forward. Now port.

Lead, leadline – a long line weighted with lead and tallow and plumbed to determine the depth of water and nature of the bottom. A *deep-sea line* is a heavier line for deeper water.

League – a nautical measurement of distance, being three nautical miles.

Lee, lee-shore, leeward – the downwind side; a ship being blown on to a lee-shore is obviously in a hazardous position.

Lie-to – to maintain minimum steerage way to ride out a gale, usually with the wind forward of the beam to minimise heavy seas breaking aboard.

Long-boat – see Appendix A.

Lordships, Their Lordships – the Lords Commissioners of the Admiralty, responsible to King and Parliament for the Navy.

Master – an officer with responsibility for the navigation of the ship, subordinate to the Lieutenant.

Masts – *Fore, Main* and *Mizzen* – the three masts of a square rigger.

Middle watch – midnight to 0400.

Orlop – the highest deck that runs the whole length of the ship.

People – ordinary name for the ship's company; that is, everyone on the ship's list except the officers.

Pink – a small square-rigged ship, often used for victualling supplies.

Point (of the compass) – 11¼ degrees of arc.

Pressed man – a man taken by the press-gang to man a naval ship, as opposed to a volunteer. Volunteers were paid more than pressed men.

Privateer – a privately-owned vessel with guns, operating against the enemy to take prizes, with or without official licence.

Puncheon – a wooden cask.

Put about – to tack or wear to put the wind on the other side.

Quarterdeck – the after part of the upper deck of a ship.

Rate – a system of classifying warships by the number of guns. E.g. *Centurion* with 60 guns was a 4ᵗʰ rate, *Wager* with 28 guns a 6ᵗʰ rate.

Reef – to reduce the sail area by tying down part of the sail with reef-points.

Scuttle – to stave in a boat or cask.

Sheet – a rope for trimming a sail to the wind.

Shrouds – rigging that takes the athwartship strain on the masts.

Sloop – now a boat with fore-and-aft mainsail and foresail, but in the eighteenth century the term was used somewhat indiscriminately for a smaller naval vessel with auxiliary duties.

Snow – a two-masted square-rigged ship.

South Sea or *South Seas* – Pacific Ocean.

Starboard – the right-hand side of a ship when facing forward.

Stave, stave in (pp. *stove*) – to break the planking of a boat or cask.

Stays – rigging that takes the fore-and-aft strain on the masts.

Steerage – in the *Wager*, the space below decks forward of the wardroom.

Studdingsail, stunsail – a fair-weather sail extending outside the square sails.

Sway – to hoist the yards to their proper place.

Tack (noun) – the rope used to hold the lower corner of a sail.

Tack (verb) – the operation of bringing the wind through the bows from one side to the other.

Tangle – kelp or other coarse seaweed.

Topgallants – the top set of sails in a square-rigged ship.

Topping-lift – the rope by which the end of a boom is hoisted or supported.

Topsails – the middle set of sails on the masts of a square-rigged ship.

Variation – the amount by which magnetic north differs from true north.

Wardroom – officers' mess.

Wear (pp. *wore*) – to turn away from the wind to put the wind through the stern and on to the other tack.

Yard – a spar that crosses a mast from which sails can be set.

Yawl – see Appendix A.

INDEX

ACKNOWLEDGEMENTS

Diego Carabias Amor and Major Chris Holt have been in effect co-authors of this book of many authors, and outstanding collaborators they have been. Many kind people in uncountable ways have greatly helped and encouraged me. They include William Allen, Amanda Barker-Mill, Paul Blunt, Lord Byron, David Carson, Angus Cheape, Professor Sondra Miley Cooney, Shirley Critchley, Susan Danforth, Señora Maria Lluïsa Farre, Guillermo Harris, Rear Admiral Richard Hill, Commander David Joel, Professor Robert Markley, Sir William Molesworth-St. Aubyn, Commander Graham Neilson, Colin and Juliet Paul, Professor Sarah Palmer, David Pole-Evans, Anthony Phillips, Lieutenant-Commander Lawrie Phillips, Anthony Terry, Andrew Torbet and Professor Glyn Williams.

The publishing team at Uniform Press have been superb, particularly Lucy Duckworth and Felicity Price-Smith.

Back inside cover image:
Spanish chart depicting the South Seas, 1744. A more detailed description can be found on page 238.